DANGEROUS

LIAISONS

DANGEROUS LIAISONS

Blacks, Gays,
and the Struggle for Equality

EDITED BY
ERIC BRANDT

THE NEW PRESS   NEW YORK

Compilation and Introduction copyright © 1999 by Eric Brandt. All rights reserved.

Published in the United States by The New Press, New York
Distributed by W. W. Norton & Company, Inc., New York

Library of Congress Cataloging-in-Publication Data

Dangerous liaisons : Blacks, gays, and the struggle for equality /
edited by Eric Brandt.
     p.   cm.
Includes bibliographical references.
ISBN 1-56584-455-6
   1. Homophobia — United States. 2. Heterosexism — United States.
3. Homophobia — Religious aspects — Christianity. 4. Afro-Americans —
Civil rights. 5. Afro-Americans — Attitudes. 6. Civil rights
movements — United States — History. 7. Gay liberation movement —
United States — History. 8. United States — Race relations.
9. United States — Politics and government. I. Brandt, Eric, 1956-
HQ76.4.U6D35 1999
305.896073 — dc21   98-56062
                                           CIP

www.thenewpress.com

9 8 7 6 5 4 3 2 1

To
Ainsworth Phillips
and to all who confront both racism and homophobia
every day of their lives

Contents

Acknowledgments

First and foremost I must acknowledge the help of my dear friend Eric Bryant, a brilliant and skillful editor at *Library Journal*. It was in conversations with him that the idea for this anthology first arose. He has given invaluable feedback, researched sources, and offered emotional support throughout the entire process. Without his selfless contributions, this anthology would not have become a reality.

Joe Wood, my editor at The New Press, offered much needed balance and invaluable insight. There were many editors who regretfully rejected my proposal for fear an anthology on such a topic would not be commercially viable. The New Press is committed to publishing in the public interest and I am grateful to them and to Joe that they were willing to take a chance that this project would be a valuable contribution to the current debate. For Joe's patience with me and care about this project I will always be grateful.

Also at The New Press, André Schiffrin, Diane Wachtell, Barbara Chuang, Grace Farrell, Janey Tannenbaum and her staff Chris Heiser, Jeff Yamaguchi, and Farley Chase, gave generously of their talents to publish this book in the best possible way. The art director Hall Smyth worked overtime to perfect a package for a complex book. I know I am very fortunate to have had such wonderful support. I could not have found a better publishing house for this book.

My excellent agent and friend Barbara Moulton was unflagging in her enthusiasm and unfailing in her advice, and I couldn't be more grateful.

From our very first meeting in his office at Columbia University's School of Law, Kendall Thomas was enthusiastic about this project and candid about his concerns regarding me. The issues in this book are too important to be dismissed because of a well-meaning but misguided editor. His challenging questions and his generous guidance have offered balance and served to keep this anthology honest.

Several gave feedback and encouragement at very early stages and throughout the process of compiling this anthology: Greg Brandenburgh, Charles Cohen, Henry Finder at the *New Yorker*, Marny Hall, Karla Jay, Richard Labonte and Ken White at A Different Light Bookstores, Caroline Pincus, Christopher Portelli at the Sexuality Information and Education Council of the United States, Barbara Smith, Urvashi Vaid at the National Gay and Lesbian Task Force, and Jim Van Buskirk at the Gay and Lesbian Center of the San Francisco Public Library. Many of their suggestions have been incorporated into this book. I will always be indebted for their kindness.

Coordinating an anthology of many contributors sometimes requires great diplomacy, and I thank my father William Brandt for his timely advice on such matters, as well as his unfailing support throughout this project.

And finally, thanks to my boyfriend Michael Carter who was always patient and reassuring as I worked on this book, and whose example has shown me more than words could say about the incredible courage and resilience it takes to be black *and* gay.

Permissions

DANGEROUS

LIAISONS

Introduction
Offering a Platform for Dialogue

According to the 1990 U.S. Census, African Americans make up 12 percent of the population; homosexuals comprise 10 percent of Americans as first determined by the Kinsey report. Though the two communities have very different histories, as minorities in America both groups face some similar challenges. It has always seemed to me that these two groups have much to learn from each other, even to gain from working together. But first they have to talk to each another. Many in both groups do not share that opinion. With this book, I hope to provide a platform for the conversation.

The experience of African Americans and the lesbian/gay/bisexual/transgendered community overlap in a number of areas; there are especially clear parallels between the oppression of blacks and gays.[1] However, the interaction of racism, heterosexism, and homophobia within and between the two communities complicates the groups' relationship. The issues have many faces, such as whether there can be a hierarchy of oppression, or what the ties are between different forms of oppression, or whether the civil rights movement needs to or should include the gay rights movement. The contributors to this anthology address many such topics and discuss them from a surprisingly wide variety of perspectives.

Indeed, given the diversity within each community—and the facticity of gay African Americans—any strict distinction made between blacks and gays is somewhat artificial. Moreover, there are many instances which suggest not a distinction but a solidarity between these two minorities. Even so, many members of both communities want to distance themselves from the opinions of the other. Some gay and lesbian organizations quietly avoid leadership by or concerns of African Americans; some African American community leaders get outraged at any comparison of movements for equal rights. The conservative right has tried to exploit of these divisions. It has attempted to turn blacks against gays where convenient, and at the same time sponsor antiaffirmative action legislation. Clearly, there is a need for a black gay dialogue.

As a student of Cornel West's at Columbia University, I remember heated classroom discussions which boiled down to whether it was blacks or gays who were *more* oppressed by the white heterosexual hegemony. Gays argued that as open homosexuals they were more oppressed because they could not marry, could not be ordained, would be passed over for advancement in their careers, were the victims of a form of genocide because of the lack of government funding of AIDS research, and were generally despised by the straight majority. Blacks argued that for gays to compare their own struggles to that of blacks was offensive. Because gays had never been enslaved, never been denied equal access to education and job opportunities, nor lived through the long history of oppression that now defined the psyche of blacks, gays would never experience the same level of oppression. Gays, when convenient, could hide, perhaps even choose their sexual proclivities, whereas blacks could never hide the color of their skin.

Such confrontations between blacks and gays were first raised to the level of national discourse during the 1993 March on Washington for Lesbian, Gay and Bi Equal Rights and Liberation. The organizers and speakers such as Larry Kramer invoked Reverend Dr. Martin Luther King, Jr.'s 1963 March on Washington for Civil Rights. Such comparisons were met with speedy and vehement reaction by distraught leaders of the black community. Gay and lesbian leaders became defensive. It then became clear to me that there was a need for a collection of thoughtful essays on the legal, social, and cultural connections between racism and homophobia, as well as the sometimes uneasy relationship between blacks and gays. I imagined a publication in which the leading minds of both communities could debate the many attendant issues surrounding the prejudices *against* blacks and gays, and *between* blacks and gays.

For years I hesitated writing the proposal for this book. I was concerned that because I am white, the credibility of such a project would be in question. But I also hesitated because the topic is such a sensitive one. Indeed, when I finally began approaching contributors, some were suspicious of my agenda. Others worried that the working title *Blacks and Gays* would appear to oppose the two communities, to suggest antagonism where they wanted to emphasize cooperation. And I suspect some of those who declined may have done so out of trepidation, fearing that publishing their position on such a sensitive subject might come back to haunt them. Indeed, many of those who did agree to contribute found the assignment a trickier challenge than they anticipated. Trying to get African Americans, gays and lesbians, and African American gays and lesbians to talk about their relationship was a project rife with danger, hence the final title: *Dangerous Liaisons.*

One of the clearest and most heinous parallels between blacks and gays is their common experience of being the target of violence. On Sunday morning, June 7, 1998, the mutilated body of a black man, James Byrd, Jr., was discovered just outside of Jasper, Texas. Mr. Byrd's torso was found at the edge of a paved road, his head and an arm in a ditch about a mile away. The night before, on his way home from a niece's bridal shower, Byrd had been picked up by three young white men, taken to some woods, where he was beaten, and then chained to their pickup truck and dragged for two miles.

On Thursday, October 11, 1998, a passing bicyclist found the burned, battered, near lifeless body of twenty-one-year-old University of Wyoming student Matthew Shepard tied to a rail fence. After being lured into a truck by two young white men, he was driven to a remote location, stripped of his shoes in near-freezing weather, lashed to a rail fence, mocked and beaten with a gun butt until comatose. At his funeral, ten days later, as his family entered the church, protesters showed up waving signs with antihomosexual messages.

The violent deaths of James Byrd, Jr. and Matthew Shepard

have recently ignited debate over a Federal Hate Crimes Protection Act. The gruesome, recorded history of racial violence is much longer than that of homophobic violence, yet the level of violence is now becoming comparable. The Anti-Violence Project in New York City reports that approximately fifty anti-gay and lesbian murders are committed each year, sixty percent of which are marked by an extraordinarily high level of gratuitous violence or "forensic overkill." Whether the result of better reporting or the greater visibility of gay people, the numbers of bias crimes against gays has risen in recent years. The *San Francisco Chronicle* recorded that bias crimes reported to the San Francisco Police Department rose by twenty-three percent from 1994 to 1995, the number of antigay crimes surpassing that of racial hate crimes for the first time. Suffering violence is unfortunately something lesbians, gay men and African Americans have in common.

To complete this grisly picture, I do well to point to Gary Comstock's landmark study of *Violence Against Lesbians and Gay Men,* where he finds that not only are lesbians and gay men the victims of violent attacks more often than the general population, but lesbians and gay men of color are (disproportionately) more often the victim of antigay/lesbian violence than are white lesbians and gay men. The racial disproportion in the general population is echoed in the gay community. Whether discussing hate crimes or racial prejudice in general, this omnipresent disproportion is an unavoidable point in our debate and is taken up by several of the contributors.

From Selma and Stonewall to California's Proposition 209 and the Defense of Marriage Act, blacks and gays continue to face struggles against political inequalities. Just as the comparison was made between the 1993 March on Washington for Lesbian, Gay and Bi Equal Rights and Liberation and Reverend Dr. Martin Luther King, Jr.'s 1963 march on Washington for Civil Rights, similar comparisons will undoubtedly be made between Louis Farrakhan's 1995 Million Man March and the upcoming gay/lesbian/bisexual/transgendered Millennium March on

Washington, D.C., in April of the year 2000. Many in both communities have bristled at any such comparisons. In his contribution to this anthology, Henry Louis Gates, Jr.'s essay *Backlash?* suggests that the outcry against any linkage between the gay rights and civil rights movements is poignantly ironic given the historical fact that the actual organizer of King's 1963 March on Washington, Bayard Rustin, was prevented from being named director of that march "in no small part because of his homosexuality—and the fear that it would be used to discredit the mobilization."

The movement away from equal rights for blacks has been gaining steam. The passage of California's antiaffirmative action Proposition 209 has set off a series of similar initiatives across the country. In the November 1998 election, Washington state voters decided to ban state-sponsored affirmative action programs. Recently a federal appeals court struck down racial preferences at the prestigious Boston Latin school, and white parents in Arlington, Virginia, are suing the school district in a challenge to its minorities admissions quotas. President Clinton's administration has publicly defended federal affirmative action programs, but a March 16, 1998, *New York Times* article claims sweeping reductions in such programs between 1996 and 1998.

For gays the success with *Romer v. Evans* in 1996, the Supreme Court's overturning of Colorado's Amendment 2, has been tempered by successful initiatives in Maine to repeal prohibitions against discrimination based on sexual orientation. A likely progay ruling on *Baehr v. Miike,* the case before the Hawaii Supreme Court on the constitutionality of same-sex marriages, was undermined with a ballot initiative in November 1998 to change the state constitution to allow the legislature to restrict marriage to heterosexual couples. And the Defense of Marriage Act signed by President Clinton during his campaign for reelection in 1996 was perceived as betrayal by many of his gay and lesbian supporters. To this day, just being a homosexual is still a punishable crime in twenty-one states.

There are a host of other shared problems, too. Bias against equal access to education and job opportunities, unequal protection by law enforcement organizations, systematic genocide, adoption rights and child-custody battles.

Clearly, alliances between gays and blacks could be useful in the struggle for equal rights. Indeed, the congressional Black Caucus has been so supportive of the rights of gays and lesbians, that in 1996 the National Gay and Lesbian Task Force presented them with an award of appreciation. Civil rights heroes Coretta Scott King and U.S. Representative John Lewis have also publicly advocated for gay rights. Many of these political alliances, as well as some of the conflicts, are explored in Keith Boykin's interview with U.S. Representative Barney Frank. Cathy Cohen and Tamara Jones discuss efforts toward alliance at the 1998 Black Radical Congress. Barbara Smith, Alisa Solomon, and Mab Segrest, offer first-hand accounts of the role of grassroots activism in the two communities.

In 1977 Anita Bryant led the Dade County "Save the Children from Homosexuality" Campaign appealing to the authority of the Christian Scriptures and the financial support of conservative churches. Twenty years later Walt Disney Co. was boycotted by the 12,000 delegates to the 1997 Southern Baptist Convention because of its "progay, antifamily practices." Moreover, president of the Christian Coalition Pat Robertson recently organized a "No Special Rights Committee" to bolster the Oregon Citizen's Alliance in their support of Oregon's Ballot Measure 9 — a proposal to amend that state's constitution in order to declare homosexuality as "abnormal, wrong, unnatural and perverse." In 1998 Robertson launched a nationwide campaign to repeal lesbian and gay civil rights protections in every state and city where they exist.

The black church was dragged into this fight after the 1993 March on Washington for Lesbian, Gay and Bi Equal Rights. There, the Traditional Values Coalition produced a video under the auspices of Citizens United for the Preservation of Civil Rights entitled *Gay Rights/Special Rights: Inside the Homo-*

sexual Agenda. Readers of this anthology will see references to this video by many of the contributors. Featuring interviews of Senator Trent Lott, Ralph Reed, Chairman of the Traditional Values Coalition Rev. Lou Sheldon, and several homophobic leaders in the black community, *Gay Rights/Special Rights* portrays homosexuality as a lascivious, morally depraved lifestyle choice. By arguing for legal recognition as a minority class, the video tries to show, homosexuals are not only attempting to advance their own un-American agenda, but also disparaging the good name of Martin Luther King and making a mockery of the civil rights movement. This video was copied and sent to hundreds of black churches across the country in a grassroots movement to eliminate any sympathy for the gay/lesbian equal rights movement felt by the black community. But there are others who offer an alternative model, such as Reverend Edwin C. Sanders II, of the African American Metropolitan Interdenominational Church in Nashville, Tennessee, who is intervewed in this collection.

An issue of common concern to blacks and gays has been the devastating spread of AIDS. In this book, Reverend Reginald G. Blaxton discusses the difficulties while on the mayor's staff in involving Washington, D.C., clergy in the fight against AIDS. Initially considered a "gay disease" in the 1980s, the demographics for highest rate of infection shifted in the 1990s. The number of new AIDS cases began dropping in the gay community as a result of an organized and systematic effort aimed at educating and protecting gays against transmission of HIV, as well as a visible and vocal activist community who advocated for new and better resources for research and treatment of the disease. A concurrent rise of rate of infection began to appear in the black and Latino communities, specifically among the poor and intravenous drug users. By 1997, the Center for Disease Control (CDC) reported that "For the first time, more new cases occurred among blacks than whites in 1996. Blacks accounted for 41% of the 68,473 new cases, whites 38% and Hispanics 19%." From the beginning of the epidemic, Reverend Blaxton informs us, the CDC's 1997 Surveillance Report counted a cumulative total of 390,692 Americans who had died of AIDS, and 132,221 of those African American—a disproportionate 30%. No longer a gay issue, the changes in opinions and prejudices attending this shift, is an important departure point in future discussion on how these two communities can join forces in fighting the AIDS epidemic.

An example of the breadth of related concerns is provided by those contributors who discuss representation of blacks and gays. The 1980s and '90s witnessed an explosion of representation of black homosexuals; the response was often equally explosive. *Tongues Untied*, directed by Marlon Riggs, was publicly assailed by Pat Buchanan in his 1992 presidential bid as a prime example of NEA misuse of public funds; *Paris is Burning* (1991), directed by Jennie Livingston about the culture of black drag queens in Harlem, and more recently the award-winning film *The Watermelon Woman* (1996), written and directed by Cheryl Dunyé, a film about the life of a black lesbian actress in early Hollywood, both funded by the NEA, have also come under much criticism because of their content.

Several contributors to this volume explore the representations of the relationship between being black and/or gay in today's society. Cheryl Clarke discusses heterosexism in the Black Arts movement and racism in white feminist poetry. Martin Duberman talks about his experience as a white gay man writing about the life of Paul Robeson. Darieck Scott looks carefully at Toni Morrison's Pulitzer Prize-winning novel *Beloved* and the blaxploitation film *Car Wash*. Robert Reid-Pharr makes some startling connections between the experience of being black and that of being gay in his reading of the poetry of Gary Fisher. Jewelle Gomez explores the phenomenon of "passing" in the movies of her youth and investigates the parallels between racial stereotypes and the stereotyping of sexualities.

Finally, this collection looks at the phenomenon of black homophobia and gay racism. Several pieces argue against the commonly held belief that homophobia is more prevalent in the black community than in society at large. A 1997 survey by the *San Jose Mercury News* of about 1,000 Californians revealed that fifty-eight percent of blacks polled felt homosexuality was morally wrong as compared to thirty-six percent of whites. Yet, there is other evidence that suggest blacks are not as homophobic as whites: a larger *New York Times*/CBS poll conducted February 9–11, 1993, found that fifty-three percnet of blacks supported equal rights for gays and lesbians, and only forty percent of whites felt the same.

One of the biggest frustrations in compiling this book was trying to find a contributor willing to discuss the phenomenon of gay racism. In her classic essay, "The Failure to Transform," Cheryl Clarke freely discusses homophobia in the black liberation movement of the early 1980s. But on the topic of racism in the history of the gay liberation movement, I was faced with a great deal of discomfort and silence. Of course, racism is undeniably present in the movement. For example, in 1970 when the Gay Liberation Front (GLF) voted to contribute money to post bail for Black Panther leaders accused of conspiring to bomb public places, detractors within the Front formed the more conservative, largely white, male, middle-class Gay Activist Alliance. This incident has been referred to by Ron Ballard, one of the black members of the GLF, as the "dirty little secret of gay liberation."

Even today, blacks are rarely included in the leadership of gay activist organizations, or targeted for participation in surveys regarding gay and lesbian issues. Examples abound, but the most obvious is the planned April 2000 Millennium March for Equality in Washington, D.C. It was announced by the Universal Fellowship of Metropolitan Community Churches, the nation's largest gay Christian denomination, and the Human Rights Campaign (HRC), the nation's largest gay rights organization. In an August 28, 1998, article in the *Washington Blade,* a weekly gay newspaper in D.C., Donna Red Wing, HRC's national field director, admitted that there were "some huge missteps" related to the initial planning process for the Millennium

March. Such missteps coupled with the HRC's endorsement of conservative Senator Alfonse D'Amato in his 1998 bid for re-election has provoked a firestorm of protest by African American lesbians and gays.

In July 1998, a coalition of Christian conservatives ran full-page ads in *The New York Times, The Washington Post,* and *USA Today* condemning homosexuality on religious and moral grounds, and featuring photos of former lesbians and gay men who claimed to have converted to heterosexuality. *NewsWatch* reported that the HRC countered with their own ad featuring "a white, God-fearing, church-going, Republican couple from Minnesota who is proud and supportive of their adult lesbian daughter." The question was raised whether the HRC was attempting to emphasize white middle-class gays, failing to use this opportunity to point out that "gays and lesbians are part of every racial and ethnic community and class." Of course, HRC is not alone in underrepresenting people of color. A summer 1998 *NewsWatch* article notes the dissatisfaction of gay people of color who feel excluded from mainstream and gay media coverage.

So, where do we go from here? I turned to three thinkers who could help point us in the right direction. In the final selections of this book, Samuel Delany, Cornel West, and Audre Lorde offer analysis and promise for greater understanding between blacks and gays.

Dangerous Liaisons is the first book to investigate the parallels and distinctions between racism and homophobia through open debate among some of our country's very best minds. In light of President Clinton's national conversation on race, the ongoing debate over a Federal Hate Crimes Protection Act, the continuing erosion or reform of affirmative action, it is my hope that the work of the contributors to this volume will not only spark controversy, but move the debate forward.

Certainly the relationship between the black and gay communities demands delicacy, caution, and thoughtfulness. But if the topic isn't engaged, if the debate isn't started, we will be a "closeted" society, internalizing racism and heterosexism until it tears us apart. In the process of compiling this collection, I worked hard to let go of any personal agendas. And by merely providing a platform for debate, I discovered a surprising breadth in the topic — from Capitol Hill to Hollywood, from advertising to poetry, from history to philosophy and faith. Rather than overlapping, the contributors exhibit a wide diversity of approaches to the intersections of race and sexuality. This is as it should be. Recognition of the diversity of both communities is one of the best weapons against unthinking stereotypes, the building blocks of persecution.

NOTES

1. After laboring over the issue, I decided to use "blacks" and "gays" as the most recognized shorthand for African Americans and the lesbian/gay/bisexual/ transgendered community (LGBT). This is not only for convenience, but also because both were terms originally meant as disparaging and were later reclaimed by each group in defiance of their oppression.

BRANCHES OF THE SAME TREE?

Blacks and Gays
Healing the Great Divide

Barbara Smith

Perhaps the most maddening question anyone can ask me is "Which do you put first: being black or being a woman, being black or being gay?" The underlying assumption is that I should prioritize one of my identities because one of them is actually more important than the rest or that I must arbitrarily choose one of them over the others for the sake of acceptance in one particular community.

I always explain that I refuse to do political work and, more importantly, to live my life in this way. All of the aspects of who I am are crucial, indivisible, and pose no inherent conflict. They only seem to be in opposition in this particular time and place, living under U.S. capitalism, a system whose functioning has always required that large groups of people be economically, racially, and sexually oppressed and that these potentially dissident groups be kept divided from each other at all costs.

I've devoted many years to making the connections between issues and communities and to forging strong working coalitions. Although this work is far from finished, it has met with some success. In 1993, however, two aspects of my identity and two communities whose freedom I've always fought for are being publicly defined as being at war with one another.

For the first time, the relationship between the African American and lesbian and gay communities is being widely debated both within and outside of movement circles. One catalyst for this discussion has been gay leaders cavalierly comparing lifting the ban on homosexuals in the military with racially desegregating the armed forces following World War II. The National Association for the Advancement of Colored People (NAACP) and other black civil rights organizations' decisions to speak out in favor of lesbian and gay rights and to support the

April 1993 march on Washington have met with protests from some sectors of the black community and have also spurred the debate.

Ironically, the group of people who are least often consulted about their perspectives on this great divide are those who are most deeply affected by it: black lesbian and gay activists. Contradictions that we have been grappling with for years, namely homophobia in the black community, racism in the lesbian and gay community, and the need for both communities to work together as allies to defeat our real enemies are suddenly on other people's minds. Because black lesbians and gays are not thought of as leaders in either movement, however, this debate has been largely framed by those who have frighteningly little and inaccurate information.

Thanks in part to the white lesbian and gay community's own public relations campaigns, black Americans view the lesbian and gay community as uniformly wealthy, highly privileged, and politically powerful, a group that has suffered nothing like the centuries of degradation caused by U.S. racism. Reverend Dennis Kuby, a civil rights activist, states in a letter to the *New York Times*: "Gays are not subject to water hoses and police dogs, denied access to lunch counters, or prevented from voting." Most blacks have no idea, however, that we are threatened with the loss of employment, of housing, and of custody of our children, and are subject to verbal abuse, gay bashing, and death at the hands of homophobes. Kuby's statement also does not acknowledge those lesbians and gays who have been subjected to all of the racist abuse he cites, because we are both black and gay. Because we are rendered invisible in both black and gay contexts, it is that much easier for the black community to oppose gay rights and to express homophobia without recognizing that these attacks and the lack of legal protections affects its own members.

The racism that has pervaded the mainstream gay movement only fuels the perceived divisions between blacks and gays. Single-issue politics, unlike lesbian and gay organizing that is consciously and strategically connected to the overall struggle for social and economic justice, do nothing to convince blacks that lesbians and gays actually care about eradicating racial oppression. At the very same time that some gays make blanket comparisons between the gay movement and the black civil rights movement, they also assume that blacks and other people of color have won all our battles and are in terrific shape in comparison with lesbians and gays.

In an interview in the *Dallas Voice* (December 1992), lesbian publisher Barbara Grier states: "We are the last minority group unfairly legislated against in the U.S." Grier's perception is of course inaccurate. Legislation that negatively affects people of color, immigrants, disabled people, and women occurs every day, especially when court decisions that undermine existing legal protections are taken into account.

In 1991, well before the relationship between the gay community and the black community was a hot topic, Andrew Sullivan, editor of the *New Republic* asserted the following in the *Advocate*:

> The truth is, our position is far worse than that of any ethnic minority or heterosexual women.
>
> Every fundamental civil right has already been granted to these groups: The issues that they discuss now involve nuances of affirmative action, comparable pay, and racial quotas. Gay people, however, still live constitutionally in the South of the '50s. . . .
>
> We are not allowed to marry—a right granted to American blacks even under slavery and never denied to heterosexuals. We are not permitted to enroll in the armed services—a right granted decades ago to blacks and to heterosexual women.
>
> Our civil rights agenda, then, should have less to do with the often superfluous minority politics of the 1991 Civil Rights Act and more to do with the vital moral fervor of the Civil Rights Act of 1964.
>
> A better strategy to bring about a society more tolerant of gay men and women would involve dropping our alliance with the current Rainbow Coalition lobby and recapturing the clarity of the original civil rights movement. The point is to rekindle the cause of Martin Luther King Jr. and not to rescue the career of Jesse Jackson.

Sullivan's cynical distortions ignore that quality of life is determined by much more than legislation. Clearly, he also knows nothing about slavery. Slaves were frequently not permitted to marry and their marriages and family relationships were not legally recognized or protected. Until 1967 when the Supreme Court decided *Loving v. Virginia*, it was illegal for blacks to marry whites in sixteen states. The armed services were rigidly segregated until after World War II. Racist abuse and denial of promotions and military honors typified the black experience in the military. Sullivan also has not noticed that joblessness, poverty, racist and sexist violence, and the lack of decent housing, health care, and education make the lives of many "ethnic minorities" and "heterosexual women" a living hell. But Sullivan doesn't care about these folks. He just wants to make sure he gets what he thinks he deserves as an upper-class white male.

Lesbians and gay men of color have been trying to push the gay movement to grasp the necessity of antiracist practice for nigh on twenty years. Except in the context of organizing within the women's movement with progressive white lesbian feminists, we haven't made much progress.

I'm particularly struck by the fact that for the most part queer theory and queer politics, which are currently so popular, offer neither substantial antiracist analysis nor practice. Queer activists' understanding of how to deal with race is usually limited to their including a few lesbians or gay men of color in their ranks, who are expected to carry out the political agenda that the white majority has already determined.

In October 1993, Lesbian Avengers from New York City traveled to several states in the Northeast on what they called a "freedom ride." Lesbians of color from Albany, New York, pointed out that the appropriation of this term was offensive because the organization had not demonstrated involvement in antiracist organizing and had made few links with people of color, including nonlesbians and nongays in the communities they planned to visit. Even when we explained that calling themselves "freedom riders" might negatively affect the coalitions we've been working to build with people of color in Albany, the group kept the name and simply made a few token changes in their press release.

These divisions are particularly dangerous at a time when the white right wing has actually targeted people of color with their homophobic message. As white lesbian activist Suzanne Pharr points out in an excellent article, "Racist Politics and Homophobia":

> Community by community, the religious Right works skillfully to divide us along fissures that already exist. It is as though they have a political seismograph to locate the racism and sexism in the lesbian and gay community, the sexism and homophobia in communities of color. While the Right is *united* by their racism, sexism, and homophobia in their goal to dominate all of us, we are divided by our own racism, sexism, and homophobia.[1]

The right's divisive strategy of enlisting the black community's support for their homophobic campaign literally hit home for me in June 1993. A black lesbian who lives in Cleveland, Ohio, where I grew up, called to tell me that a group of black ministers had placed a virulently homophobic article in the *Call and Post*, Cleveland's black newspaper.

Entitled "The Black Church Position Statement on Homosexuality," the ministers condemn "HOMOSEXUALITY (including bisexual as well as gay or lesbian sexual activity) as a lifestyle that is contrary to the teachings of the Bible." Although they claim to have tolerance and compassion for homosexuals, their ultimate goal is to bring about "restoration," that is, changing lesbians and gays back into heterosexuals in order "to restore such individuals back into harmony with God's will." One of the several sources they cite to prove that such "restoration" is possible is the *Traditional Values Foundation Talking Points, 1993*, a publication of the Traditional Values Coalition.

The ministers also held a meeting and announced their goal to gather 100,000 signatures in Cleveland in opposition to the federal civil rights bill, HB 431, and to take their campaign to

Detroit and Pittsburgh. A major spokesperson for the ministers, Reverend Marvin McMichol, is the minister of Antioch Baptist Church, the church I was raised in and of which the women in my family were pillars. Antioch was on a number of levels one of the most progressive congregations in Cleveland, especially because of the political leadership it provided at a time when black people were not allowed to participate in any aspect of Cleveland's civic life.

McMichol states, "It is our fundamental, reasoned belief that there is no comparison between the status of blacks and women, and the status of gays and lesbians." He explains that being black or being female is an "ontological reality . . . a fact that cannot be hidden," whereas "homosexuality is a chosen lifestyle . . . defined by behavior not ontological reality."

By coincidence, I met Reverend McMichol in May when Naomi Jaffe, an activist friend from Albany, and I did a presentation on black and Jewish relations at the invitation of Cleveland's New Jewish Agenda. Antioch Baptist Church and a Jewish synagogue cosponsored the event. My cousin had informed me that McMichol was a very important person in Cleveland and that he had just stepped down as head of the NAACP. Naomi and I were struck by his coldness to us throughout the evening in sharp contrast to the kind reception we received from both the black and Jewish participants who were mostly elder women. We guessed that it was because of his homophobia and sexism. Little did we know at the time how right we were.

When I first got news of what was going on in my hometown, I was emotionally devastated. It would have been bad enough to find out about a major black-led homophobic campaign in any city in this country, but this place wasn't an abstraction, it was where I came from. It was while growing up in Cleveland that I first felt attraction toward women and it was also in Cleveland that I grasped the impossibility of ever acting on those feelings. Cleveland is a huge city with a small-town mentality. I wanted to get out even before I dreamed of using the word *lesbian* to describe who I was. College provided my escape. Now I was being challenged to deal with homophobia, dead up, in the black community at home.

I enlisted the help of the National Gay and Lesbian Task Force (NGLTF) and Scot Nakagawa who runs their Fight the Right office in Portland, Oregon, and of members of the Feminist Action Network (FAN), the multiracial political group to which I belong in Albany. Throughout the summer we were in constant contact with people in Cleveland. FAN drafted a counter-petition for them to circulate and in early September several of us went there following NGLTF's and Stonewall Cincinnati's Fight the Right Midwest Summit. Unfortunately, by the time we arrived, the group that had been meeting in Cleveland had fallen apart.

We had several meetings, primarily with black lesbians, but found very few people who were willing to confront through direct action the severe threat right in their midst. Remaining closeted, a reluctance to deal with black people in Cleveland's inner city, and the fact that Cleveland's white lesbian and gay community had never proven particularly supportive of antiracist work were all factors that hampered black lesbian and gay organizing. Ironically, racial segregation seemed to characterize the gay community, just as it did (and does) the city as a whole. The situation in Cleveland was very familiar to me, however, because I've faced many of the same roadblocks in attempts to do political work against racism and homophobia in my own community of Albany.

I cannot say that our effort to support a visible challenge to the ministers in Cleveland was particularly successful. The right wing's ability to speak to the concerns and play on the fears of those it wishes to recruit; the lack of visionary political leadership among both black and white lesbians and gays both nationally and locally; and the difficulty of countering homophobia in a black context, especially when it is justified by religious pronouncements, make this kind of organizing exceedingly hard. But we had better learn to do it quickly and extremely well if we do not want the pseudo-Christian right wing to end up running this country.

Since returning from Cleveland we have been exploring the possibility of launching a nationwide petition campaign to gather at least 100,000 signatures from black people who support lesbian and gay rights. One black woman, Janet Perkins, a heterosexual Christian who works with the Women's Project in Little Rock, Arkansas, has already spoken out. In a courageous article entitled "The Religious Right: Dividing the African American Community" Perkins takes on the ministers in Cleveland and the entire black church. She calls for black church members to practice love instead of condemnation. She writes:

> These African American ministers fail to understand they have been drawn into a plot that has as its mission to further separate, divide and place additional pressure on African Americans so they are unable to come together to work on the problems of the community . . .
>
> What is needed in our community is a unity and bond that can't be broken by anyone. We must see every aspect of our community as valuable and worth protecting, and yes we must give full membership to our sisters and brothers who are homosexual. For all these years we have seen them, now we must start to hear them and respect them for who they are.[2]

This is the kind of risk taking and integrity that makes all the difference. Perkins publicly declares herself an ally who we can depend on. I hope in the months to come the gay, lesbian, and black movements in this country will likewise challenge themselves to close this great divide, which they can only do by working toward an unbreakable unity, a bond across races, nationalities, sexual orientations, and classes that up until now our movements have never achieved.

I wrote this article for Gay Community News *in 1993. Unfortunately, the "great divide" between the lesbian and gay community and the black community has not markedly improved since then. In August 1997 Alveda King, a niece of Martin Luther King, Jr., denounced California legislation designed to crack down on an-*

tigay discrimination. She stated, "To equate homosexuality with race is to give a death sentence to civil rights."[3] A few weeks later gospel singers Angie and Debbie Winans released a song entitled "It's Not Natural" that condemned homosexuality as unnatural and antifamily. King's and the Winans's public homophobia was met with vigorous protests from black lesbians and gays from other segments of the lesbian, gay, and black communities.

In contrast, organizing among lesbian and gay people of color has flourished in the Capital Region during the same period, catalyzed in part by the racial terrorism aimed at a number of us in 1995. An umbrella coalition of four organizations, In Our Own Voices, is providing autonomous political leadership and support for people of color. Cleveland's black lesbian and gay community has made similarly significant strides with the formation of the African American Lesbian, Gay, and Bisexual Caucus in 1995 and the publication of a newsletter. The homophobic campaign initiated by black ministers in Cleveland in the summer of 1993 and the connections I began to make there with black lesbians and gays in response to this crisis, were important factors in my decision to do research in Cleveland for my study of African American lesbian and gay history.

Nationally, the National Black Lesbian and Gay Leadership Forum continues to build the scope of its critically important work. Under its auspices, the extraordinary activist Mandy Carter has traveled extensively as a field organizer to work with black lesbians and gays, especially in areas where organized homophobic campaigns are under way. The National Gay and Lesbian Task Force continues to work in coalition with communities of color. One aspect of these efforts is their annual Honoring Our Allies program which has recognized the members of the Congressional Black Caucus (who have the most consistently supportive voting record, compared to all the other members of congress, for example, Democrats or women, on legislation affecting lesbians and gays); the government of South Africa for becoming the first nation in history to protect the rights of lesbians and gays in its constitution; and Coretta Scott King for her decades as an ally to the lesbian, gay, bisexual, and transgendered community.

NOTES

1. Suzanne Pharr,"Racist Politics and Homophobia," *Transformation,* July/Aug 1993.
2. Jane Perkins, "The Religious Right," *Transformation,* Sept./Oct. 1993.
3. Cassandra Sweet, "King's Niece Denounces Gay Rights," *Associated Press,* 20 Aug. 1997.

Blacklash?

Henry Louis Gates, Jr.

For some veterans of the civil rights era, it's a matter of stolen prestige. "It is a misappropriation for members of the gay leadership to identify the April 25 march on Washington with the Rev. Dr. Martin Luther King Jr.'s 1963 mobilization," one such veteran, the Reverend Dennis G. Kuby, wrote in a letter to the editor that appeared in the *Times* on the day of the march. Four days later, testifying before the Senate Armed Services Committee's hearings on the issue of gays in the military, Lieutenant General Calvin Waller, United States Army (retired), was more vociferous. General Waller, who, as General Norman Schwarzkopf's second-in-command, was the highest-ranking black officer in the Gulf War's theatre of operations, contemptuously dismissed any linkage between the gay rights and civil rights movements. "I had no choice regarding my race when I was delivered from my mother's womb," General Waller said. "To compare my service in America's armed forces with the integration of avowed homosexuals is personally offensive to me." This sentiment—that gays are pretenders to a throne of disadvantage that properly belongs to black Americans, that their relation to the rhetoric of civil rights is one of unearned opportunism—is surprisingly widespread. "The backlash is on the streets among blacks and black pastors who do not want to be aligned with homosexuals," the Revered Lou Sheldon, chairman of the' Traditional Values Coalition, crowed to the *Times* in the aftermath of the march.

That the National Association for the Advancement of Colored People endorsed the April 25 march made the insult all the deeper for those who disparage the gay rights movement as the politics of imposture—Liberace in Rosa Parks drag. "Gays are not subject to water hoses or police dogs, denied access to lunch counters or prevented from voting," the Reverend Mr. Kuby as-

serted. On the contrary, "most gays are perceived as well educated, socially mobile and financially comfortable." Even some
of those sympathetic to gay rights are unhappy with the models
of oppression and victimhood which they take to be enshrined
in the civil rights discourse that many gay advocates have
adopted. For those blacks and whites who viewed last month's
march on Washington with skepticism, to be gay is merely an
inconvenience; to be black is to inherit a legacy of hardship and
inequity. For them, there's no comparison. But the reason the
national conversation on the subject has reached an impasse
isn't that there's simply no comparison; it's that there's no
simple comparison.

Prejudices, of course, don't exist in the abstract; they all
come with distinctive and distinguishing historical peculiarities.
In short, they have content as well as form. Underplaying the
differences blinds us to the signature traits of other forms of social hatred. Indeed, in judging other prejudices by the one you
know best you may fail to recognize those other prejudices *as*
prejudices.

To take a quick and fairly obvious example, it has been observed that while antiblack racism charges its object with inferi-
ority, anti-Semitism charges its object with iniquity. The racist
believes that blacks are incapable of running anything by themselves. The anti-Semite believes (in one popular bit of folklore)
that thirteen rabbis rule the world.

How do gays fit into this scheme? Uneasily. Take that hard-
ridden analogy between blacks and gays. Much of the ongoing
debate over gay rights has fixated, and foundered, on the vexed
distinction between "status" and "behavior." The paradox here
can be formulated as follows: Most people think of racial identity as a matter of (racial) status, but they respond to it as behavior. Most people think of sexual identity as a matter of (sexual)
behavior, but they respond to it as status. Accordingly, people
who fear and dislike blacks are typically preoccupied with the
threat that they think blacks' aggressive behavior poses to them.
Hence they're inclined to make exceptions for the kindly, "civi-

lized" blacks: that's why "the Cosby Show" could be so popular among white South Africans. By contrast, the repugnance that many people feel toward gays concerns, in the first instance, the status ascribed to them. Disapproval of a sexual practice is transmuted into the demonization of a sexual species.

In other respects, too, antigay propaganda sounds less like antiblack rhetoric than like classical anti-Jewish rhetoric: both evoke the image of the small, cliquish minority that nevertheless commands disproportionate and sinister worldly influence. More broadly, attitudes toward homosexuals are bound up with sexism and the attitudes toward gender that feminism, with impressive, though only partial, success, asks us to reexamine.

That doesn't mean that the race analogy is without merit, or that there are no relevant points of comparison. Just as blacks have historically been represented as sexually uncontrollable beasts, ready to pounce on an unwilling victim with little provocation, a similar vision of the predatory homosexual has been insinuated, often quite subtly, into the defense of the ban on gays in the military.

But can gays really claim anything like the "victim status" inherited by black Americans? "They admit to holding positions in the highest levels of power in education, government, business, and entertainment," Martin Mawyer, the president of the Christian Action Network, complains, "yet in the same breath, they claim to be suffering discrimination in employment." Actually, the question itself is a sand trap. First, why should oppression, however it's measured, be a prerequisite for legal protection? Surely there's a consensus that it would be wrongful, and unlawful, for someone to discriminate against Unitarians in housing or employment, however secure American Unitarians were as a group. Granted, no one can legislate affection or approval. But the simple fact that people enjoy legal protection from religious discrimination neither confers nor requires victimization. Why is the case of sexual orientation any different?

Second, trying to establish a pecking order of oppression is generally a waste of time: that's something we learned from a long-standing dialogue in the feminist movement. People figured out that you could speak of the subordination of women without claiming, absurdly, that every woman (Margaret Thatcher, say) was subordinate to every man. Now, the single greatest predictor of people's economic success is the economic and educational level of their parents. Because gays, like women, seem to be evenly distributed among classes and races, the compounding effect of transgenerational poverty, which is the largest factor in the relative deprivation of black America, simply doesn't apply. Much of black suffering stems from historical racism; most gay suffering stems from contemporary hatred. It's also the case that the marketing surveys showing that gays have a higher than average income and education level are generally designed to impress potential advertisers in gay publications; quite possibly, the surveys reveal the characteristics only of gays who are willing to identify themselves as such in a questionnaire. Few people would be surprised to learn that secretiveness on this matter varies inversely with education and income level.

What makes the race analogy complicated is that gays, as demographic composites, do indeed "have it better" than blacks—and yet in many ways contemporary homophobia is more virulent than contemporary racism. According to one monitoring group, one in four gay men has been physically assaulted as a result of his perceived sexual orientation; about fifty percent have been threatened with violence. (For lesbians, the incidence is lower but still disturbing.) A moral consensus now exists in this country that discriminating against blacks as teachers, priests, or tenants is simply wrong. (That doesn't mean it doesn't happen.) For much of the country , however, the moral legitimacy of homosexuals, as homosexuals, remains very much in question. When Bill Crews, for the past nine years the mayor of the well-scrubbed hamlet of Melbourne, Iowa, returned home after the April 25 march, at which he had publicly disclosed his homosexuality for the first time, he found "Melbourne hates Gays" and "No Faggots" spray-painted on his house. What makes the closet so crowded is that gays are, as a rule, still socialized—usually by their nearest and dearest—into shame.

Mainstream religious figures—ranging from Catholic archbishops to orthodox rabbis—continue to enjoin us to "hate the sin": it has been a long time since anyone respectable urged us to, as it were, hate the skin. Jimmy Swaggart, on the other hand, could assure his millions of followers that the Bible says homosexuals are "worthy of death" and get away with it. Similar access to mass media is not available to those who voice equivalent attitudes toward blacks. In short, measured by their position in society, gays on the average seem privileged relative to blacks; measured by the acceptance of hostile attitudes toward them, gays are worse off than blacks. So are they as "oppressed"? The question presupposes a measuring rod that does not and cannot exist.

To complicate matters further, disapproval of homosexuality has been a characteristic of much of the black nationalist ideology that has reappeared in the aftermath of the civil rights era. "Homosexuality is a deviation from Afrocentric thought, because it makes the person evaluate his own physical needs above the teachings of national consciousness," writes Dr. Molefi Kete Asante, of Temple University, who directs the black studies program there, one of the country's largest. Asante believes that "we can no longer allow our social lives to be controlled by European decadence," and argues that "the redemptive power of Afrocentricity" provides hope of a cure for those so afflicted, through (the formulation has a regrettably fascist ring) "the submergence of their own wills into the collective will of our people."

In the end, the plaintive rhetoric of the Reverend Mr. Kuby and those civil rights veterans who share his sense of unease is notable for a small but significant omission: any reference to those blacks who are gay. And in this immediate context one particular black gay man comes to mind. Actually, it's curious that those who feel that the example of the 1963 march on Washington has been misappropriated seem to have forgotten about him, because it was he, after all, who organized that heroic march. His name, of course, was Bayard Rustin, and it's quite likely that if he had been alive he would have attended the march on Washington thirty years later.

By a poignant historical irony, it was in no small part because of his homosexuality—and the fear that it would be used to discredit the mobilization—that Rustin was prevented from being named director of the 1963 march; the title went to A. Philip Randolph, and he accepted it only on the condition that he could then deputize Rustin to do the arduous work of coordinating the mass protest. Rustin accepted the terms readily. In 1963, it was necessary to choose which of two unreasoning prejudices to resist, and Rustin chose without bitterness or recrimination. Thirty years later, people marched so his successors wouldn't have to make that costly choice.

The Failure to Transform: Homophobia in the Black Community

Cheryl Clarke

That there is homophobia among black people in America is largely reflective of the homophobic culture in which we live. The following passage from the proposed "Family Protection Act," a venomous bill before the U.S. Congress, vividly demonstrates the depth of the ruling class" fear and hatred of homosexuals, homosexuality, and the homosexual potential in everyone (themselves included).

> No federal funds may be made available under any provision of federal law to any public or private individual, group, foundation, commission, corporation, association, or other entity for the purpose of advocating, promoting, or suggesting homosexuality, male or female, as a lifestyle.[1]

Yet, we cannot rationalize the disease of homophobia among black people as the white man's fault, for to do so is to absolve ourselves of our responsibility to transform ourselves. When I took my black lesbian feminist self to the First National Plenary Conference on Self-Determination (December 4, 5, 6, 1981) in New York City, thinking surely that this proclaimed "historic meeting of the Black Liberation Movement" must include black lesbian feminists, I was struck by a passage from the printed flyer left on every seat:

> Revolutionary nationalists and genuine communists cannot uphold homosexuality in the leadership of the Black Liberation Movement nor uphold it as a correct practice. Homosexuality is a genocidal practice . . . Homosexuality does not produce children . . . Homosexuality does not birth new warriors for liberation . . . homosexuality cannot be upheld as correct or revolutionary practice. . . . the practice of homosexuality is an accelerating threat to our survival as a people and as a nation.

Compare these two statements — the first from the ultra(white)-right and the second from self-proclaimed black "revolutionaries and genuine communists." Both reflect a decidedly similar pathology: homophobia. If I were a "revolutionary nationalist" or even a "genuine communist," I would be concerned if my political vision in any way supported the designs of my oppressors, the custodians of white male privilege. But it is these black macho intellectuals and politicos, these heirs of Malcolm X, who have never expanded Malcolm's revolutionary ideals beyond the day of his death, who consciously or unwittingly have absorbed the homophobia of their patriarchal slavemasters. It is they who attempt to propagate homophobia throughout the entire black community. And it is they whom I will address in this writing.

Since 1965, the era which marked a resurgence of radical black consciousness in the United States, many black people of the post-World War II generation began an all-consuming process of rejecting the values of WASP America and embracing our African and Afro-American traditions and culture. In complete contrast to the conservative black bourgeoisie and to bourgeois reformist civil rights proponents, the advocates of Black Power demanded progressive remedies to the accumulated ills of black folk in America, viewed racism as international in scope, rescued Afro-American culture from anonymity, and elevated the black man to the pedestal of authority in the black liberation movement. In order to participate in this movement one had to be black (of course), be male oriented, and embrace a spectrum of black nationalist, separatist, Pan Africanist sentiments, beliefs, and goals. Rejection of white people was essential as well as rejection of so-called white values, which included anything from reading Kenneth Clark's *Civilization* to eating a TV dinner.

Although the cult of Black Power spurned the assimilationist goals of the politically conservative black bourgeoisie, its devotees, nevertheless, held firmly to the value of heterosexual and male superiority. As Michele Wallace states in her controversial essay, "Black Macho" (1979):

> . . . the contemporary black man no longer exists for his people or even for himself . . . He has become a martyr. And he has arrived in this place, not because of the dependency inflicted upon him in slavery, but because his black perspective, like the white perspective, supported the notion that manhood is more valuable than anything else.[2]

It is ironic that the Black Power movement could transform the consciousness of an entire generation of black people regarding black self-determination and, at the same time, fail so miserably in understanding the sexual politics of the movement and of black people across the board.

Speaking of the "sexual-racial antagonisms" dividing the Student Nonviolent Coordinating Committee during the 1960s, Manning Marable assesses the dilemma of the black movement of that era:

> . . . The prevailing popular culture of racism, the sexist stereotypes held by black men and women, and the psychological patterns of dependency which exploitation creates over several generations could not be uprooted easily. In the end the Movement may have failed to create a new interracial society in the South because its advocates had first failed to transform themselves.[3]

Like all Americans, black Americans live in a sexually repressive culture. And we have made all manner of compromise regarding our sexuality in order to live here. We have expended much energy trying to debunk the racist mythology which says our sexuality is depraved. Unfortunately, many of us have overcompensated and assimilated the Puritan value that sex is for procreation, occurs only between men and women, and is only valid within the confines of heterosexual marriage. And, of course, like everyone else in America who is ambivalent in these respects, black folk have to live with the contradictions of this limited sexual system by repressing or closeting any other sexual/erotic urges, feelings, or desires.

Dennis Altman, in his pivotal work, *Homosexuality: Oppression and Liberation* (1971), says the following of Western culture:

> The repression of polymorphous perversity in Western societies has two major components: the removal of the erotic from all areas of life other than the explicitly sexual and the denial of our inherent bisexuality.[4]

That Western culture is limiting, few can deny. A tremendous amount of pressure is brought to bear on men, women, and children to be heterosexual to the exclusion of every other erotic impulse. I do not begrudge heterosexuals their right to express themselves, but rabid sexual preference is a stone drag on anybody's part. That the black community is homophobic and rabidly heterosexual is a reflection of the black movement's failure to "transform" its proponents with regard to the boundless potential of human sexuality. And this failure has prevented critical collaboration with politically motivated black lesbians and gay men. Time and again homophobia sabotages coalitions, divides would-be comrades, and retards the mental restructuring, essential to revolution, which black people need so desperately.

The concept of the black family has been exploited since the publication of the infamous Moynihan report, *The Negro Family: A Case for National Action* (1965). Because the insular, privatized nuclear family is upheld as the model of Western family stability, all other forms—for example, the extended family, the female-headed family, the lesbian family—are devalued. Many black people, especially middle-class black people, have accepted the male-dominated nuclear family model, though we have had to modify it because black women usually must work outside the home. Though "revolutionary nationalists and genuine communists" have not accepted the nuclear family model per se, they have accepted African and Eastern patriarchal forms of the family, including polygamy (offering the specious rationalization that there are more black women than black men). Homosexuality is viewed as a threat to the continued existence of the heterosexual family, because homosexual unions do not, in and of themselves, produce offspring—as if one's only function within a family, within a relationship, or in sex were to produce offspring. Black family lifestyles and homosexual lifestyles are not antithetical. Most black lesbians and gay men grew up in families and are still critically involved with their families. Many black lesbians and gay men are raising children. Why must the black family be so strictly viewed as the result of a heterosexual dyad? And finally, why is the black male so-called left so vehement in its propagation of these destructive beliefs, and why have its proponents given such relentless expression to the homophobic potential in the mass of black people? Because the participation of open black lesbians and gay men in the black so-called liberation movement is a threat to the continued hegemony of dogmatic, doctrinaire black men who have failed to reject the Western institution of heterosexuality and the Christian fundamentalist notion of sex as "sin," no matter what doctrine or guru they subscribe to. Homophobic black intellectuals and politicos are so charged with messianic fervor that they seem like a perversion of the W. E. B. Du Bois concept of the "Talented Tenth," the hypothesis that "the Negro race . . . is going to be saved by its exceptional men." Indeed, this homophobic cult of black men seems to view itself as the "exceptional men" who will save the black liberation movement from homosexual "contamination." Furthermore, the black intellectual/political man, by dint of his knowledge, training, and male privilege—and in spite of racism—has access to numerous bourgeois resources (such as television, radio, the stage, the podium, publications, and schools) whereby he can advance his reactionary ideologies and make his opinions known to the public at large.

Let us examine the rhetoric and ravings of a few notable black heterosexuals.

Chairman Baraka, Imamu Baraka, LeRoi Jones—whatever patriarchal designation he assumes—is a rabid homophobe. Wherever he makes his homophobic statements, his sexist invective is not far behind. From his early works on, this chameleon, the patriarch of the "new black poetry" of the 1960s, has viewed homosexuality as a symbol of a decadent establishment, as defectiveness, as weakness, as a strictly white male flaw.

In his first book of poems, *Preface to a Twenty Volume Suicide Note* (1961), in which he reveals himself as a versatile though imitative poet, Jones is homophobic and woman hating. In a wildly imagistic poem, "To a Publisher . . . cut out," he free-associates:

> . . . Charlie Brown spent most of his time whacking his doodle, or having weird relations with that dopey hound of his (though that's a definite improvement over . . . that filthy little lesbian he's hung up with).[5]

In the same poem, Jones debunks the myth of the black woman's superior sexual prowess: "I have slept with almost every mediocre colored woman/On 23rd St. . . . [6]

In his notorious essay "American Sexual Reference: Black Male" (1965), Jones lays the ultimate disparagement on the American white man and white woman:

> Most American white men are trained to be fags. . . . That red flush, those silk blue faggot eyes. So white women become men-things, a weird combination sucking male juices to build a navel orange, which is themselves.[7]

But Jones is at his heterosexist best in the essay "Black Woman" (1971), which should have been titled, "One Black Macho Man's Narcissistic Fantasy." He commands the black woman, with arrogant condescension, to "complement" her man, to "inspire" her man.[8] He is laughable in his smugness, his heterosexist presumptions—to say nothing of his obvious contempt for women. It seems that his homophobic and misogynist attitudes have not abated since he embraced Marxism. LeRoi-Imamu-Chairman-Jones-Baraka is an irreversible homophobe. Methinks he protests too much.

In another classic example of sixties-style black woman ha-

tred, playwright Ed Bullins attempts a portrayal of a lesbian relationship in *Clara's Ole Man* (1965).[9] The action is set in the
North Philadelphia flat of Clara and Big Girl, Clara's "ole man"
who is stereotypically "butch." Clara and Big Girl are not disparaged by their "ghetto" community, symbolized by two older,
alcoholic black women who stay upstairs and by three juvenile
delinquents, Stoogie, Bama, and Hoss, who take refuge from a
police chase in the couple's apartment, a familiar haunt. It is
only Jack, an outsider and an ex-marine in pursuit of upward
mobility through "college prep courses," who is too narcissistic
to understand the obvious bond between the two women. Jack,
whose intention is to date Clara, "retches" when he realizes
Clara and big Girl are lovers. *Clara's Ole Man* is a substanceless
rendering of the poor black community, a caricature of lesbianism, and a perpetuation of the stereotype of the pathological
black community. But Ed Bullins gained a great deal of currency
among black and white "avant-garde" intellectuals for his ability
to replicate and create caricatures of black life.

In that same year (1965), a pivotal year in the political development of black people, Calvin Hernton discusses the interre-
lationship of sex and racism in his popular book, *Sex and
Racism in America.* Hernton does not address the issue of homosexuality in any of his four essays, "The White Woman,"
"The Negro Male," "The White Male," and "The Negro
Woman." In several homophobic asides Hernton is alternately
dismayed by, presumptuous about, and intrigued by his obser-
vations of homosexual behavior:

> The extent to which some white women are attracted to Negro lesbians
> is immensely revealing — even the Negro lesbian is a "man." It is not an
> uncommon sight (in Greenwich Village, for instance) to see these
> "men" exploiting this image of themselves to the zenith.[10]
>
> . . . One man who seemed *effeminate* put coins into the jukebox,
> *swished* along side of me.[11]
>
> He had the appearance of a businessman or a politician — except
> for his eyes, which seemed to hold some dark secret, something in
> them that made me wonder . . . maybe this man was a homo-
> sexual.[12]

We can see from the few passages cited above that homophobia in the black community has not only a decidedly bourgeois character but also a markedly male imprint. Which is not to say, however, that homophobia is limited to the psyche of the black intellectual male, but only that it is he who institutionalizes the illness within our political/intellectual community. And rest assured, we can find his homophobic counterpart in black women, who are, for the most part, afraid of risking the displeasure of their homophobic brothers were they to address, seriously and in a principled way, homosexuality. Black bourgeois female intellectuals practice homophobia by omission more often than rabid homophobia.

Michele Wallace's *Black Macho and the Myth of the Superwoman* is a most obvious example. This brave and scathing analysis of the sexual politics of the black political community after 1965 fails to treat the issues of gay liberation, black lesbianism, or homophobia vis-à-vis the black liberation or the women's liberation movement. In "Black Macho," the opening essay, Wallace addresses the homophobia of Eldridge Cleaver and Amiri Baraka, but she neither calls it "homophobia" nor criticizes these attitudes as a failing of the black liberation movement. For the sake of her own argument regarding the black macho neurosis, Wallace exploits the popular conception of homosexuality as passivity, the willingness to be fucked (preferably by a white man, according to Cleaver). It is then seen as antithetical to the concept of black macho, the object of which is to do the fucking. Wallace does not debunk this stereotype of male homosexuality. In her less effective essay, "The Myth of the Superwoman," Wallace omits any mention of black lesbians. In 1979, when asked at a public lecture at Rutgers University in New Jersey why the book had not addressed the issues of homosexuality and homophobia, the author responded that she was not an "expert" on either issue. But Wallace, by her own admission, was also not an "expert" on the issues she *did* address in her book.

The black lesbian is not only absent from the pages of black political analysis, her image as a character in literature and her role as a writer are blotted out from or trivialized in literary criticism written by black women. Mary Helen Washington's otherwise useful anthologies are a prime example of this omission of black lesbianism and black lesbian writers. In both *Black Eyed Susans* (1975) and *Midnight Birds* (1980), the editor examines the varied roles black women have played in the black community and how these roles are more authentically depicted in the fiction of black women than in the fiction of black men.

In her introduction to *Midnight Birds*, Washington speaks of the major themes of the material presented in this anthology: "women's reconciliation with one another," antagonism with men, "areas of commonality among black and white women." Now, one would think with all the mention of these women-identified themes that there would be a lesbian story or two in the anthology. But, again, we are disappointed. There is no mention of lesbianism in the introduction, there are no open lesbian contributors to the anthology, and there is no lesbian story in the collection. And yet, we know there is certainly plenty of available work by black lesbian writers. For example, Audre Lorde's lesbian fiction piece, "Tar Beach," which appeared in *Conditions: Five, The Black Women's Issue* in 1979 — prior to the publication of *Midnight Birds* — would have powerfully enhanced the collection. Washington knows that black lesbian writers exist. In a footnote to the previously mentioned introduction,[13] Washington credits Barbara Smith's essay, "Toward a Black Feminist Criticism" in *Conditions: Two* (1977), as one of two pieces of writing which has challenged and shaped her thinking. Smith is a lesbian and she writes about lesbianism. The other piece Washington refers to, Adrienne Rich's "Disloyal to Civilization: Feminism, Racism, Gynephobia" is written by a lesbian as well.[14]

One of the most recent books to appear in the name of feminism is bell hooks' *Ain't I A Woman: Black Women and Feminism*. Hooks seems to purposely ignore the existence and central contributions of black lesbians to the feminist movement. Aside from a gross lack of depth in her analysis of the current women's movement in America, the most resounding shortcoming of this work of modern feminism is its omission of any discussion of lesbian feminism, the radicalizing impact of which distinguishes this era of feminism from the previous eras. Hooks does not even mention the word *lesbian* in her book. This is unbearable. Ain't lesbians women, too? Homophobia in the black movement and in the women's movement is not treated, yet lesbians historically have been silenced and repressed in both. In her statement, "Attacking heterosexuality does little to strengthen the self-concept of the masses of women who desire to be with men,"[15] hooks delivers a backhanded slap at lesbian feminists, a considerable number of whom are black. Hooks would have done well to attack the institution of heterosexuality, as it is a prime tool of black women's oppression in America. Like the previously discussed writers, hooks fears alienating the black community cum the black bourgeois intellectual/political establishment. And there is the fear of transformation, the fear that the word will generate the deed. Like her black male counterpart, the black woman intellectual is afraid to relinquish heterosexual privilege. So little else is guaranteed black people.

I must confess that, in spite of the undeniably homophobic pronouncements of black intellectuals, I sometimes become impatient with the accusations of homophobia hurled at the black community by many gay men and lesbians, as if the whole black community were more homophobic than the heterosexist culture we live in. The entire black community gets blamed for the reactionary postures of a few petite bourgeois intellectuals and politicos. Because no one has bothered to study the black community's attitudes on homosexuals, homosexuality, or homosexual lifestyles, it is not accurate to attribute homophobia to the mass of black people.

Prior to the growth of the contemporary black middle class, which has some access to the white world, the black community—because of segregation North and South—was even

more diverse, encompassing a world of black folk of every persuasion, profession, status, and lifestyle. There have always
been upwardly mobile blacks, but until the late 1950s and early
sixties there had never been so many opportunities to reap the
tenuous fruits of affluence outside the traditional black community. The cordoning off of all types of black people into a single
community because of race may be one influence on black attitudes toward difference.

The poor and working-class black community, historically
more radical and realistic than the reformist and conservative
black middle class and the atavistic, "blacker than thou" (bourgeois) nationalists, has often tolerated an individual's lifestyle
prerogatives, even when that lifestyle was disparaged by the prevailing culture. Though lesbians and gay men were exotic subjects of curiosity, they were accepted as part of the community
(neighborhood) — or at least, there were no manifestos calling
for their exclusion from the community.

I can recall being about twelve years old when I first saw a
black lesbian couple. I was walking down the street with my best
friend, Kathy. I saw two young women walking together in the
opposite direction. One wore a doo-rag, a Banlon button-down,
and high-top sneakers. The other woman wore pink brush roll-
ers, spit curls plastered with geech, an Oxford-tailored shirt, a
mohair sweater, fitted skirt with a kick pleat, black stockings,
and the famous I. Miller flat, sling-back shoe, the most prestigious pair of kicks any Dee Cee black girl could own. I asked
Kathy, "Who are they?" "Bulldaggers," she answered. "What's
that?" I asked again. "You know, they go with each other,"
Kathy responded. "Why?" I continued. "Protection," Kathy
said casually. "Protection?" I repeated. "Yeah, at least they
won't get pregnant," Kathy explained.

It is my belief that poor black communities have often accepted those who would be outcast by the ruling culture — many
times to spite the white man, but mainly because the conditions
of our lives have made us empathic. And, as it stands now, the
black political community seems bereft of that humanity which

has always been a tradition among Afro-American freedom fighters, the most illustrious of whom have come from the grass-roots.

As a group and as individuals, black lesbians and gay men — sometimes obvious and sometimes not — have been as diverse as the communities we've lived in. Like most other people, we have been workers, church-goers, parents, hustlers, and upwardly mobile. Since black gay men and lesbians have always been viable contributors to our communities, it is exceedingly painful for us to face public denunciation from black folk — the very group who should be championing our liberation. And because of the level of homophobia in the culture in general, many black gay men and lesbians remain in the closet, passing as heterosexuals. Thus, when public denunciations of our lifestyles are made by other black people, we remain silent in the face of their hostility and ignorance. The toll taken on us because we repress our rage and hurt makes us distrustful of all people whom we cannot identify as lesbian or gay. Also, for those of us who are isolated from the gay or lesbian community, the toll is greater self-hate, self-blame, and belief in the illness theory of homosexuality.

In the face of this, open and proud black gay men and lesbians must take an assertive stand against the blatant homophobia expressed by members of the black intellectual and political community, who consider themselves custodians of the revolution. For if we will not tolerate the homophobia of the culture in general, we cannot tolerate it from black people, no matter what their positions in the black liberation movement. Homophobia is a measure of how far removed we are from the psychological transformation we so desperately need to engender. The expression of homophobic sentiments, the threatening political postures assumed by black radicals and progressives of the nationalist/communist ilk, and the seeming lack of any willingness to understand the politics of gay and lesbian liberation collude with the dominant white male culture to repress not only gay men and lesbians, but also to repress a natural part of all human beings, namely the bisexual potential in us all. Homophobia divides black people as political allies, it cuts off political growth, stifles revolution, and perpetuates patriarchal domination.

The arguments I have presented are not definitive. I hope that others may take some of the issues raised in this essay into consideration for further study. The sexual politics of the black liberation movement have yet to be addressed by its advocates. We will continue to fail to transform ourselves until we reconcile the unequal distribution of power in our political community accorded on the basis of gender and sexual choice. Visions of black liberation which exclude lesbians and gay men bore and repel me, for as a black lesbian I am obligated and dedicated to destroying heterosexual supremacy by "suggesting, promoting, and advocating" the rights of gay men and lesbians wherever we are. And we are everywhere. As political black people, we bear the twin responsibilities of transforming the social, political, and economic systems of oppression as they affect all our people—not only the heterosexuals—and of transforming the corresponding psychological structure that feeds into these oppressive systems. The more homophobic we are as a people the further removed we are from any kind of revolution. Not only must black lesbians and gay men be committed to destroying homophobia, but *all* black people must be committed to working out and rooting out homophobia by engaging in dialogue with the advocates of gay and lesbian liberation, educating ourselves about gay and lesbian politics, confronting and correcting homophobic attitudes, and understanding how these attitudes prevent the liberation of the total being.

NOTES

1. U.S. Congress, *Family Protection Act,* 1981, S. 1378, H.R. 3955 , 9.
2. Michele Wallace, *Black Macho and the Myth of the Superwoman* (New York: Dial Press, 1979), 79.
3. Manning Marable, *From the Grassroots* (New York: Challenge Press, 1980), 125.
4. Dennis Altman, *Homosexuality: Oppression and Liberation* (New York: New York University Press, 1971), 79.

5. LeRoi Jones, *Preface to a Twenty Volume Suicide Note* (New York: Totem/Corinth, 1961), 19.

6. Ibid.

7. LeRoi Jones, "American Sexual Reference: Black Male," *Home* (New York: William Morrow and Co., Inc., 1966), 216.

8. Imamu Amiri Baraka, "Black Woman," *Raise Race Rays Raze: Essays Since 1965* (New York: Random House, 1971).

9. Ed Bullins, *Five Plays by Ed Bullins* (New York: Bobbs-Merrill Co., Inc., 1968).

10. Calvin Hernton, *Sex and Racism in America* (New York: Grove press, 1965), 113.

11. Ibid., 114.

12. Ibid., 89. Emphasis added.

13. Mary Helen Washington, *Midnight Birds* (New York: Anchor Books, 1980), xxv.

14. Adrienne Rich, "Disloyal to Civilization: Feminism, Racism, Gynephobia," *On Lies, Secrets, and Silence* (New York: W.W. Norton, 1979).

15. bell hooks, *Ain't I A Woman: Black Women and Feminism* (Boston: South End Press, 1981), 191.

Race and the Invisible Dyke

Mab Segrest

> *I am an invisible man . . . I am invisible, understand, simply be-*
> *cause people refuse to see me. . . . When people approach me, they see*
> *only my surroundings, themselves, or figments of their imagination—*
> *indeed, everything and anything except me.*
> —Ralph Ellison, *The Invisible Man*

I didn't know the word "homosexual" until I read it when I was eleven or twelve, in the early 1960s, in an article in *Life* magazine, one of the first treatments of the urban gay sub-culture in the mainstream media. In the back corner of my brain in which I allowed such conversations, it occurred to me that the word might explain a lot. But my problem was not that I was not seen; more that I was not named. Or, the names available carried such lethal stigma. Queer: alone, outside community, outside family, outside love, the only one. Genuine invisibility would have been a relief; instead, I had my painfully visible efforts at invisibility, futile efforts to suck all my energy back in: a child of the universe, trying to be a black hole. I had little means to figure the "curious abrupt questions [that] stirred within me," as the great faggot poet of democracy Walt Whitman wrote, questions of how "I had received identity in my body,/that I was I knew was of my body, and what I knew I should be I knew I should be of my body."[1]

So the struggle to fix elusive language to the slippery category of sexual identity has been a central preoccupation of my life, as it has been of many lesbians and gay men of my generation. It is a struggle I enter into again with the drafts of this text, long over-due but still littering my study unfinished; I shuffle through them in the early hours of the morning, trying to remember what it was I meant to say. This morning I pull out Eve Sedgwick's *Epistemology of the Closet* and recall that I had wanted to extend her project of developing an "alternative analytical axis — call it sexuality."[2]

Sedgwick distinguishes sexuality ("an array of acts, expectations, narratives, pleasures, identity-formations and knowledges . . . that tends to cluster most densely around certain genital sensations") from gender ("rigidly dichotomized social production and reproduction of male and female identities and behaviors"),[3] into which it easily slips. My difficulty, I realize, is to distinguish sexuality from race (a rigidly dichotomized social production and reproduction of white and "colored" identities and behaviors), a particularity of my location as a southern woman born circa 1949.

As an adolescent, with no one available to translate for or with me the language of my body, I began to translate it myself into the language of race. African Americans all around me were rising against ontological erasure as much as they were against Jim Crow. When I was thirteen in 1963 I lay on my belly underneath some shrubs to watch several black children my age walk across the breezeway at my high school, surrounded by hundreds of state troopers sent by George Wallace to keep my school from integrating. I have circled back many times to my moment of identity with the three black children inside the circle of force, a "queer" empathy with their aloneness. It has since occurred to me that they might instead have felt a huge sense of power and pride together at having braved the troopers, after the President of the United States threatened to federalize the National Guard in their behalf. But to me, they were lonely because I was lonely and we were all surrounded by mirrors of hard distorting glass.

I saw also, clearly, how race and sex and white people's confusions about both were hopelessly intermingled. Even from within my white family, I could see that the black uprising all around me was deeply spiritual in its challenge to the morality of white supremacist culture. But I heard white people defending that culture by attacking the sexual morality of the civil rights movement. The Selma to Montgomery march, one of the great ethical pilgrimages of the twentieth century, was dismissed as an occasion for white nuns to have sex with black men on the state capitol grounds, leaving used condoms in the bushes. Viola Luizzo, the white woman from Detroit who was murdered by Klansmen driving marchers back from Montgomery, was dismissed as a whore. Even at thirteen, it was clear to me that part of the struggle was over contending views of righteousness: a prurient and constrictive sexual ethic that could be used to justify murder over against an expansive ethic of liberation that was challenging deep violence in the culture.[4]

In the years after this, as a generation of lesbians and gay men have gained our own acknowledged presence and language, I have found myself puzzled and frustrated at how the movement against homophobia and heterosexism and for gay/lesbian liberation could grow up often so seemingly separate from the movement against racism and for the liberation of people of color. Indeed, there is a vocal presence in both communities conniving to maintain the separation. For example, Andrew Sullivan, a senior editor at *The New Republic* and most recent poster boy for that cliché, the affluent white gay male, wrote, "The truth is, our position [as gay people] is far worse than that of any ethnic minority or heterosexual women," a sentence the syntax of which makes gay and ethnic minorities mutually exclusive and the content of which shows his oblivion to any reality that is not white. On the other side of the barricade, the Reverend Marvin McMichol, a black minister in Cleveland, asserts: "It is our fundamental, reasoned belief that there is no comparison between the status of blacks and women, and the status of gays and lesbians," the former being "an ontological reality . . . a fact that cannot be hidden"; the latter being "a chosen lifestyle . . . defined by behavior." Reverend McMichol likewise obliterates the womanness of lesbians and the existence of lesbian and gay people of color, illustrating his oblivion to the gay reality he presumes to define.[5]

The Christian right's "wedge strategies" feed such definitional schisms, most viciously in the video *Gay Rights/Special Rights*, which uses such devotees of black freedom struggles as

Mississippi Senator Trent Lott and Reagan's Attorney General Ed Meese (who did as much as he could to dismantle affirmative action) to argue that because gayness is behavior based, gay people do not deserve or need civil rights protections. These are reserved for minorities whose identities are based on "immutable characteristics." The video uses black spokespeople to reinforce the white message that gay people have "hijacked" the civil rights movement, which has in fact been subjected to decades of terrorist attack by the likes of Lott and Meese.[6]

I am puzzled, as always, by the opposition of blackness and gayness: "the fact (of skin pigment) that cannot be hidden" (McMichol) versus "the open secret . . . the epistemology of the closet (Sedgwick)." Of course, it's not so simple. Blackness signifies much more than dark skin, given the sexual history of slavery, in which any slavemaster had sexual access to black women, and any offspring "followed the condition of the mother" into slavery, however light the child's skin. Passing as white under a regime of white supremacy was every bit as much a temptation and strategy as passing as straight under heterosexist regimes, and neither comes without cost.

Nor is "invisibility" only a category of gay life. Ralph Ellison begins his classic novel in my hometown of Tuskegee, Alabama, with a metaphor I totally understand: "I am an invisible man." Racism, like homophobia, is predicated on ontological erasure, an invisibility located not so much in the "biochemical accident of my epidermis," as Ellison's narrator explains, as in the eye and consciousness of the racist (or homophobic) beholder, "a matter of the construction of their inner eye."

"I am invisible, understand, simply because people refuse to see me. . . ." writes Ellison. "When people approach me, they see only my surroundings, themselves, or figments of their imagination—indeed, everything and anything except me."[7] Like Ellison, as a child in Tuskegee I knew there was something about me, elusive as fog, that people around me acted out of but never explained. I wondered "whether [I wasn't] simply a figure in a nightmare which the sleeper tries with all his strength to destroy." People bumped against me and my aching need to convince myself that I "existed in the world, part of all the sound and anguish" of having and of being a body.

Racism in the gay community and homophobia in the black community are realities, as are the deliberately divisive tactics of the right. But is there also something in the category of "civil rights" that causes confusion and disjunction about the complexity of "having and being a body"? Have the praxes of our movements—their political discourse of civil rights and related strategies of legal protection—somehow hijacked us all?

It is no accident that the civil rights movement gave me ways to understand my sexuality. "Civil rights" is the dominant discourse—which is to say the most complex embodiment of identity, intersection, and disjunction—for translating among race, gender, and sexual orientation in the twentieth-century United States. The civil rights movement was the mid-twentieth-century incarnation of four hundred years of freedom struggles of African people on this continent. The struggle against slavery—the racism that generated it and that it in turn generated—encompassed slave resistance and rebellion; the abolition movement; the Civil War; the brief period of Reconstruction when there was a glimmer of a possibility of racial and economic democracy; the reinstitution of white supremacy with Jim Crow segregation, voter disenfranchisement, and the racist terrorism of lynching and the Klan at the end of the nineteenth century. In 1954, *Brown v. Board of Education* challenged school segregation, and campaigns across the South targeted segregated public facilities such as buses and restaurants and hotels. Highly visible campaigns in Birmingham and Selma resulted in the two civil rights acts that by 1965 opened up the vote and eliminated the legally enforced systems of segregation put in place at the beginning of the century.

When I encountered the civil rights movement from beneath the bushes looking out at my former high school at thirteen, its impact to me was revolutionary. Not that this movement was monolithic. We knew there was King and the Southern Christian Leadership Conference leading the demonstrations in Selma; young SNCC workers were attempting to integrate our churches and registering poor black voters out in the country, a strategy at odds with the more black middle-class emphasis of the Tuskegee Improvement Association; the Black Panthers were rumored to be stealing weapons out of the National Guard Armory, stockpiling them, we feared, for open warfare. But it was all "radical" to me, because it shook my culture and my family to the root, because our racism went that deep. I left Alabama after undergraduate school, fleeing the racism as much as the (still unnamed) homophobia. I went to graduate school, came out as a lesbian, and in the 1980s started a "career" in political organizing. Second-wave feminism had given me the context to come out finally as a lesbian; and I learned how women's struggles grew up within, alongside, and at times in opposition to black struggles.

Now, in the 1980s and 1990s, after nearly twenty years of activism, I hear that gay people such as myself are "hijacking" the civil rights movement.

Lesbian and gay movements from the 1970s to this day do make claims using civil rights laws and legal concepts that emerged from antiracist struggles. The movement against hate violence is one example of the efforts to extend "civil rights" to include sexual orientation. During the 1980s, a group of activists—of whom I was one—worked with North Carolinians Against Racist and Religious Violence to document an epidemic of racist and homophobic violence. We also worked in communities under Klan siege and pressured law enforcement to bring perpetrators of hate violence to justice. At the same time, The Center for Constitutional Law pioneered a legal strategy against white supremacist groups and racist attackers using the anti-Klan statutes and the Fourteenth Amendment.

All of the federal protections, such as they were, applied to race, and none to sexual orientation. In 1983, moreover, national civil rights groups generally did not include homophobic violence in discussions of "hate violence," a discourse that was emerging as the Reagan administration's effects became more deadly. In North Carolina we could handily document hundreds of brutal acts perpetrated against blacks, Native Americans, gay people, and Jews. Violence was the bloody common thread among stigmatized identities. A profusion of white supremacist groups marched throughout the state with their pedagogy of hate, explicating the links among queers, kikes, niggers, commies, and so forth.

Kevin Berrill was doing his ground-breaking work on antigay violence with the National Gay and Lesbian Task Force, documentation that would lead the Reagan Justice Department to conclude, then censor the conclusion, that homosexuals were the most frequent victims of hate crimes. The Center for Democratic Renewal was able to link homophobia to the range of hate crimes,[8] and other national monitoring and response groups followed suit. In 1990, a civil rights coalition in which the National Gay and Lesbian Task Force played a major role lobbied Congress to pass the Hate Crimes Statistics Act. "It was the first measure to put the federal government on the record as opposing violence against gay men and lesbians in any way," Urvashi Vaid, then Director of NGLTF, explains.[9] It was an important victory, albeit a symbolic one, since being counted for a hate crime was not the same as being protected against one. Moreover, the measure has had the long-term, negative effect of putting the definition of the problem into increasingly conservative federal hands.

National gay rights organizations in the 1970s lobbied to get a Gay Rights Bill introduced into Congress, the passage of which would give lesbians and gay men protections against homophobic discrimination that was similar to gender and race: discrimination in employment, public housing, and access to public facilities; and against hate violence. Failing to secure the bill's passage, gay lobbyists have whittled this down to a bill outlawing job discrimination based on homophobia/heterosexism. In 1997, it came within one vote of passing in the House. Gay civil rights strategies have moved more successfully at the municipal level, where many cities passed ordinances including gay people as a protected class. It was these successes that the right targeted in a series of ballot initiatives pioneered in such places as Oregon and Colorado, with the arguments that gayness was a "behavior-based lifestyle" and thus any rights we might gain were "special rights."

Pressing myself to understand the historical nexus in which antiracist advances became available to antihomophobic struggles, in 1994 I went to a local bookstore and bought two textbooks on constitutional law and read the rights sections through. I saw how the particular struggles of African Americans that resulted in the Thirteenth, Fourteenth, and Fifteenth amendments have repeatedly resulted in the codification of legal concepts that have extended far beyond the African American community to other groups. In 1954, *Hernandez v. Texas* explained, "Community prejudices are not static, and from time to time other differences from the community norm may define other groups which need the same protection. The Fourteenth Amendment is not directed solely against discrimination . . . based upon differences between 'white' and 'Negro.'"[10] While some of these groups are also economically exploited (such as other people of color and women), people in other categories have rights protected without necessarily having a group history of economic exploitation or what *Gay Rights/Special Rights* called "immutable characteristics." Any group seeking to use the Fourteenth Amendment to gain constitutional status must, by definition, compare itself to African Americans to get in the door of the Constitution.[11]

In 1995, the Supreme Court's decision in *Romer v. Evans* finally acknowledged the Fourteenth Amendment rights of lesbians and gay male citizens. The Supreme Court declared that gay people are not "strangers to the law." Justice Kennedy wrote, "We find nothing special in the protections Amendment 2 withholds. These are protections taken for granted by most people either because they already have them or do not need them; these are protections against exclusion from an almost limitless number of transactions and endeavors that constitute ordinary civil life in a free society." Constitutional experts were quick to explain that the ruling does not necessarily challenge the current policy on homosexuals in the military or the question of "gay marriage," nor did it provide affirmative rights for gay people.[12]

The civil rights paradigm fits gay experience at the points where that experience intersects with the experience of women and people of color. "Equal protection" arguments can apply for lesbians and gay men to discrimination in housing and jobs and freedom from hate violence; to police brutality and political repression, all of which are also tactics used against people of color. Sodomy laws in half the states (and all the southern states) make lesbians and gay men second-class citizens, also by my way of thinking a violation of equal protection, although they were upheld in *Hardwick v. Bowers* in 1986, a case from Georgia.

But there are also places where gay experience does not fit the historic experience of the African American community about which much of the civil rights language emerged. Visible lesbian and gay communities and political movements are fairly recent developments in the United States. Gay people as gay people did not need the Thirteenth Amendment, through which African Americans won their centuries-long struggle to abolish slavery. Although many white lesbians and gay men are subjected to employment discrimination, being born into straight families has protected us from being ghettoized as a super-exploited class over decades and generations, as had often happened with people of color, so that there is less of a case, in my opinion, for affirmative action for gay people. Gay people likewise did not need the Fifteenth Amendment's protection of voting, because gay people as such have never been legally prohibited from voting although lesbians as women have and lesbian and gay African Americans and Indians have as people of color.

Urvashi Vaid argues that the shift to a "rights-based movement" from earlier "liberation-based" gay and lesbian movement was inherently conservative, a mainstreaming strategy aimed at winning acceptance on heterosexual terms. Vaid sees the more conservative "civil rights strategy" moving gay and lesbian liberation away from a more radical integration of gay people into the broad movements for social change that emerged from the 1960s—ironically, the very movements that gave birth to the terms of the civil rights strategy. Civil rights strategies consolidated gay people as an identity (read "minority") group rather than looking—as the early liberation thrust did—at sexuality as a shaper of various and fluid sexual identities.

Lesbian and gay movements made claims using many laws and legal concepts that emerged from antiracist struggles at the same time that increasingly conservative courts were erasing those civil rights. Simultaneously, legal scholars of color began to challenge seriously the reigning legal ideologies about race built in the 1960s and 1970s. "Critical race theorists" such as Derrick Bell, Richard Delgado, Mari Matsuda, and Kimberlé Crenshaw began to chart the coopting of the radical legal tradition of the civil rights movement:

> Racial justice was embraced in the American mainstream in terms that excluded radical or fundamental challenges to status quo institutional practices in American society by treating the exercise of racial power as rare and aberrational rather than as systemic and ingrained. . . . Along with the suppression of explicit white racism (the widely celebrated aim of civil rights reform), the dominant legal conception of racism as a discrete and identifiable act of prejudice based on skin color placed virtually the entire range of everyday social practice in America—social practices developed and maintained throughout the period of formal American apartheid—beyond the scope of critical examination or legal remediation.[13]

Not coming from contexts of struggle, many middle- class white gay people did not realize how fragile were the gains to people of color given a virulent racist backlash and a declining economy.

Within the range of "everyday social practice" in America that lies beyond race and gender-based antidiscrimination law are also most elements of the messy question of sex. How can gay people persuade others to pass a federal law protecting our civil rights when they are wondering whether we eat shit and rape children, as right-wing videos suggest? How do we have that conversation in any public way, on our own terms?

Civil rights will remain a powerful paradigm for ameliorating the effects of systemic discrimination based on race, gender, and sexual orientation in the United States in the foreseeable future. Movements for "civil rights" and against "hate violence" will remain places where coalitions of people from various racial/ethnic, gender, and sexual communities will come together to get to know each other and figure out how to join efforts in the work for social change.

These rights frameworks require us, however, to prove our belonging by proving our victimhood. We gain "strict judicial scrutiny" in Fourteenth Amendment cases by establishing ourselves as a "special [discriminated] class." Many gay people responded to the right-wing film *Gay Rights/Special Rights* by clamoring to prove we are a "real [read: persecuted] minority," denied rights held as the preserve of the "majority," variously constituted as white, male, propertied, and straight. We can hardly expect communities subjected to brutal attack not to employ legal defenses using the only Constitution available. With these victim arguments, we could persuade a good many people that we should not to be mutilated, tortured, or brutally attacked, barely asserting our right to life. Liberty and the pursuit of happiness, which in biblical terms some of my friends call "fullness of life," are quite another matter. Attaining those and a more genuine democracy in the United States will require more transformative frameworks, and movements, than those structured currently under the U.S. Constitution.

NOTES

1. Walt Whitman, "Crossing Brooklyn Ferry," in *Modern Poets: An Introduction to Poetry*, edited by Richard Ellmann and Robert O'Clair (New York: Norton, 1976), 4.

2. Eve Sedgwick, *Epistemology of the Closet* (Berkeley: University of California Press, 1990), 32.

3. Ibid., 29, 27.

4. For earlier versions of this narrative, see my "Southern Women Writing: Towards a Literature of Wholeness," in *My Mama's Dead Squirrel: Lesbian Essays on Southern Culture* (Ithaca: Firebrand, 1985), 20; and *Memoir of a Race Traitor* (Boston: South End, 1995), 21–25.

5. Both are quoted in Barbara Smith, "Blacks and Gays: Healing the Great Divide," in *Eyes Right: Challenging the Right Wing Backlash*, edited by Chip Berlet (Boston: South End, 1995), 264, 276.

6. For a longer analysis of *Gay Rights/Special Rights* see my essay, "Visibility and Backlash," in *The Question of Equality: Lesbian and Gay Politics in America since Stonewall*, edited by David Deitcher (New York: Simon & Schuster, 1995), 83–122.

7. Ralph Ellison, *The Invisible Man* (New York: Vintage, 1972), 3.

8. See Segrest and Leonard Zeskind, *Quarantines and Death: The Far Right's Homophobic Agenda* (Atlanta: Center for Democratic Renewal, 1988).

9. Urvashi Vaid, *Virtual Equality: The Mainstreaming of Gay & Lesbian Liberation* (New York: Anchor Books, 1995), 11.

10. Hernandez v. Texas, 347 U.S. 475 (1954); see *Constitutional Law: Cases and Materials*, 9th edition, edited by William Cohen and Jonathan D. Varat (Westbury, N.Y.: Foundation Press, 1993), 720.

11. Native Americans, on the other hand, engaged in open warfare against encroaching white supremacy, the outcome settled by treaties between nations claiming sovereignty, rather than "citizens" claiming civil rights.

12. Linda Greenhouse, "Gay Rights Law Can't Be Banned, High Court Rules," *New York Times*, 21 May 1996, p. 1, C19.

13. "Introduction," *Critical Race Theory: The Key Writings That Formed the Movement*, edited by Kimberlé Crenshaw, Neil Gotanda, Gary Pellar, Kendall Thomas (New York: The New Press, 1995), xiv, xv.

In Struggle

Nothing Special: The Specious Attack on Civil Rights

Alisa Solomon

You can't get colder than February in Augusta, Maine, but a little fire and brimstone was enough to warm the crowd of 300 people who had turned up on the steps of the state capitol for a rally supporting an important state-wide referendum. Proponents of the referendum hoped to end recognition of homosexuals as a protected class thereby overturning a gay rights bill that the legislature had passed a few months before. Drawing more people than any other proreferendum gathering, and making headlines less than two weeks before the vote, the event was the most successful photo-op the initiators of the referendum — the Christian Coalition and Maine's Christian Civic League — had yet pulled off. The key to this triumph? The featured speaker: Alveda King, a niece of the Reverend Martin Luther King, Jr.

As the crowd knelt on the cold capitol steps, King led them in praying that homosexuals would "turn from their wicked ways." And in a speech following the prayer, she explained her reason for making the trip from Atlanta to join the referendum effort: "God hates racism," she said. "And God hates homosexuality." That only stood to reason, given the central rhetorical strategy the Christian Coalition employed throughout the campaign. Marshalling the charge that gay rights are "special rights" — a tactic honed in antigay campaigns around the country over the last decade — the forces in Maine essentially equated homosexuality with racism.

And they won, despite pre-election polls that showed a staggering majority opposing the measure and despite an antireferendum coalition that counted strong support among elected officials, newspaper editorial pages, and civil rights, education, labor, and religious organizations around the state. Less than a third of the electorate turned out to vote (many pundits blamed the week's massive ice storm) and gay rights went down fifty-one to forty-nine percent. Not only did Maine thereby become the first state in the nation to reject a gay rights law enacted by its legislature, Portland's 1992 gay rights ordinance was rendered illegal, and the domestic partner benefits granted by some state universities became suspect.

Devastating as this victory has been within Maine, it has perilous implications that reach far beyond the state borders: implications for the future of the gay movement nationally; for the increasingly cynical battle over who carries—and defines—the moral legacy of the black civil rights movement; and even for the contested nature of the relationship between the American state and its polity. The "special rights" argument that came to full fruition in the Northeast, and will continue to fuel right-wing activism in ever more sophisticated invocations, attacks the very core of the civil rights protections in whose name the antigay forces claim to be acting. What's more, the right's political strategy threatens democracy itself, as it puts minority rights to majority vote. Voter initiatives, such as the referendum in Maine, may look democratic, but they are an easily manipulable means of making an end-run around legislatures, a useful tool— especially when combined with the specter of sodomy—for undermining civil rights laws of every stripe. It's no accident that the anti-gay forces in Maine took an Orwellian cue from the antiaffirmative action movement in California. The West Coast organization that is helping states across the United States craft ballot measures to outlaw that civil rights act calls itself the American Civil Rights Initiative; the eastern effort to repeal gay inclusion in the state's human rights law took the name Equal Rights for Maine. Alveda King may think she's striking a blow for Christian decency–and even for black dignity—when she allows the name she happens to have to do symbolic service in the holy war against "special rights." But in fact she is being used in a far-reaching effort to dismantle the very structures her uncle gave his life to build. To the far right—which looks less and less "far" as the center shifts rightward in Congress, the courts, and state legislatures around the country—all civil rights are "special." Those who stand with African Americans or with gays—and certainly with or within both groups—must understand the nefarious ways in which the right exploits the "special rights" polemic in a divide-and-conquer tactic to do damage to both causes.

The "special rights" argument works on a variety of levels, calling class resentment into play and rerouting it toward convenient scapegoats by appealing to basic paradigms of prejudice. It's a commonplace that bigotry toward scapegoats takes similar sex-panicked forms, often painting the pariah group as sexual predators, going after "our" children and women. Charges against rapacious Jews in Europe or Chinese railroad workers in this country are typical instances, and the gruesome history of lynching, among other attacks, tells the relentless story of such accusations against African American men in the United States. In the case of women—as the crusade against "witches" or the portrayal of African American women as insatiable jezebels illustrates, to cite only two examples—the sexual dysfunction of a detested group is figured as an incurable, out-of-control, over-the-top lust that infects the body politic like a spreading rash. As James Weldon Johnson once put it, "at the core of the heart of the race problem is the sex problem."

Given this use of sexual excess and perversion as a way of designating a group as derelict, how easy it is to whip up disgust for homosexuals. Never mind that heterosexuals do the same sorts of things in bed. The traditional template of demonization can be easily laid over queer culture—as the right's propaganda film *The Gay Agenda* makes all too clear. Featuring raunchy footage of a couple of San Francisco Gay Pride parades—drag nuns wagging dildos, S/M "slaves" crawling on the pavement as their "masters" brandish whips, near-naked buff boys grinding to disco music, the delegation of the North American Man-Boy Love Association interspersed with images of children—the film was produced by the Oregon Citizen Alliance (OCA) as part of its 1992 campaign to pass Measure 9, a ballot initiative seeking to amend the state constitution to declare homosexuality "abnormal, wrong, unnatural, and perverse," and forbid state agencies and schools to "promote, encourage or facilitate" homosexuality. Though the referendum was defeated, the film was distributed nationally by the Christian Coalition, including to every member of Congress, to make a defiant declaration in the escalating queer-bashing culture war. Never mind, again, that one could easily hash together raunchy footage of, say, heterosexual frat parties and girlie shows to similar effect. The OCA propaganda pic ingeniously appeals directly to the old paradigm of prejudice and then overlays one more: The right invokes the tropes of European anti-Semitism by painting gays as a privileged class, earning far more than heterosexuals and having powerful allies in government and media through whom they control those institutions. "Do such people deserve or need the protection of special laws?" the Right thunders. And folks who feel economically insecure and politically shut out can easily be stirred to answer with a resounding "No."

Such rhetoric is especially effective in a place like Maine, where the median income is well below the national average. Sparsely populated, the state has pockets of extreme poverty, and is dotted with rural outposts that tend to be more conservative than its urban centers. Days before the 1998 referendum, a local shoe factory employing hundreds of workers for decades announced it was moving south of the border. "Special rights" plays all too well in such areas. Such was the case in Oregon, too, where OCA regional organizer, John Leon, trumped up local timber workers, many of whom were unemployed and others of whom were just barely hanging on in a failing lumber industry, with the specter of losing their livelihoods to queer body-snatchers. Making no mention of the decades of forest overcutting that have debilitated the industry nor of increasing automation or the exportation of mill jobs to Mexico, Leon stirred their insecurity by showing *The Gay Agenda*. Afterwards, according to press reports at the time, he'd warn, "If sexual orientation is included in the civil rights laws, that would mean special privileges and hiring quotas. Some timber workers in Corvallis said the other day: 'Maybe it's good if Measure 9 loses. Then we can go over to the next town and say we are homos and they'll have to give us a job!'"

You don't have to have perfect political pitch to hear the attack on affirmative action as a rumbling obbligato beneath the homophobia theme. Indeed, much of the language crafted around the antigay efforts of the early 1990s paved the way for the rollback of affirmative action legislation. The wording of Colorado's antigay Amendment 2, which was passed by voters in 1992 (but struck down by the Supreme Court) is telling: The amendment called for forbidding the government from enacting any statutes that would treat homosexuals, lesbians, or bisexuals as a class entitled to "minority status, quota preferences, protected status or claims of discrimination." Similarly, an OCA leaflet put out by its "No Special Rights" Committee offers "Pro-family Answers to Pro-gay Questions." If one is asked why homosexuals shouldn't have the same basic rights as everyone else, the respondent is instructed to reply:

> Again, homosexuals already have the same basic rights as everyone else: the right to vote, to own property, to freely assemble, to worship, etc. However, homosexuals want special rights to be granted to their behavior. They want their choice of homosexuality to be given the same civil rights protections and preferences as being born Black or Hispanic. This would be like granting affirmative action quotas to celibates or polygamists just because they claimed to be born that way.

While this twisted text seems to defend the principle of civil rights protections for "real" minorities, such as blacks and Hispanics, it quickly slides into equating those protections with "affirmative action quotas"—never mind that there have never been any affirmative action demands in any proposals for gay rights legislation. The very mention of civil rights offers an opening for its opponents to define affirmative action as a quota system, that is, to define civil rights protections themselves as the conferring of unfair advantages.

Of course, these are not the angles that are played when the right seeks black support for its homophobic campaign. "Special rights" has a different sinister ring in the propaganda made especially for the African American community. It evokes the salaciousness of queer sexuality and then, instead of moving to the specter of hiring preferences, hammers that homos are making off with a sacred mantle that belongs to blacks.

Under another specious name — Citizens United for the Preservation of Civil Rights — the Traditional Values Coalition produced a video like *The Gay Agenda* in 1993 targeted at the black community. This film, *Gay Rights/Special Rights: Inside the Homosexual Agenda* was sent to hundreds of black churches across the country. It argues, essentially, that to demand protection from discrimination in employment, housing, public accommodations, and other such spheres, is to claim to be like African Americans, to whose efforts America owes such antidiscrimination laws. The argument essentially goes like this: Gays are affluent and powerful and don't need any legal protections. Besides, they don't have to stay gay the way a black person has to stay black. Theirs is an identity based on behavior, not on an immutable characteristic such as race, and that behavior is disgusting and immoral to boot. To include them in civil rights protections, then, is to insult and degrade African Americans. Thus the gay movement wears political blackface to wring "special rights" from the state. And thus, gays not only defy nature with their unspeakable sexual behavior, they are also racist. The genius of this propaganda is that on top of appealing to "religious" (that is, homophobic) objections to homosexuality, it gives African Americans a political justification for resenting gays.

Of course it's easy enough to blow holes in the premises of this argument. For starters, it assumes that all homosexuals are well-to-do men, closing out the possibility that anyone gay might also be female, poor, someone other than a white Anglo-Saxon Christian, even — heavens forfend! — black. Moreover, if immutability were a requirement for civil rights protections, discrimination on the basis of religious belief would be acceptable—especially against converts.

But more important, perhaps, than refuting this argument is recognizing how it, too, constructs a debilitating description of the black civil rights movement as it seeks to drive a wedge between the gay and black movements not just to defeat gays, but also to defeat blacks. This isn't to say that the right's heavily funded and nationally orchestrated attack on gays is merely a Trojan horse concealing a separate purpose; these attacks have devastating material and ideological consequences for the gay movement and, indeed, for the daily lives of gay men and lesbians. Still, there is a wider purpose. The right is targeting gays in its broader effort to redefine the concept of the American state and its relationship to—and its responsibilities toward—its citizens. Thus the right is primarily engaged, most of all, in redefining the citizenry itself, and who may belong to it.

For reasons already suggested, it's easy to set up gays as a screen on which to project anxieties over America's ever-changing national identity. Through its various attacks—on gays, immigrants, African Americans—the right insists on "deserving" citizens who must demonstrate their worthiness of constitutional protections. The rhetorical tropes aimed at exclusion of these "aliens" and "cheats" are almost interchangeably applied to all three groups. Queers, for example, are derided in the same terms as the "welfare queen," who is, of course, always figured as black. Both are depicted as sexually incontinent, immoral beings who try to trick the state out of scarce resources. "Special rights," forged in the cauldron of antigay initiatives, became an instrumental phrase in the restructuring of "welfare as we know it." Arguments on the floor of the Senate for the Defense of Marriage Act, which defined matrimony as a status that could be conferred only on a heterosexual couple, sounded the same fear and loathing as the welfare reform debates: both sought to draw strict lines around what constitutes an American family unit.

What's more, the welfare reform effort relied, in turn, on the increasingly mainstream disdain for public spending of any sort—a view made popular by the right's relentless assault on the National Endowment for the Arts. Pat Buchanan's campaign ads in the 1992 presidential race went the furthest, perhaps, in reproaching the government for spending taxpayers' dollars on "glorifying homosexuality." In one infamous commercial, an appalled voiceover spoke over frames from Marlon Riggs's elegiac film *Tongues Untied* that showed men dancing, charging then-President Bush with "wast[ing] our tax dollars on pornographic and blasphemous art too shocking to show" (as if people who appreciate such work don't also pay taxes). As Riggs said at the time, in this ad, Buchanan's "anti-quota race-baiting . . . fused with a brazen display of anti-gay bigotry." But it was not only Buchanan, of course, who coupled racism and homophobia in his denunciation of public spending. No other candidates in 1992 had the decency or courage to publicly reject Buchanan's crass appeals to prejudice, and since then, his blatant bias has become political commonplace—as ordinary as quips castigating commies during the height of the Cold War. Fulminating against queer artists—and especially against queer artists of color—has proven to be a surefire way to inflame public opinion against the principle of public funding. It's a short leap from the assertion that artists can say what they like just so long as "we" don't have to pay for it, to the argument that people can live as they like so long as "we" don't have to help them when they fall on hard times. And there's no leap required to move across the bridge of sexual "misconduct" to the position that people can do what they like so long as "America" doesn't have confer "special rights" on them. Anyone whose sexual behavior cannot be maritally contained—homosexuals and unwed mothers, most of all—are cast out from civil protections, and in the right's fantasy, from citizenry itself.

It would be simplistic however—and politically naive and enfeebling—for progressives to credit the right alone for its victories against civil rights principles, and for its ability to coopt the language, symbols, and even heroes of the black civil rights movement. The right has been assisted by liberal revisionism of the civil rights legacy and increasingly, even by an increasingly dominant conservatism within the contemporary gay rights movement. On the one hand, as many historians and social critics have observed, the civil rights movement has been widely embraced as a heroic struggle precisely because it has been denuded of its radical challenge to racial power. Over the last forty years, the basic principle that it's wrong to discriminate against people on the basis of race has seeped into the American mainstream like rain into dry earth. The only trouble is, what constitutes discrimination, and how best to remedy it, has been diluted by America's abiding myth of meritocracy. Insisting that the goal of civil rights legislation is to make skin color—or other characteristics distinguishing minorities—not matter at all, mainstream civil rights discourse derides any remedy that recognizes race in an attempt to overturn centuries of institutional black suppression as reverse discrimination," which is another name for "special rights." Thus, notwithstanding white supremacist movements and occasional campaigns for public office by the likes of David Duke, America has generally clasped civil rights principles to its bosom—as long as the measures they support are seen as answering deliberate, demonstrable, individual acts of discrimination. Radical redistribution of institutional power has been written out of this liberal vision. Thus emptied, an appealing image of the nobility and decency of the civil rights movement has become a commodity everyone with a cause wants to claim. Absurdly, then, the moral imprimatur of the civil rights movement has been reduced to an advertising slogan battled over by groups across the political spectrum. Alveda King's visit to Maine could be read as the Christian Coalition's retort to a statement supporting gay rights that Coretta Scott King had offered two years earlier, when Maine battled the right's first effort to outlaw gay rights laws across that state.

Increasingly, the gay movement itself is predicated on liberal versions of civil rights. Since 1969 at least, when the Gay Activist Alliance split off from the Gay Liberation Front to focus on an exclusive gay rights agenda in contrast to the GLF, which opposed the Vietnam War and supported the Black Panthers as integral parts of its own struggle, the gay movement was animated by two currents: assimilationist and liberationist. Arguably, as the country has tilted rightward, the assimilationist agenda has become dominant, some might even say hegemonic. Legislative efforts at gay inclusion in civil rights statutes — such as the one in Maine — are often made through campaigns exhorting the public to recognize that gay people are just like everyone else, and therefore deserving of protections against discrimination in employment, public accommodations, and so on. There's nothing special about gay people, this tactic maintains, so there's nothing special about gay civil rights. What's more, this argument not only rejects a sexual liberation agenda that stands firmly with — indeed, sees itself as part of — other liberation struggles; it frantically denies that sexual liberation has anything to do with gay rights. The conservative wing of the gay movement is, in fact, currently poised to make the essential assimilationist gesture: stigmatizing queer sexuality. In early 1998, the Universal Fellowship of Metropolitan Community Churches (MCC), the nation's largest gay Christian denomination — with 225,000 members — and the Human Rights Campaign, the nation's largest gay rights lobby, announced joint plans to produce the "Millennium March for Equality" in Washington, DC in April 2000. The theme these organizers chose is "faith and family" and the purpose of the demonstration, said MCC's founder, the Reverend Troy Perry, "is to show Middle America that we're mature people who work, just like them." And the way to do that, he added, was to avoid the nudity and flamboyance that has marked pockets of other gay gatherings and, instead, to emphasize gay church-affiliation (never mind all those who don't go to churches, but to mosques, synagogues, ashrams, Radical Faerie Circles, or nowhere at all) and to "put our children on stage."

Certainly reaching people through the communities and values they hold dear is just plain good organizing, and there's

nothing inherently superior about gay people who don't participate in organized religion or the gay baby boom. But to build a
movement on the basis of baby raising or belief is another kind
of politics altogether. It's fundamentalism.

How do march organizers defend their sectarian approach?
How else, but by invoking the role of the black church in the
civil rights movement. Only they've got it backwards. African
Americans didn't march on the capitol to prove they loved Jesus
as much as white folks; that was hardly the moral basis of their
claim to equality. The Christian movements of the '90s, on the
other hand, turn political rallies into revival meetings, making
demands not on the state, but on the demonstrators themselves.
The Millennium March thus buys into the right's ideal of the
"deserving" citizen; indeed, the purpose of the march is to demonstrate such dessert. Though it lowers the bar some, like
Alveda King, the Millennium March prays that homosexuals
"turn from their wicked ways," thus they will be worthy of being
granted basic civil rights. Disastrously, then, the conservative
wing of the gay movement supports the premises of the "special
rights" rhetoric that has so damaged our cause, and worse, is
lining up to join the assault on civil rights in general.

Blacks and Gays in Conflict: An Interview with U.S. Representative Barney Frank

Keith Boykin

A few years ago when I was doing research for my first book, I stumbled across a piece of information that challenged a widely held belief about blacks and gays. While browsing through the main reading room of the Library of Congress, I came across a public opinion poll about gays in the military. The survey, conducted by Gallup in April 1993, found that sixty-one percent of blacks favored lifting the ban on gays in the military while only forty-two percent of whites responded the same way.

Because the plan to lift the ban was so closely connected with President Clinton, I thought the racial discrepancy might have been explained by the black community's strong support for Clinton in the 1992 election. But when the respondents were asked about other gay issues not associated with the Clinton administration, the racial divergence remained. For example, eighty-five percent of blacks felt that homosexuals should have equal rights in terms of job opportunities, as compared to seventy-nine percent of whites. On virtually every question, blacks were more likely than whites to support civil rights protections for gays and lesbians. Other polls, both before and after Clinton's term began, supported these results. Soon I began to challenge my own assumptions about black support for gay rights.

Despite a few high-profile exceptions, black leaders have been out front in their support for civil rights protections for gays and lesbians. Civil rights leaders such as Jesse Jackson, Joseph Lowery, and Coretta Scott King have joined with black political leaders such as Kweisi Mfume, Marion Barry, and

David Dinkins to support laws that would end sexual orientation discrimination in the workplace. In South Africa, Nelson Mandela and the African National Congress have created the world's first constitution that specifically outlaws sexual orientation bias. In our own country, the Congressional Black Caucus has distinguished itself with a strong record of support on gay and lesbian issues. In fact, some black members of Congress, such as Representative John Lewis, have been the gay community's strongest allies, even fighting to oppose restrictions on same-sex marriage.

Perhaps no one in the gay community is more familiar with the black community's leadership on these issues than Representative Barney Frank of Massachusetts, one of two openly gay members of the U.S. Congress. I sat down with Representative Frank in that context, to talk about the perceptions and misperceptions of blacks and gays in conflict. As we observe renewed efforts by right-wing ideologues to drive a wedge between blacks and gays, it seems an appropriate occasion to explore the question of black support for gay rights.

KEITH BOYKIN: The first question I would like to start with is what does it mean to be gay in America today. And there are a lot of different definitions and interpretations, but I wonder if you could offer me what you think it means to be gay in America today.

REP. FRANK: It means, obviously different people will give different interpretations, to be the victim of a prejudice which seems to me to be diminishing. And it's an interesting kind of prejudice. It's prejudice which people have been able to duck for a long time externally, but I think people now realize the price of that was pretty severe internally. Gay people, more than any other victim of prejudice, have never liked being gay. Obviously, you could conceal your being gay much more easily than you could conceal your gender or your race and also more easily in fact than you could conceal your religion, although I suppose if you really want to conceal your religion it might be even easier.

But today what it means is, I think, to be grappling, for a lot of people, with how much of a choice to make to confront the prejudice. Obviously, what's happening is that people have been moving from hiding the fact that they're gay. Thirty years ago there was a very, very small number of gay men and lesbians who would acknowledge their sexual orientation—to the point now where I think the majority have told, at least some straight people.

BOYKIN: You think the majority of gay people have told [someone]?

FRANK: At least some straight people, yes. It may not be a large number, but it's made a qualitative difference, I think, between, some and none. And I think thirty years ago the tendency was for people to have told no one. So I think that's the dominating factor today in being gay in America, that is, dealing with a prejudice which is diminishing but it's still there and to some extent you have some control over how much of it to expose yourself to. And I think that's the interesting fact that people have to deal with.

BOYKIN: As a member of Congress, you've been somewhat privileged in your experiences, but how have you been personally affected by homophobia in your lifetime?

FRANK: Well, for the first forty years or so of my life I wasn't affected by it by other people. The wounds were self-inflicted. That is, I, until I was 40 years old, just didn't want to tell anybody—or almost forty, thirty-nine. So the damage I felt was internal and psychic. And since then, of course, I didn't really start to tell other people until I was a member of Congress . . . because I had been in kind of an important position and I really told almost no one that I was gay. I think I told a few friends and my siblings in the months before I decided to run for Congress, and since running for Congress is when I really told people, before then I hadn't really experienced it a great deal. I suppose there might have been more political options open to me had I not been gay. I might have cast my own political career differently. I might have been thinking earlier of maybe running for governor or maybe running for a House [of Representatives] leadership position or thinking of a Cabinet job. One of those things. On the other hand, it may also have helped me because it helped me focus and say, "Hey, you don't have to worry about ambition at this point. All you want to do is stay where you are." I continued to pay the price of not being fully open until 1987. I did stupid things. So for me, even after I began to tell other people, the price I paid has been almost exclusively an internal one, first a kind of psychic pain and then doing these stupid things, and trying to resolve a half-in, half-out situation.

BOYKIN: And do you feel that as a member of Congress or as an influential person in the public domain you have even more of an obligation to do something to come out of the closet?

FRANK: Yes, I do. I think when you can help other people at a relatively low price to yourself you ought to do that. I mean, you aren't obligated to commit suicide if someone is drowning and you can't swim, you're not really obligated to jump in. On the other hand, if a small child is floundering in two feet of water, you have absolutely no right to stay out. And for me, it's somewhere in between. I do think for me not to have acknowledged being gay would have been to deny a lot of vulnerable people help they could have gotten.

BOYKIN: One of the issues I'm getting at is the whole question of the relationship between blacks and gays and those who are part of both groups, and there's a perception that black people are more homophobic than nonblack people. Is that your perception?

FRANK: Oh absolutely not. I've spent twenty-three years as an elected official. I think elected officials are pretty good indicators on the whole of the feelings of the public. This notion that elected officials don't pay attention to public opinion is silly.

And of the demographic groups in the U.S. House of Representatives, none, none comes as close to being progay and lesbian as the Congressional Black Caucus. I think the experience of having lived in a society in which you are discriminated against forges a common bond. The fact is that the Congressional Black Caucus has been, with no close second, the most supportive group for gays and lesbians. Women and Jewish members are also much more supportive than the average, but neither group comes close to the Congressional Black Caucus. When a member of the Congressional Black Caucus votes no, it's like really exceptional. So I don't think that group would survive if there was broad homophobia. Secondly, the two cities in the United States tied for the most progay are San Francisco and Washington, D.C. In the case of Washington, D.C., you have a very large white male gay population for a variety of reasons, but the majority is still African American, and if the black population in Washington were homophobic, you wouldn't have this virtual unanimity of support.

When you look at Anacostia [a predominantly black section of Washington, D.C.], Marion Barry, who has always been identified as a very progay candidate, just chews up Wilhemnia Rolark [for a seat on the City Council], who had been the antigay candidate. Now he didn't beat her because he was progay, but if in fact, homophobia were as strong here among the African American population, Marion Barry could not have devastated Wilhemenia Rolark by that kind of margin in a virtually all-black ward.

BOYKIN: So where does this perception come from?

FRANK: I don't know where. Part of it may be a class thing—that is, that people who are lower in the socioeconomic scale are more explicit in expressing their prejudices. And if you are a gay man, you are more likely given where you live in a big city to come in contact with blacks in that socioeconomic stratum than whites, so it may just be a proximity thing in gentrification.

There have probably been more cases of gay men moving into what have been black neighborhoods, but that's just a guess. It may also be partly this — a few prominent ministers who may be especially outspoken, but in general I think [the assumption about black homophobia is] demonstrably wrong and I haven't heard a lot about it.

BOYKIN: I've interviewed a number of people, both black gay and lesbian people who've said to me, pretty much that they don't think that white gay and lesbian people understand, particularly white gay men. They just don't understand black lesbian and gay people. And I think there's a great deal of frustration and, in some sense, just a hands-off approach, that they just don't really care to deal with the white gay community anymore. What do you think is behind all that?

FRANK: I have no idea. It seems to me quite stupid to use this as a reason not to praticipate in the organizations that are fighting for gay and lesbian rights. It does not seem to be very sensible to let this become a reason for not participating in the political effort to defeat anti-gay and lesbian prejudice, and in fact it seems to me to play into the hands of the people who are against us. I've heard criticism of organizations where there aren't enough [black people], but well, I know of no organization that hasn't tried actively to bring other people in it. And I just think that criticism is always a stupid one, whether it's women or African Americans or whoever it is that's complaining. You get organizations where people, they act like they want to be there and they decide to do it, and then other people stay out of it. I have no idea why people argue the way they do. And I don't know what it means when they say people don't understand black gay people. I don't understand what that means.

BOYKIN: Well, part of it is the assertion that there's a great deal of racism still in the gay white community and that people who are gay and white don't seem to think of themselves as having any racism in them because of the fact that they're gay.

Frank: Well, some of them do and some of them don't. It seems to me an equally dumb statement for people to characterize all white people. In fact, certainly if you were going to look in America, the gay and lesbian organizations and the gay and lesbian elected officials are much more likely to be aligned with black elected officials on race matters. The Congressional Black Caucus is very progay, but if you look at the lesbian and gay elected officials, they are overwhelmingly people who've been very supportive of a whole range of issues that black people say are important. So I just think that's a dumb statement with nothing behind it, but I can say I've read some of these things and to some sense they're self-fulfilling prophecies [when people say] "they don't want me there so I won't go." It seems to me just typical of the tendency of human beings to find reasons to fight with each other for no good reason over small differences.

Boykin: Now the Family Research Council and the Traditional Values Coalition and other groups like that have made an effort to drive a wedge between the black community and the gay community, and one of the arguments they make is that the gay community is arguing that blacks and gays are the same. Whether it be the struggles or the types of oppression, they're the same. Is that an argument that you believe?

Frank: Oh, I believe, as I said earlier, there are some elements of being discriminated against that are common, that victims of discrimination have a lot in common. Now obviously blacks have had much more serious economic discrimination, [and] they couldn't have hidden if they wanted to. Gays have been able by hiding to avoid that, so in that sense there's a difference, but in some areas it seems to be quite similar. In some instances, as for example, the discrimination in the military is very, very similar. The rationale is virtually identical. And actually that is something where I have been disappointed in the vehemence with which [some] blacks have denounced the notion that there are any similarities in the struggles. The answer is that there are some similarities and some differences. I think if you read, for instance, Taylor Branch's book about Martin Luther King and think back to the relationship blacks had with John Kennedy, it's very similar to the relationship of gays with Bill Clinton, so there are some similarities and some differences. I remember the first time I encountered the argument was in 1973. I filed a gay rights bill in the Massachusetts House and at the first hearing, Royal Bolling, Jr., who was a black state representative, said "I know what you're talking about because I'm black and it's very similar," and I was very pleased by that. And people make other comparisons. I mean people compare being Jewish to being a woman to being black, and there are similarities and differences. And I think that's the sensible answer there—some things are the same and some aren't.

BOYKIN: Well, in terms of the arguments that people use to justify homophobia and racism, are those closer to the same? I mean, you mentioned the military. . . .

FRANK: The argument for segregation in the military and kicking gays out is identical. It is not that these are bad people. In fact, they would be very well behaved and very capable. But there is a dislike of them among the majority that would make their presence disruptive and therefore they should be excluded. You can take arguments that they used in '48 and the arguments that are used in '93 and I think they are identical.

BOYKIN: But does that comparison apply anywhere else outside of the military?

FRANK: Yes, I think there are some elements in common. I haven't thought about others, but that was the most recent one we had. Well, obviously it would be in housing discrimination. There is also a common religious element to both. It's not fashionable anymore, but if you go back to the '40s and '50s when the segregation fight was raging, religion was used very often to justify discrimination and segregation, and it's used obviously similarly with gay people.

BOYKIN: There's also a great deal of concern within some communities about coalition building and the value of coalitions, and particularly with regard to black and gay organizations and communities, and some people just don't see that such coalitions benefit black people or black organizations. What would you say to a black person or a black community or a black organization struggling with the question of whether they should be engaged in a coalition with a gay group or community?

FRANK: You mean a straight black organization?

BOYKIN: Yes.

FRANK: Fighting discrimination is a moral obligation and that I suppose if you wanted to calculate now in terms of whether it's good or bad for you, it might be good or bad. Aligning yourself with a particular prejudice might help you fight another one. There's no question about that. It might help gay organizations in some parts of the country if they were explicitly racist or stayed away from integration. If you argued purely on self-interest, people argue that with the Jews, too. The right-wing people like Irving Kristol have said to Jews, "What are you hanging out with the blacks for?" Irving Kristol has written articles saying it's time for Jews to break off this alliance with black people and instead to move over to the Christian right because they've got more power in this country and they'll be able to move it better. The answer is, that may or may not be the case, but it seems to me it's a moral obligation to fight for freedom.

In the end, I do think that people make a mistake, even practically, because I think the arguments against discrimination are common. The arguments for it may be different, but the arguments against it are the same ultimately, which is, it is unfair to judge an individual on anything other than his or her merits. And I think it's very hard to start making arguments to fight discrimination in one case and then allow it in another. But I would hope people wouldn't even make that kind of translation. If that's the case, well then if blacks are told, "Well, hey, don't hang out with the gay people because that could be bad for you" and Jews will be saying "Well, why don't you stop hanging out with the black people" and then the women's groups will probably be saying, "Well, we're the biggest group, why should we be hanging out with any of these minority groups? Let's just head right out."

BOYKIN: And then eventually everyone splinters off?

FRANK: Yes, I think people have more to gain by coming together. Especially since it may just be statistical. You know, maybe there's no logic to it at all. I think there is some logic to it. It is in fact the case that the most virulent opponents of the agenda that African Americans have and that gay people have and that feminist groups have are all the same people. So the logic may or may not be that great, I think it is, but I think statistically that's the way things work out.

BOYKIN: Thank you for your time.

FRANK: You're welcome.

Fighting Homophobia versus Challenging Heterosexism: "The Failure to Transform" Revisited

Cathy J. Cohen and Tamara Jones

I. THE FAILURE TO TRANSFORM . . . STILL?

In 1983, Cheryl Clarke published a very important essay entitled "The Failure to Transform: Homophobia in the Black Community."[1] It is considered a classic because it is one of the first articles to turn a critical eye on the topic of homophobia in the black community, and because it places the issue in the larger framework of homophobia in the dominant society. In fact, Clarke beings her essay by reminding the reader that the existence of "homophobia among black people in America is largely reflective of the homophobic culture in which we live."[2] She rightly reminds us that black communities — even their most nationalistic and seemingly autonomous segments — are in constant dialogue, struggle, and negotiation with the dominant culture as well as with other cultures existing in the United States.[3] Clarke goes on to attack those who would place same-sex relationships or sex outside the boundaries of blackness. In this age of advanced communication technologies, pervasive market capitalism, and unbridled consumerism, most of our social products simultaneously exist both "inside" bounded communities and "outside" in the larger society. Whether the subject is rap music, the development of mathematics, or homosexuality, delimiting the boundaries of ownership is not only a largely futile project, but can be downright destructive, useful only to those who seek to exclude people or establish their superiority over them.

Clarke also tackles head-on arguments which excuse practices of domination and oppression *within* marginalized communities as legacies of dominant institutions, attitudes, and practices. She notes that "we cannot rationalize the disease of homophobia among black people as the white man's fault, for to do so is to absolve ourselves of our responsibility to transform ourselves."[4] While Clarke's discussion of the origins of homophobia contextualizes the discussion, the essential question of the essay is the revolutionary purpose of black activists, which she sees as inextricably joined to the production and practice of a true liberatory analysis that understands the intersection of systems of oppression and thus the necessity of fighting on multiple fronts.[5] For Clarke, the "failure to transform" is rooted in the contradictions inherent among revolutionary identities, rhetoric, and practice, especially as manifested in the conservative, homophobic, and patriarchal analyses offered by such "revolutionaries." She quotes a passage from a leaflet placed on every chair at the First National Plenary Conference on Self-Determination (December 4–6, 1981):

> Revolutionary nationalists and genuine communists cannot uphold homosexuality in the leadership of the Black Liberation Movement nor uphold it as a correct practice. Homosexuality is a genocidal practice. . . . Homosexuality does not produce children. . . . Homosexuality does not birth new warriors for liberation . . . homosexuality cannot be upheld as correct or revolutionary practice. . . . The practice of homosexuality is an accelerating threat to our survival as a people and as a nation.[6]

It is important to acknowledge that there were some lesbians, gay men, feminists, antiwar, black power, and similar activists who created alternative analyses and practices in response to the political challenges of the time. Motivated in part by the practical needs for alliances in an environment of COINTELPRO infiltration and brutality, a few activists developed different and less damning ways of relating to the gay movement, gay activists and the topic of homosexuality. It was, for example, Huey Newton who wrote in "A Letter from Huey to the Revolutionary

Brothers and Sisters about the Women's Liberation and Gay Liberations Movements," that homosexuals might be "the most oppressed people in the society" as well as "the most revolutionary."[7] However, in spite of such periodic counterdevelopments in the ideological and practiced homophobia of political activists of that time, the overwhelming tendency among self-stated revolutionaries was to embrace the homophobia present in the dominant society, tagging lesbian and gay life-style yet another example of "bourgeois decadence."[8]

Our goal is not to enumerate, once again, the many traditional examples of homophobia and heterosexism in black communities. Instead we start from an apparent shift in the sexual language of black leftists. We believe that there has been a change in the way a significant number of black activists on the left talk about homophobia. We infer, perhaps hopefully and somewhat naively, that this signals some change in popular attitudes toward black nonheterosexuality. However, we also think the new political and academic rhetoric fails to reflect a deep understanding of heterosexism as a normative system. Although the picture of homophobia as an oppressive barrier that must be torn down has become a feature of leftist stump speeches and articles, we question the degree to which these same authors and speakers understand the ways in which homophobia and heterosexism are rooted in the everyday experiences of black people, and are manifestations of interlocking systems of oppression. We are left pondering the degree to which heterosexism and patriarch are recognized as systemic threats to black communities, as devastating and irreducible as market capitalism and racism.

Like Cheryl Clarke before us, we direct our comments to the black left because it is with them that we hope to find a more informed understanding of the multiple forms of oppression confronting black people. The black left in the United States has historically demonstrated the courage to speak and to fight against oppression, usually rooting their struggle in the fight for better living conditions for poor and working-class black people. The leading figures and organizations have been many and as personally different from each other as the ideologies they represent: Paul Robeson, Ella Baker, Fannie Lou Hamer, Audre Lorde, the Black Panther Party, the National Coalition of Black Lesbians and Gays, and the Combahee River Collective, to name just a few. Yet they are all united in their commitment to improving substantially the lives of black and other marginal peoples. Two of the central goals of black politics are the critical examination and radical transformation of *all* areas of black and social and institutional life, and realization of a radical egalitarian and just society. These are precisely the conditions necessary to overcome black heterosexism and homophobia. Thus, we believe that the successful transformation of black communities is most likely to originate among those who identify as members of the black left.

The most recent evidence of such bounded transformation on the part of the black left was demonstrated at the Black Radical Congress. The congress was held in Chicago on Juneteenth 1998 and drew over 2,000 participants.[9] Its founders conceived of it as an attempt to bridge the many ideological divides that exist on the black left while at the same time introducing the masses of black people to a progressive and in some cases revolutionary way of thinking about their conditions and their power. We have chosen the Black Radical Congress as a case to briefly explore because we both were active participants in the planning process for and activities of the congress and can comment on the event with some authority. We also have chosen to examine the congress because it provides an example of the limitations of the black left's current dealing with homophobia and heterosexism as well as the promise for a truly radical intersectional analysis as the basis of struggle. After detailing some of the activity leading to the congress, we turn our attention to the impact of heterosexism on black communities. It is our contention that a truly radical analysis of the condition of black communities necessitates a focus on the impact of heterosexism, homophobia, and patriarchy on the structure, thinking, and actions evident in black communities. We end the essay with a call for intersectional politics to fight not only heterosexism, but the multiple systems of oppression facing all marginal people.

II. INCLUSION AS THE FIRST STEP?

The congress was born in 1996 when five activists—Barbara Ransby, Bill Fletcher, Leith Millings, Manning Marable, and Abdul Alkalimat—set in motion a two-year process that would culminate in the largest gathering of black radicals in over twenty-five years. Concern over the absence of a coherent left voice and presence in black communities in recent years, coupled with a rising conservative dominance of national institutions and policies, prompted these five individuals to act. From the beginning, they committed themselves and the congress to the inclusion of black leftists across the ideological spectrum. "Unity without uniformity" was the rallying cry as black feminists, revolutionary nationalists, communists, socialists, and others on the left struggled together to plan the congress. Those of us who came as visible lesbians and gay men were hopeful but wary. Would our historical exclusion and silence be repeated here? Even among ourselves, there were differences.

The most important activity of this new group was the drafting of a set of principles which would define the congress and its work. Clearly, the agreed-on principles would have to pay respect to the fundamental principles of all the participating groups. Not surprisingly, a struggle ensued over the place of homophobia and heterosexism in the congress's principles, but also over the relevance of addressing issues of sexism, patriarchy, self-determination, and globalization in the context of black liberation.

It seemed clear to us at the time that the struggles over feminist and lesbian and gay politics took on a different nature and tone than other points of disagreement. Brothers felt quite empowered in proclaiming that black radical politics needed to be defined primarily in terms of "bread and butter issues," and that the "masses" of black people simply would not understand what we meant by patriarchy or heterosexism (which led us to wonder how the "masses" nonetheless understood terms such as proletariat or bourgeoisie).[10] The presumed foreign status of these issues and politics, outside of what black people knew, experienced, and were familiar with, generally characterized the debates. Eventually, however, we all made compromises, and the Black Radical Congress's Principles of Unity were agreed on. Listed below is the preamble to the congress and the final version of the principles. The reader may wish to especially note Principles 3 and 4.

> The Black Radical Congress will convene to establish a "center without walls" for transformative politics. Despite diverse tendencies within Black radicalism, we are united in opposition to all forms of oppression, including class exploitation, racism, patriarchy, homophobia, anti-immigrant prejudice and imperialism. At our gathering we will propose actions and set forward paths. The Congress is not intended to replace or displace existing organizations, parties or campaigns but will contribute to mobilizing formal and ad hoc organizations, as well as unaffiliated individuals, around common concerns and pursuant of common goals.
>
> 1) We recognize the diverse historical tendencies in the Black radical tradition, including revolutionary nationalism, feminism and socialism; 2) The technological revolution and market globalization have changed the economy, labor force and class formation in ways that need to inform our analysis and strategies. The increased class polarization created by these developments demand that we, as Black radicals, ally ourselves with the most oppressed sectors of our communities and society at large; 3) Gender and sexuality can no longer be viewed solely as personal issues but must be a basic part of our analyses, politics and struggles; 4) We reject racial and biological determinism, Black patriarchy and Black capitalism as solutions to the problems facing Black people; 5) We must see the struggle in global terms; 6) We need to meet people where they are, taking seriously identity politics and single issue reform groups, at the same time that we push for a larger vision that links these struggles; 7) We must be democratic, inclusive in our dealings with one another, making room for constructive criticism and honest dissent within our ranks. There

must be open venues for civil and comradely debates to occur; 8) Our discussions should be informed not only by a critique of the status quo, but by serious efforts to forge a creative vision of a new society; 9) We cannot limit ourselves to electoral politics — we must identify multiple sites of struggle; 10) We must overcome divisions within the Black radical forces, such as those of generation, region and occupation. We must forge a common language that is accessible and relevant; 11) Black radicals must build a national front of radical forces in our communities to strengthen radicalism as the legitimate voice of Black working and poor people, and to foster organized resistance.[11]

In many ways the struggle to win these acknowledgments of the work, lives, and issues of feminists, lesbians, gays, bisexuals, and queers in black communities were not unlike other previous attempts in our history to gain such recognition and access within black communities. We have no doubt that black lesbians and gay male activists who helped to create progressive organizations such as the National Coalition of Black Lesbians and Gays and the Combahee River Collective — individuals who committed themselves to the liberation of black people while simultaneously embracing their lesbian, gay and queer identities — also confronted similar arguments that strove to place them outside of black communities and black politics. Thus, the fight to place the lives of black lesbians, gay men, bisexuals, transgender people squarely in the center of the black experience in the United States is a struggle that has a long history and continues to be waged on multiple fronts.

As witnessed by the Black Radical Congress's principles of unity, clearly these moments of internal contestation had had some cumulative effect, both on those Lesbian/Gay/Bisexual/ Transgendered (LGBT) folk whose authenticity was being debated and on those who never before had to interrogate and explain publicly their thinking on "the homosexual question" and black lesbian and gay men in particular. It would be disingenuous not to confess the overwhelming emotions we both felt locating our black lesbian selves in the center of struggles to liberate black communities in front of nearly 2,000 black activists and backed by a document (the Principles of Unity) that declared that we had a right to be there. Neither one of us had ever experienced anything comparable. But the elation and great hope we felt was balanced by a general wariness, and even a little fear, that our sexual identities and interests would be summarily rejected. Balance of course ruled the day with our feelings of acceptance continuously tempered by those who repeatedly sought to reopen the discussion on the principles of unity or complained that feminists were "dominating" the "woman question."

The Congress ended with an agreement to propose and vote on a national structure and campaign. Participants were committed to continuing the work started at this historic event. Because the Congress's work is unfinished so too is our assessment of how effective and long lasting its commitment to principles three and four will be. Moreover, while our pledge to the organization remains steadfast, many questions remain: Should we interpret the inclusion of homophobia among the list of oppressions as a signal of real transformation? Does the inclusion of feminism as part of the contemporary black radical tradition signal a new popular understanding of gender and sexuality that extends beyond the realm of the personal? And most importantly, had our many debates, discussions and arguments around these issues truly transformed anyone's thinking?

As stated earlier, our general sense is that members of the Congress and other black leftists seemed to have moved beyond Clarke's indictment of black revolutionaries, understanding the fight against homophobia as something they must embrace, at least rhetorically, if only to appear consistent. For many this was not just a rhetorical transformation, but a process in which they began, possibly for the first time, to associate blackness with gayness, making the characterization of gay struggles as external and European activity, no longer possible. Yet even as many took steps to redefine lesbian, gay and queer struggles as internal to black communities, they did not take the next step and define these battles as central to the liberation of all black people. Still missing from many who identify as black leftist is a deeper understanding of heterosexism as a system of oppression that threatens the health and empowerment of black people. Without making heterosexism central to an intersectional analysis of struggle, the fight to radically transform black people's lives will never be complete.

Below we turn our attention to the reality of heterosexism in black communities and the intersectional politics needed to fight such oppression.

III. THE IMPACT OF HETEROSEXISM ON BLACK COMMUNITIES

Black communities have changed dramatically in the last fifteen years since Cheryl Clarke's essay was written. The gap between the middle class and the working poor has widened as economic opportunities have become more accessible for those blacks with the training and resources to take advantage of them. A mobilized and organized black gay "movement," at times more cultural and social than political, also increased "out" black LGBT visibility in our neighborhoods. Globalization and immigration have introduced new cultural forms and identities into black communities in this country. Of course, differences in class, sexual, and national identities have always been present in black communities. But in recent decades these groups, and others like them, have used collective action to achieve a new level of cohesion, visibility, and political salience. Each has tried, with varying degrees of success, to impact public discussions and agenda formation. In these and in many other ways can we measure the diversity of black people. Thus, to speak of a single black community is to risk ignoring our internal differences and the ways in which those differences shape our political challenges and strategies.

However, heterosexism still blantly rejects critical aspects of black diversity. Heterosexism presumes and legitimizes only a single set of sexual and general relationships: the sexual union between a man and a woman, and the social relations which flow out of that union. Many black institutions are afflicted with this myopia, unable (and unwilling) to see the real problems and strengths of the people they supposedly serve. These institutions have become so defined by heterosexist values that their visions of black empowerment are inextricably linked to heterosexist practices. For example, when HIV/AIDS rose to public attention in the early '80s, evidence soon mounted to the threat which the disease posed to black communities. Yet the reluctance and fear of acknowledging black gay men, injection drug users, sex workers, and their clients, led many black churches and public officials to deny that AIDS posed any threat to black people. It is important to realize that the motive for this inaction can be traced to the close identification of AIDS with social identities and practices which have posed the most direct challenge to heterosexism. Transmission of the virus through male-to-male sex certainly means that there are other sexual realities than male-to-female sex. The existence of sex workers points to the uncomfortable fact (for some) that sex is subject to commercialization, and in so doing negates the fantasy that sex only occurs, or is only possible, between monogamous partners. In short, AIDS forced recognition that the realities of sex and gender in black communities went far beyond any single Judeo-Christian model.

Of those who had the most access to the media, pulpits, and other information sources within black communities, these were difficult admissions to make. To talk about black people's sexual and gender diversity was seen as an act of normalization for identities and practices which they believed to be destructive. Instead, they seized the opportunity to reinforce monogamous heterosexual marital relationships by presenting them as the surest way for black people to be protected from the epidemic. In this moment of crisis, the political responses of many black leaders were guided by heterosexist ideological constructs, rather than the everyday realities of black people's lives.

Consequently, our leading organizations and officials refused to push for public policy, institutional responses, and the fiscal resources necessary to protect black people from this threat.

The damaging effects of appeals to traditional family structures offered as a response to the "crisis" within black communities extends well beyond issues of AIDS. Heterosexism normalizes certain family structures by privileging a state-recognized relationship between a heterosexual man and woman, and in so doing marks as deviant the hundreds of thousands of black families that do not match this model. From nineteenth-century slave codes, through the Moynihan report of the 1960s, to current attacks against poor women levied by the Work & Personal Responsibility Act, black communities have been denounced for the prevalence of nontraditional family structures—even when those structures are themselves the product of racist laws and policies. The image of the traditional nuclear family has thus been used as a weapon against all black people. But it is important to recognize the deployment of this idealized family structure recently by those on the right to both attack heterosexual, single black women and to demonize lesbians and gays, denying them equal rights such as the right to marry. This is a powerful point of connection between black lesbians and gay men and our home communities.

In its full force, heterosexism is not satisfied with merely categorizing behaviors as deviant or normal, but works systematically to (re)produce conformity to "normalcy." Heterosexism thus requires that black communities engage in continuous policing of members by each other.[12] It demands an environment of constant surveillance in which individual members must adhere to strict codes of conduct or risk being attacked. Specific gender roles are an inevitable consequence of a heterosexist belief system. Women are believed to have certain rights and privileges as a function of their biological gender, and the same holds true for men. In many black communities, this view is expressed in an ideology of "complementarity," which often traces this gender division and specialization to (supposed) historical African practices. Thus while there is no evidence to support the assertion of homogeneously heterosexual African societies, such arguments denounce black gay men and lesbians as not being truly black or African because our very sexual identities transgress heterosexist gender roles and relationships.[13]

Black women—straight or gay—are particularly subject to surveillance and control in a black heterosexist system. Black women are frequently chastised and punished for behaviors that go unremarked when done by black men. Even more unbelievably, black women's very survival has also been used against us. For example, single-headed households are regarded as a triumph of personal will and commitment when undertaken by black men, but seen as a pathology and a mark of the community's weakness when headed by black women.[14] The patriarchal values which underlie heterosexism see nothing remarkable about women who take care of children and who run households, for that is their "natural role", however, men who undertake responsibilities traditionally associated with women are seen as exceptional. The irony here, of course, is that women who take on traditional male roles are not accorded the same praise and appreciation. Some lesbians are denounced precisely because we are viewed as relinquishing our "femininity" and as being too "mannish." Straight black women can also be seen as a threat to black masculinity, as usurpers of black male leadership (in the home, at the job, etc.). Black women—whatever our sexual identity—are castigated unless our identities and actions are primarily defined in subordinate relations to black men. This unremitting censure is necessary to reinforce a system which is unable to value female identities and accomplishments unless they are centrally informed by heterosexist social relations. Heterosexism and patriarchy thus results in increased freedoms for black men (mitigated by race) while severely limiting the freedoms of black women.

Many of those who decry rights for black LGBTs often justify their homophobia and heterosexism in terms of protecting the welfare of black children. Yet it seems to us that it is heterosex-

ism and homophobia which are themselves limiting and threatening the lives of our children. There is the immediate threat to
the lives and physical well-being of young black people who either voluntarily or involuntarily are identified as gay, lesbian,
bisexual, or transgender. Others have written very effectively
about the increased suicide rate among such youth.[15] However,
less documented are the instances in which young black lesbians, gay, bisexual, and transgender folk are hunted down on city
streets, in parks, and even in their own homes and brutalized
and murdered because of their sexual identities.

This threat to the lives of young black people posed by heterosexism extends into the entire community, including those
who identify as heterosexual or "straight." The assumptions
underlying heterosexism and homophobia constrain, influence,
and determine the actions and attitudes of all black people.
Ideas that men have a right to women's bodies; that every
woman is in search and need of a man; and that men are to be
privileged in all relationships permeate our children's lives. Undoubtedly, it was some combination of these fatal myths, tied
together, dispersed, reproduced, and made culturally relevant
through intersecting systems of heterosexism, patriarchy, racism, and capitalism, that led to the killing of Tamika Thomas in
Chicago, Illinois, in early 1998. Ms. Thomas was killed as she
attempted to defend her friend from a sexist attack. Historian
and activist Barbara Ransby comments:

> Tamika Thomas, the working class mother of a young child, was shot
> to death outside a North Side theater in Chicago. She wasn't shot to
> death for drugs or money or anything as common or tangible as that.
> She was killed because she came to the aid of her friend who was
> fondled by a stranger while leaving the theater. [Ms. Harris] turned
> around and slapped the man. A fight ensued and he killed her. This
> says something about random violence, but it also says something
> about the politics of gender and sexuality in our community. The
> young man obviously felt she had no right to physically thwart his at-
> tack. After all, the most pervasive public image of black women is of
> gyrating, insatiable sex machines. . . . The young man was prob-
> ably shocked and enraged that this woman would slap him simply be-

cause he tried to "get some." Isn't that what women are there for?
Clearly, this is an extreme case but smaller insults to black women's
bodies occur every day. Sexual harassment and violence toward black
women is commonplace compounded by the reality of racism and the
vulnerability and lack of resources poor women experience.[16]

As Ransby suggests, the killing of Ms. Thomas may seem like
an extreme case, but everyday women remain in physically and
emotionally abusive relationships as they attempt to fulfill heterosexist and patriarchal narratives as well as emulate capitalist
commercials about what it is to be a woman in this society.
Clearly, material concerns with finding a job, supporting family
and friends, and just having a decent place to live and food to eat
will consume a significant part of their energies, but these are
not the only issues that shape women's lives. Concerns over
whether she will be beaten, raped, or harassed on a daily basis
just for walking down the street or, worse yet, for failing to con-
form to communal and societal standard of feminine and heterosexual appearances will also confront her. As we have argued
above, young black women learn that the development of their
individual characters, intellect, and independent strength must
at all times be secondary to their dependence and obedience to
black men. Or to put it in the words of a recent declaration from
the Southern Baptist Convention, a woman must "submit herself graciously to the servant leadership of her husband . . . ,"
with a minimum of protest.[17] Thus, liberation from class exploitation while critical will not alone improve the totality of black
women's lives. Needed is a more complex understanding of the
intersection of oppressions, including heterosexism and patriarchy in black communities.

The same can be said of the young black men we raise in our
communities. Heterosexist notions of black masculinity offer an
anemic selection of possibilities for young black men. The consumer industries which drive popular culture (music, advertising, television) deluge our communities with images of black
men as violent, abusive, selfish, and super-materialistic. These
qualities tend to become even more exaggerated in relation to

women or femininity. Against this backdrop, the few alternative images of black masculinity which are put forward simply cannot compete. Any embrace by black men of qualities that are defined under heterosexism as belonging primarily to the domain of women, and be immediately counter balanced by super-"masculine" traits which leave no doubt that the character in question is a "real" man. In addition, when structural constraints prevent black men from living up to certain heterosexist norms reinforced by consumer culture, many exaggerate other dimensions of their masculinity. Men are supposed to be economically independent. Unemployed black men are thus under pressure to demonstrate their masculinity in other, sometimes dangerous and destructive, ways. Our young men get the messages being "hard" is better than being "soft," and while they must "respect" and "protect" their women (male partners, of course, are simply out of the question) they must never be led by her. The result is another generation of men struggling to maintain gender fictions dictated by a heterosexist system unconcerned about their realities.

Finally, we would be remiss if when speaking to those of the black left we did not directly discuss, even briefly, the important role of class in manifestations of heterosexism and homophobia in black communities. Here we define class not only as levels of individual and family income, but also include considerations of access to influential institutions. This two-pronged approach is necessary to account properly for the complex ways in which money and power function in contemporary black communities and their effects on struggles over black sexuality.

There have always been individuals and families within black communities who have managed to gain a greater degree of economic success and attendant privileges. One such privilege, for those who would have it, has been a leading role in black organizations, elected office, and public discussions. In our resource-poor communities, money plays a powerful role in shaping black institutional behaviors and commitments. For example, affluent blacks are much more likely to be represented on governing boards and executive committees. But wealth has not been the only route to positions of influence within black communities. A few grassroots organizers and activists have also risen to positions of widespread visibility and leadership as a result of their perceived or actual hard work in pursuit of black empowerment. This emergent group of community leaders, however, is overwhelmingly male, (publicly) heterosexual and most often middle class with high levels of formal education. As recognized "activists" and "spokespersons," this group enjoys a greater degree of access to resources which shape political agendas and actions. Unequal distributions of money and institutional access have thus combined to produce a power elite that is marked by its failure to represent black gender and sexual diversity among its members and their public statements.

Even more disturbing than the fundamental unfairness that money and gender play in defining the development of black leadership are the ways in which many who profess to oppose class exploitation unashamedly and uncritically embrace and reproduce heterosexist and homophobic rhetoric and practices in market capitalism's image. This is not surprising as capitalism and heterosexism both share, as do most systems, several features which are centrally responsible for their oppressive effects. First, both systems rely on the creation and maintenance of clearly defined roles and sets of relationships among participants. Specialization and categorization are what allow these systems to work at their best. There may be instances of overlapping positions or role switching, but such acts cannot be reproduced on a mass scale without presenting a radical challenge to the system as a whole, and thus are tolerated in closely limited contexts. The marking and policing of boundaries is an essential aspect of this role distinction.

Second, concomitant with role differentiation, both heterosexism and capitalism share a distribution scheme which links institutional power to resource ownership. Under a capitalist system, resources are commonly measured by capital or those things which can produce money; the more resources or money one controls, the more powerful is one considered. Under heterosexism, power is assigned on the basis of one's ability to adhere to behaviors and appearances associated with traditional gender roles; the greater the match, the more social power one has. In both systems, those who possess the least amounts of the favored resources—those who are poor or among the working class under capitalism, and those who are visibly lesbian, gay, bisexual, transgender, or queer under heterosexism—are the most marginalized and subject to acts of repression and containment. Not surprisingly, those who are most valued often use their power to reinforce their positions of privilege and to perpetuate the marginal status of those who are not.

Third, both capitalist and heterosexist systems rely on continuous surveillance to ensure that individuals behave in ways which further the systems' values: profit and gender marking. It is not uncommon to hear of cameras installed on factory floors, locked doors to prevent unauthorized movement of workers, prowling supervisors who "keep an eye" on productivity levels, and even company policies which ban activities that might lead workers to form unions or engage in other forms of collective bargaining. Nor are we unfamiliar with the ways in which those who are gender suspect are quickly labelled "faggot," "Zami," "queer", "bulldagger," and are targeted for verbal and physical abuse. On the playground, at work, in church, and in our neighborhoods, behaviors that challenge traditional gender norms are quickly marked as deviant in order to protect and engender more acceptable gender identities and behavior.

These common characteristics leave no room in which to pursue economic and social justice for blacks at the expense of gender and sexual liberation. Black leftists who define themselves in opposition to market capitalism and the exploitation it produces run the risk of reproducing capitalism's oppressive logic and social environment when they leave unexamined and uncriticized their own heterosexist beliefs and behaviors. We cannot afford to be a house divided against itself. Even those who declare they are committed to black gay liberation and call for "toleration" and an end to gay bashing and murders must realize this is simply not enough. Black people need a liberatory politics that includes a deep understanding of how heterosexism operates *as a system* of oppression, both independently and in conjunction with other such systems. We need a black liberatory politics which affirms black lesbian, gay, bisexual, and transgener sexualities. We need a black liberatory politics that understands the roles sexuality and gender play in reinforcing the oppression rooted in many black communities. It is this liberatory, intersectional black politics we briefly discuss in the concluding section.

IV. INTERSECTIONAL POLITICS

The fight against male chauvinism is a class struggle — that's hard for people to understand. To understand male chauvinism one has to understand that it is interlocked with racism. . . . In other words the idea of saying "keep a woman in her place" is only a short step away from saying "keep a nigger in his place"
— Bobby Seale, Black Panther Party,
Interview in *The Guardian*, February 1970.

We have argued in this essay that the problem of homophobia within the black community is itself a manifestation of the deeper problem of heterosexism which subjugates not only black lesbians, gays, and queers but also severely limits the lives of black heterosexual women and men. Indeed, heterosexist beliefs, values, and practices pervade every aspect of black life, and attempts to hold all black men and women accountable to their own set of gender and sex norms, even when these norms fail to reflect the collective interests and individual realities of black people. In this context, fighting homophobia and heterosexism should be at the center of any black social justice politics.

Black lesbians, gay men, transgender, and queer folks still struggle, however, to find ways to talk to black heterosexuals about heterosexism and homophobia. What things must we say and how must we say it so that such discussions will produce new insights, behaviors, and connections? What evens must occur in collective levels before we confront the crisis of heterosexism currently gripping our communities? Must our mothers, sisters, partners, and friends be demeaned, beaten, or raped for not holding to some mythic narrative of womanhood, or must our fathers, sons, partners, and friends be incarcerated, beaten, or killed trying to define and defend their "manhood" before we take serious the pervasive and perverse reach of patriarchy and heterosexism?

It is our belief that those who practice intersectional politics are best positioned to confront and address homophobia, heterosexism, and patriarchy among black people. As detailed by women of color feminist authors such as Kimberlé Crenshaw, Deborah King, Patricia Hill Collins, or the women of the Combahee River Collective, an intersectional approach to liberatory politics seriously examines the ways in which race, sexuality, gender, class, citizenship status, and other significant social dimensions all combine to define the experiences, identities, and political challenges of black people.[18] Intersectional politics rejects the argument that any one dimension is always more important than the other; that race, for example, always outweighs gender and sexuality. Intersectionality is rooted in the complex interweaving of the political categories of race, gender, and sexuality, the lived experiences of black people under such categories; and the development of a political consciousness that links the two. It demands an understanding of how systems of injustice (such as heterosexism and racism) structure our society at both the macro- and micro-levels, and how they work both independently and together. Fundamentally, it means being prepared to show the connections among seemingly unrelated events that are rooted in heterosexism. For example, intersectionality means being able to identify the meta-narratives of gender-role ascription that helps explain and challenge the political correlation between the woman who is killed fighting back against her violent husband and the fifteen-year-old boy who is teased and beaten by his classmates for being a "sissy."

For those of us on the black left we must always ensure that our political analyses and actions are rooted in the everyday lived experiences of black people, in particular poor and working-class black people. It is also essential, however, that we pay attention to how different social, political, cultural contexts, and identities affect expressions of blackness in our communities. This requires that we become comfortable with the differences and pluralities that exist within black communities. Traditionally, we have feared those differences and the tensions they have produced, leading us to ignore them or to seek ways to impose one "right" way over the others. Rather, we need to ask what has produced these observed differences. It is really "natural" to be one way and not another, or is our degree of comfort with a particular group a product of its control of our main institutions and resources? More specifically, we have to ask how the exclusion of black lesbian, gay, bisexual, and transgender people reflects and supports our broader political goals; this is a crucial, though often unexplored, public discussion. As black leftists, what kind of society are we really fighting for? As black LGBT left activists, we also need to develop multiple languages or ways of talking about our issues, or we risk having our issues perceived as irrelevant by the majority of blacks.

Overcoming homophobia in black communities requires that we also commit ourselves to the broader struggle against heterosexism in black communities. Because dominant gender norms define our common oppressions, the fate of black lesbian, gay, bisexual, and transgender people is inextricably joined to the fate of heterosexual black women and men. Our joint social freedom will signal the freedom of all black people. We must remember, however, that fighting heterosexism also requires a critical engagement with capitalist ideology because of the ways in which it reinforces the logic of heterosexism. And although the problem of capitalism is pervasive in black communities, even among those sectors commonly identified as "radical," we must avoid the trap of denouncing capitalist work practices even as we affirm and embrace its logic in other areas of our lives.

The work to transform black communities, to confront and eradicate heterosexist and homophobic thinking among black social agents, has been gaining momentum in the fifteen years since Cheryl Clarke's essay was first published. There are sites of action where black LGBTs are both developing and deploying this intersectional and transformative politics; groups such as the Audre Lorde Project (currently the nation's only Center for Lesbian, Gay, Bisexual, Two-Spirit, & Transgender People of Color Communities), and the Black Radical Congress's Feminist Caucus are but two examples of the intersectional and transformative work that is being done. That's the good news. But there remains much more work to be done before black communities are transformed into sites of radical inclusivity, widespread democracy, and full empowerment.

NOTES

1. Cheryl Clarke, "The Failure to Transform: Homophobia in the Black Community," in *Home Girls: A Black Feminist Anthology*, edited by Barbara Smith (New York: Kitchen Table: Women of Color Press, 1983), 197-208.
2. Ibid., 197.
3. Throughout the text we use the term homophobia meaning the hatred, fear, and loathing of gay men, lesbians, bisexuals, transgender, and queer people. Heterosexism in this text refers to the systemic and imposed normalization of heterosexual relationships (those between one man and one woman) as natural, right, and the only acceptable family and intimate form of relating. Particularly, as a form of male authority where the husband, father, and male children are presumed to dominate the family structure, is closely tied to heterosexism. Finally, we should remember that not all heterosexual relationships are treated equally. And thus, heterosexual privilege as with patriarchal privilege is mitigated by hierarchies around race, class, and sexuality.
4. Ibid., 197.
5. Some have undoubtedly found fault with Clarke's collapsing of distinction among the large continuum of revolutionary activists in black communities.
6. Ibid., 198.
7. Huey Newton, "A Letter from Huey to the Revolutionary Brothers and Sisters about the Women's Liberation and Gay Liberation Movements," *We Are Everywhere: A Historical Sourcebook of Gay and Lesbian Politics*, M. Blasius and S. Phelan (eds.). (New York: Routledge, 1997), 404-406.
8. Robin Podolsky, "Sacrificing Queers and Other 'Proletarian' Artifacts," *Radical America*, vol. 25, no. 1; (January 1991), 53-60.

9. "Juneteenth is the oldest known celebration of the ending of slavery. Dating back to 1865, it was on June 19 that the Union soldiers, led by Major General Gordon Grander, landed at Galveston, Texas, with news that the war had ended and that all slaves were now free. Note that this was two and a half years after President Lincoln's Emancipation Proclamation — which had become official on January 1, 1863. The Emancipation Proclamation had little impact on the Texans because of the minimal number of Union troops to enforce the new Executive order." (June-teenth.com,http:www.juneteenth.com/history.htm)

10. Interestingly, we witnessed only men making these arguments

11. From the document "Black Radical Congress: The Fight for Human Rights Democracy and Economic Justice in the 21st Century."

12. We want to highlight the point that the policing of heterosexism occurs not only outside black communities by right-wing politicians and Christian conservatives, but also can be found from those we would call our own. For example, much of the rhetoric surrounding the Million Man March highlighted the rightful role of men as breadwinner and leader in their families and communities. Again, the family in all its patriarchal and heterosexist glory is offered as the key to emancipation for black people. But this time the argument is being made not by the Promise Keepers or the Regan/Bush/Clinton administrations, but by the Nation of Islam.

13. E. Frances White, "Africa on My Mind: Gender, Counter Discourse and African-American Nationalism," *Journal of Women's History*, vol. 2, no. 1 (spring 1990), 73–97.

14. See for example, William Julius Wilson. *The Truly Disadvantaged: The Inner City, the Underclass, and Public Policy.* (Chicago: University of Chicago Press, 1987).

15. Scott L. Hershberger and Anthony R. D'Augelli, "The Impact of Victimization on the Mental Health and Suicidality of Lesbian, Gay Male and Bisexual Youths," *Development Psychology,* vol. 31, no. 1; (January 1995) and, Paul Gibson, "Gay and Lesbian Youth Suicide," *Report of the Secretary's Task Force on Youth Suicide,*, vol. 3. *Prevention and Intervention in Youth Suicide* (Washington, D.C.: U.S. Department of Health and Human Services, 1989).

16. From email document "Isn't All that Feminist Crap Irrelevant to Real Black Women?" 30 April 1998.

17. *The Associated Press*, Wednesday, 10 June 1998.

18. Kimberlé Crenshaw, "Mapping the Margins: Intersectionality, Identity Politics, and Violence Against Women of Color," *Stanford Law Review* vol. 43 (July 1991), 1241–99; Deborah K. King, "Multiple Jeopardy, Multiple Consciousness: The Context of a Black Feminist Ideology," in *Black Women in America*, edited by M.R. Malson, E. Mudimbe-Boy; J. F. O'Barr and M. Voyer (Chicago: University of Chicago Press, 1988), 265–95; Patricia Hill Collins, *Back Feminist Thought* (New York: Routledge, 1991); Combahee River Collective, "The Combahee River Collective Statement," in *Home Girls: A Black Feminist Anthology*, edited by B. Smith (New York: Kitchen Table: Women of Color Press, 1983), 272–82.

"Jesus Wept":
Reflections on HIV Dis-ease
and the Churches of Black Folk

Reginald Glenn Blaxton

The title of this essay, from Saint John's Gospel (11:35), recapitulates the shortest verse in the Christian scriptures, and one of only two instances in which Jesus of Nazareth was reported to have cried in public. The story is heavily freighted with theological interpretation and dogmatic significance, but a kernel of historical truth can still be detected by the careful reader.

An itinerant religious teacher and charismatic healer,[1] Jesus, on arriving in the village of Bethany at the home of intimate friends—a highly unusual family unit in that time and place, consisting of three adult siblings[2]—receives confirmation that Lazarus, the brother of Mary and Martha, has died from an unspecified illness four days earlier. According to the narrative:

> When Jesus saw [Mary] weeping, and the Jews who came with her also weeping, he was deeply moved in spirit and troubled; and he said, "Where have you laid him?" They said to him, "Lord, come and see." Jesus wept. (John 11:33–35)

It is a pastor's commonplace that people may weep for a variety of reasons. But, according to the story, the tears of all the participants in the encounter, including Jesus's, are tears of grief and sorrow.

Tears of bereavement are a physiological indication that the initial period of shock and denial following the death of a loved one has passed; that there is a conscious, painful recognition of the profundity of one's loss; and that the often difficult and demanding work of accepting significant change in personal and social circumstances has begun.[3] Weeping is also an indication, even in the case of false or affected "crocodile tears," of the integral connection of body, mind, and spirit.

This essay, on reflection, was conceived more than a decade ago during the first years of the AIDS epidemic, when public health officials in Washington, D.C., and elsewhere noticed the reluctance of religious community leaders to be/become involved, as *community* leaders,[4] in reducing the fear and panic attending the lethal outbreak of HIV, a family of viruses of unknown origin.[5]

In 1984, I was appointed to the staff of the Mayor of Washington, D.C., with broad liaison and outreach responsibilities to a large and diverse religious community in the metropolitan area. The staff position of Special Assistant for Religious Affairs in a government committed to the constitutional principle of church-state separation is at least unusual and possibly unique.

Implicit in the establishment of such a position is the recognition by an elected official that people of faith, and the institutions that embody and publicly represent their spiritual challenges, disciplines, and commitments—that is to say, their worldviews—can and do contribute in extraordinary ways to the quality of life of the jurisdictions in which they are located.

Needless to say, most successful politicians in a representative democracy, whatever their views of the relationship of spiritual life to social concerns, tend to be realists who can count; they view the religious community as an aggregation of present (and future) constituents, who are likely on election day to return the favor of targeted constituent liaison and outreach in the common currency of electoral exchange: votes.

(By way of comparison, at the time of my appointment, the Reagan White House contained an Office of Public Liaison, with several individuals paid from public funds, who exercised similar functions and responsibilities in respect of the significant political influence of religious conservatives.)

A few months after starting work, in 1985, I received a request for assistance from Jim Graham, the administrator of the district's Whitman-Walker Clinic, which had been started in 1973 as a free clinic for gay men and lesbians. Because the first cases of sickness reported to the federal Centers for Disease Control were detected in young homosexual men, Whitman-Walker was the health organization best positioned to be the city's premier AIDS education and service agency. In addition, the clinic enjoyed the confidence and support of the mayor and the council of the district.

At the time, his request seemed simple enough; he asked for assistance in identifying local clergy to serve on a religious community advisory panel to counsel the clinic on the most effective ways of stimulating religious community involvement in the AIDS crisis.

I suspect that most African Americans and many others are aware that Washington is the oldest and longest-established majority-black city in the country.[6] The city's government, which combines state, county, and municipal functions, has been led mainly by black men and women since the advent of limited home rule, subject to congressional oversight and review, in 1975.

The city's Christian religious community, which is the focus of this paper, also has unusual characteristics. There are, for example, at least five "first" Baptist churches, four of which are predominantly black congregations. There are at least six churches formally designated as "cathedrals," which are traditionally associated with the ministry of bishops; and four religious dignitaries who, within the ecclesiastical traditions they represent, claim some variation of the title "Bishop of Washington." There are many more pastors who are styled "bishop" by their parishioners.[7]

Over the years, many of the larger denominations, black and white, have built or designated "national" churches in the nation's capital.[8] AME church members, for example, will probably be aware that the first church of African Methodism, "Mother Bethel," founded by Richard Allen in 1794,[9] is located in Philadelphia; the "National Cathedral of African Methodism," the Metropolitan AME Church, is located in downtown D.C.

Altogether, there are over 800 established congregations, large and small, within the city limits, and roughly double that number including the immediate suburbs of Maryland and Virginia. The vast majority of Christian congregations in Washington are predominantly African American, and most of them are led by African Americans. Consistent with the profile of black church membership nationally, most African Americans in Washington are members of Baptist congregations; the second largest cohort consists of black Christians who claim membership in one of the several denominations of the Methodist tradition.[10]

This concentration of black religious traditions, personnel, related organizations, and, in the Howard University School of Divinity (a member of an ecumenical consortium of theological schools in the metropolitan area), an institution of theological education which has educated black clerics and lay leaders for 128 years, is rivaled nationally only by the religious community of another eastern city with a black political establishment, Atlanta, Georgia.

The clinic director, then, was pursuing the active involvement of African American clergy with ties to local congregations in AIDS education, prevention, social support, and care initiatives. Why? In 1985, it was already evident to public health officials monitoring new infection and mortality rates that African Americans, who make up twelve percent of the American population, were disproportionately represented among the sick, the dying, and the dead.[11]

For many people of faith, within and outside the Christian tradition, recollection of the early years of the epidemic will be painful and unpleasant, and long-term memory, a mixed blessing. For where death is sudden and unexpected; where the brute fact of human mortality has been unconsciously denied;[12] when there has been little opportunity for emotional preparation; when the finality of death cuts short the possibility of reconciling dis-eased interpersonal and social relationships, weeping may be a sign of conflict, and anger-laden emotion. Weeping, an expression of personal, intrapsychic freedom from emotional and culturally determined constraints,[13] in such circumstances embodies and expresses the complexity of sorrow in the face of human mortality.

Too, for people of faith, recollection of the early years of the HIV/AIDS epidemic will be painful because, from the perspective of the dying, their companions and caregivers, friends and families, it is demonstrably true with few exceptions across the denominational spectrum, that the clerical leadership of the American religious community increased significantly the final suffering of people with AIDS.[14]

Far from responding to the sick and dying with that immediate compassion for "the poor" — a biblical category describing the economically, physically, *and* sociopolitically disadvantaged[15] — signified in the life, teaching, and healing ministry of Jesus of Nazareth (*Jesus wept!*), the intentional response of most communities of faith represented, rather, the shadow side of American religious life: a harsh public piety unmixed with compassion or empathy; a proud and defensive moralism untouched by modern historical and scientific method, learning, and insight; and a punitive and rejecting posture toward the sick and suffering grounded in a "religious" belief that persons with AIDS (PWAs) were, in some essential sense, morally deficient, and, in consequence, deserving of suffering and death.[16]

In fact, it was confidently asserted by many American religious leaders, from 1981 to about 1987, some of them influential in the formulation of public policy at the federal level,[17] that suffering and death from HIV infection represented the condign will of a righteous God.[18] The sick and dying—with the possible exception of HIV-infected hemophiliacs and infants who, inconsistently, were said (and judged) to be "innocent" victims—were only reaping the consequences of irresponsible, "unnatural" conduct and lifestyles. The Christian scriptures were cited to justify the harshness of the verdict.[19]

R. Jay Wallace, a philosopher, in a discussion of free will and accountability, has persuasively argued that "[p]eople who are morally responsible may be made to answer for their actions, in the sense that their actions render them liable to certain kinds of distinctively moral responses." In addition to simple blame, he cites a range of sanctioning responses, such as avoidance, reproach, scolding, denunciation, remonstration, and (at the limit) punishment.[20]

All these moral responses are evident in early reactions of the religious community to persons with AIDS; and the range of reactions thus deployed constitutes the phenomenon I have termed "HIV dis-ease." Indeed, if moralism was not *the* dominant religious interpretation of, and response to, HIV/AIDS in the early days of the epidemic, it was the most clearly articulated, and the theological viewpoint publicly proclaimed with the most energy. And, according to polling data, it was widely believed by the American people.[21]

As a moral judgment, it had many public advantages. It was not so much simple—a critical inconsistency has been noted above—as simplistic and uncomplicated. It was the kind of emotionally charged message easily tailored to the requirements of the media of mass communication—television and direct mail—at which religious conservatives have demonstrated exceptional proficiency.[22] The judgment was consistent with a century-long battle with "godless" rationalism of various kinds, with infidelity to "religious" values, and with the immorality of a society which, it was plausibly alleged, had strayed from the moral and spiritual tutelage (and social control) of church officials.

Moreover, it appealed to centuries-long popular prejudices about social deviants, which, even in seemingly secular form and content, were grounded in traditional evangelical Protestant (and Catholic) religious doctrines concerning sickness and sin, sexuality, suffering, and death.[23] It has long been noted that Americans profess and demonstrate a high degree of religiosity.[24] It would have been unusual if the public—including, tragically, the HIV-infected, their advocates and caregivers—had failed to be influenced and affected by the clear disapprobation and sense of moral revulsion[25] informing traditional religious teaching.

In the popular mind, and certainly in the religious community, the early identification of the threat of AIDS (originally called GRIDS: Gay-Related Immune Deficiency Syndrome) with the sexual practices of gay men, stuck long after French and American researchers had separately identified the HIV family of viruses in 1983.[26] With the upheaval in sexual mores in the 1960s, under the pressure of rapid secularization and unprecedented societal change, the AIDS phenomenon was, in a certain sense, seen as God-sent—as condign judgment on morally irresponsible behavior—by many theologically conservative religious leaders.

In a gesture of ecumenical détente, this conservative moral/theological interpretation of "sin" and suffering, well grounded in the Christian scriptures *and* in both Catholic and evangelical Protestant church traditions, was allowed to pass from pulpit to pew into the public square without significant challenge or correction by more "liberal" religious authorities. Their critique of the "orthodox" interpretation of HIV/AIDS bore, to theological conservatives, all the signs of continuing a capitulation by religious authorities to the social and moral decay and decline of American society.[27]

Also, the "progressive" position on the meaning of AIDS bore an additional liability. Although the "liberal" analysis was well grounded in the historical-critical method, it was not—and, indeed, it *is* not—rooted in the "plain" interpretation of the scriptures. It was therefore unlikely to have much appeal to biblical literalists. Moreover, it seemed to rely on the kind of *political* thinking and reflection which, in orthodox hindsight and interpretation, had produced all manner of contemporary social ills, immorality (meaning *sexual* immorality, as in common definition and usage), and irresponsible behavior.

For reasons that I explore below, the African American religious tradition is, despite its public image as an activist institution, demonstrably more conservative than its white evangelical Protestant counterpart.[28] The four or five denominations most Americans would readily identify as "the black church,"[29] are steeped, historically, in the ethos of evangelical Protestantism. African Americans, further, tend on average to be more conservative on a range of social issues, *other than issues of racial justice*, than white Americans.[30]

There is good reason to expect, given this religious and social conservatism, that many African Americans would find "orthodox" arguments cogent and appealing. Because conservative analysis and arguments are based in sources of ecclesiastical authority—the Bible, church doctrine and discipline, the preacher—to which black Christians have historically accorded great respect, I should not have been surprised, in retrospect, when fourteen clergymen out of fifteen contacted, all of whom served sizable, well-established congregations, declined to be involved in any way with the work of the clinic.[31]

Given their unapologetically conservative theological posture, why did the clinic administrator even bother to seek the involvement of black religious leaders in this cause (and with a health clinic "owned" by the city's white gay community),[32] when resistance and rejection might have been more realistically expected? Similarly, if the initial reaction of the fourteen black ministers represented their best understanding of the ethical requirements of their several church traditions, how do we account for the *official* shift in religious community attitudes, across denominational lines, after about 1987?[33] What social and political potentialities did the clinic director recognize in the ministers and in the congregations they serve and lead? And from the ministers's perspective, what actual or potential threat to the integrity of their worldview and religious self-understanding did the clinic director's bid for assistance entail?

The answers to these questions, I believe, speak to the current state of African American communities of faith in the urban context, their capacity to adapt to novel challenges, their critical awareness and self-awareness, and their future as *the* most important social institution in black communities and neighborhoods.

While this is not an essay in spirituality, the questions have, of necessity, a spiritual dimension; for *all* questions of human challenge, expectation, commitment, and response are related to the world of Spirit, a world of invisible potentialities, of things unseen. The answers indicate, I suspect, whether, and to what extent, the African American religious community still embodies, and how adequately it contextualizes, the deepest needs, hopes, concerns, and aspirations of African Americans.

By the end of 1985, 12,568 Americans had died from the complications of HIV/AIDS. According to the Centers for Disease Control, 3,420 of them were African Americans.

I

What, then, did the clinic director see when he looked to the leadership of the black church community for counsel and assistance?

Black Christian faith communities, since the rise of the independent church movement in the late eighteenth century,[34] have been the nursery and training ground for most black civic and religious leaders. Black churches have made original and distinctive contributions to American culture. Most contemporary secular music styles—jazz, rock and roll, pop, R&B, soul, hip-hop—have been influenced by the rhythms and improvisational inventiveness of black religious music forms. The imagination, style, and sheer communication skill of the black preacher are instantly recognizable in much American rhetoric and oratory.[35]

Financial contributions to black churches from a relatively poor people represent the primary form of charitable giving in African American communities and neighborhoods.[36] Anecdotal evidence suggests that black churches were the original venue for the development of minority entrepreneurial initiative, talent, and ability.[37]

Perhaps more than anything else, religious institutions owned and/or controlled by black people, against the social backdrop of chronic legal discrimination and customary racial prejudice, have nurtured and encouraged the self-respect[38] of their parishioners. Minority clergy have taken the preaching and religious traditions of their white coreligionists, and, in an act of invention and cultural recreation, reformed them for use as spiritual resources supportive of black pride and achievement. Black church leaders have produced, over two centuries, some of the most scathing moral critiques of, and made the most pointed appeals to, the nation's sense of social justice and fair play.[39]

In the popular mind, black and white, the African American churches' involvement in the civil rights movement of the 1950s and 1960s—exemplified preeminently in the ministry and martyrdom of the Reverend Martin Luther King, Jr.—has clothed its religious teaching and institutional practice with a moral authority and credibility[40] generally missing today from mainline Protestant church bodies. In fact, perhaps due to the power of television to amplify their preaching, teaching, and social criticism, black clergy are seen—and more important, in my experience, tend to see themselves—as religiously committed social activists.

The problem today, reflected in the fourteen black clerics' inability to confront the challenge and consequences of HIV/AIDS for their community, is that even among black religious institutions, there is no necessary relationship between religious teaching and social ethics and activism, *outside of the consistent concern for racial justice*. And, according to philosopher of religion and social critic Cornel West, because the black church lacks a critical awareness and self-awareness, there has been little to make the multiple connections between the ethics of the struggle for racial justice, and a host of contemporary sociopolitical concerns.[41]

Historically, black religious denominations that are typically considered "the black church," have developed within, and in tension with, the matrix of traditional (white) Christian doctrine in its evangelical Protestant form. To the extent that the churches of black folk are churches, rather than spiritually grounded protest movements, the emphasis on traditional sources of ecclesiastical authority — scripture, doctrine, discipline, liturgical practice, and ordained professionals who are accredited to interpret and teach doctrine *correctly* — is not likely to enhance future engagements with contemporary sociopolitical problems and moral/theological analyses that do not take, as their point of departure, orthodox Christian teaching.

In the increasingly faint afterglow of the civil rights era, it is important to remember that this is not a new point of view; it has been an ongoing criticism of black church life, proffered by several black leaders, many of whom remained active church members. In this regard, the early career (and spiritual journey) of the abolitionist Frederick Douglass is illustrative.

According to William McFeely, a recent biographer, Douglass, who was "sexton, steward, class leader, clerk, and local preacher" in Zion Chapel, a congregation of the AME Zion Church in New Bedford, Massachusetts in 1839:

> [s]oon after he took to the field for antislavery . . . wrote a candid letter to his fellow communicants . . . saying . . . that he had to cut loose from the church "because he had found the American church, writ large, to be a bulwark of American slavery." His affection for the chapel that had been his and [his wife] Anna's never faltered, but Frederick Douglass was now committed to a new faith, one for which he could speak the word.[42]

Or again, commenting on antebellum black church life in the North, and Douglass's restlessness (a spiritual condition, in the view of the Fifth-century C.E. bishop and church doctor Augustine of Hippo Regius in north Africa)[43] "for something more than the respectability of black New Bedford," McFeely says:

> [t]he churches not only gave their members religious nourishment but also provided them with the opportunities to raise their confidence by

talking together of both personal and public concerns—moral improvement, it was called. Temperance, attractive less for its assault on
alcoholism than as a mark of respectability, one accepted by proper
white middle-class neighbors, was among the chief of the public concerns. *So was antislavery, but many proper black church groups
shunned it as too controversial.*[44]

McFeely comments, Douglass found "he could not marry the
two religions, Christianity and antislavery, though one led to the
other."[45] Under intense personal pressure to use the resources
of faith, in its Methodist form and "African" coloration, to effect
direct social and political change, Douglass's critical discovery
confirms the wisdom of H. Richard Niebuhr's insight into
Methodism, originally a reform movement largely of poor
people within the Church of England. Neibuhr observes:

> The ethics which [Methodism] had in mind was not the social ethics of
> [William Law's] "The Serious Call" and of Moravian piety. It was in
> one sense of the word much more of a religious and less of an ethical
> movement. . . . The religious interest preceded the social, and so-
> cial idealism remained more or less incidental, while the hope of a thor-
> oughgoing social reconstruction was almost entirely absent. . . . the
> socially beneficial results of Methodism were never designed . . .
> they accrued as mere by-products of the movement.[46]

Douglass, to be sure, never renounced the black church, in the
sense that his name was removed from membership rolls; indeed, his "affection" for African Methodism remained constant
throughout his life.

A photograph of the interior of Metropolitan AME Church,
which he joined after moving to Washington, still adorns the
west sitting room of his home in the Anacostia section of Washington. Two gigantic candelabra, Douglass's gift to the church,
still flank the communion rail at Metropolitan. When his final
rites were held at Metropolitan in 1895, distinguished African
American clergy from the AME, AME Zion, CME, Baptist,
Presbyterian, and Episcopal churches participated.[47]

But in a sense not reflected in membership records, I contend
Douglass had "left" the black church many years before. A

questing spirit, and his critical perception of the distance between faith and works, between creed and deed, led him to do so. The caesura between religious teaching and the lived experience of communicants such as Douglass identifies a perennial problem of American religious institutional life: the problem of credibility.[48] The institutions of black religious life are—and have been—subject to this concern.

Gary Marx, a sociologist who has studied the "confused" relationship between the religious attitudes and beliefs of black Christians, and their social attitudes and commitments, has raised important questions concerning the "activist" posture and popular perception of black religious institutions. Seeking to clarify the relationship between religion and political radicalism, the area of Douglass's concern, he conducted, in 1964, a nationwide study of African Americans living in metropolitan areas, asking them questions about religious beliefs and behavior in the context of the civil rights struggle.[49]

Marx measured "conventional" militancy, as distinct from civil rights protest related to black nationalism, by asking questions about patience over the speed of integration, opposition to discrimination in public facilities and the sale of property, perception of barriers to black advancement, support of civil rights demonstrations, and expressed willingness to take part in a demonstration. His findings? Marx concludes:

> In an overall sense even for those who belong to . . . conventional churches [rather than sects, as sociologically defined], the greater the religious involvement, whether measured in terms of ritual activity, orthodoxy of religious belief, subjective importance of religion, or the three taken together, the lower the degree of militancy.[50]

Also, contrary to popular perception and expectation, the study found that black "individuals in largely white denominations (Episcopalian, Presbyterian, United Church of Christ and Roman Catholic) are those most likely to be militant, in spite of the perhaps greater civil rights activism of the Negro denominations. This pattern emerged even when social class was held constant."[51]

A footnote concerning the social attitudes of black clergy is also worth quoting at length:

> . . . few studies . . . have focused on the Negro minister. [Daniel] Thompson notes that in New Orleans Negro ministers constitute the largest segment of the Negro leadership class (a grouping which is not necessarily the same as "protest leaders") but that "the vast majority of ministers are primarily interested in their pastoral role . . . their sermons are essentially biblical, dealing only tangentially with social issues." Daniel Thompson, *The Negro Leadership Class* (Englewood Cliffs, New Jersey: Prentice-Hall, 1963). Studies of the Negro ministry in Detroit and Richmond, California also stress that only a small fraction of Negro clergymen show any active involvement with the civil rights struggle. R.L. Johnstone, *Militant and Conservative Community Leadership Among Negro Clergymen*, Ph.D. dissertation, University of Michigan, Ann Arbor, 1963, and J. Bloom, *The Negro Church and the Search for Equality*, M.A. thesis, University of California, Berkeley, Department of Sociology, 1966.[52]

It is true the studies cited, though conducted at the height of civil rights achievement and optimism, are thirty years old; and, as Marx notes, "many militant people are nevertheless religious," as the example of Frederick Douglass serves to demonstrate. It is possible that, with the rise of the black power movement in the late 1960s, attitudes toward social change have deepened and intensified among the following generation of African American clerical leaders.[53]

I would suggest, however, that when the clinic director looked to the black clergy leadership of Washington to become involved in AIDS prevention and service delivery work, his vision and expectations (and mine) had already been unduly influenced by an image, an *impression* of black clerical activism, rather than its reality.[54] The examples of black clergy, many of whom earned their public reputations as civil rights activists and used the name recognition civil rights leadership afforded them to gain purchase on political careers—Jesse Jackson, Walter Fauntroy, Andrew Young come readily to mind—were exceptional. Their exceptionality did not mirror black clerical reality on the ground.[55]

More typical of the views of the majority of black clergy on the subject of AIDS, in a sermon redolent of HIV dis-ease, was the biblical interpretation and theological analysis of a pastor in New York City:

> For the theology of AIDS, I hear Jesus saying, it is better for a man to go into life all maimed and blind than to have his members cast into hell's fire.
>
> I dare say, on the theology of AIDS, those folks who know they are going to die may get right with God more than those folks who we are dealing with who don't know they are going to die . . .
>
> You can't come up and tell me clearly, here is the position of the church; the church has got to work that out.
>
> We got to show love, compassion, and care, and yet not get ourselves caught up with aiding and abetting doing things that God clearly condemns.[56]

One would be hard pressed to say that this minister has misunderstood or misrepresented the biblical texts (Matthew 5:29f; Mark 9:43f) he cites with literal precision. The point, rather, is that traditionalist black Christians, clerical and lay, will most likely be willing to support explicit and targeted AIDS education and prevention efforts to the extent that their moral worldviews remain undisturbed by the challenge of HIV dis-ease.[57]

A global calamity,[58] the HIV/AIDS phenomenon touches in many Americans deep reservoirs of guilt about the moral status of contemporary sexual attitudes and behaviors. Guilt, in turn, provokes profound questions about the appropriate relationship of religion and culture,[59] and unsettling fears, common to *every* human being, about the goodness of created, embodied existence, the moral meaning of sickness and plague, and the inevitability, for every human being, of death. Clearly, HIV disease also cuts across other fault lines in a society deeply divided along lines of race, class, gender, and sexual orientation.

There is today a scholarly consensus as to the nature of the conflict experienced by the American religious community in the early years of the HIV/AIDS epidemic. The immediate conflict centered on the venereal transmission of HIV, and on the moral status of the sexual behavior of gay men. In a broader context, however, the clinic's request exposed the anxiety of church leaders, and, in my view, the contextual inadequacy of contemporary church teaching on the topic of sexuality generally, and on the moral legitimacy of bodily pleasure specifically.[60]

In the nineteenth century, the fluid physicality of black people (compared to the physical rigidity of whites), was frequently commented on with amazement by whites.[61] In particular, the exuberant and ecstatic expression and effect of the *movement* of Spirit on the bodies of the faithful is a typical, and in popular consciousness, defining feature of black church liturgical practice.

Assuredly an African survival, *unfettered* ease of physical movement which might be a safe form of spiritual self-expression in the church setting,[62] might also prove socially dangerous, if misinterpreted by racist whites, as it often was, as evidence of presumed black hypersexuality.[63] And the charge of hypersexuality leveled by clerics at oppressed people, has been used over centuries,[64] particularly during times of plague,[65] as an instrument of sociopolitical and spiritual domination. In this sense, the churches of black folk were originally the guardians and guarantors of the human right of (black) people to have, value, and express a culturally different, legitimately moral sense and understanding of human sexuality.

Similarly, drugs, which chemically induce changes in brain chemistry and conscious awareness, are used for the sensate pleasure they provide. Different cultures draw quite arbitrary distinctions between licit and illicit drugs; but the fact remains that people smoke cigarettes, marijuana and crack/cocaine, drink alcohol, shoot up heroin, snort cocaine, gulp caffeinated coffee and cola products, and take barbiturates because doing so, finally, is a pleasurable experience.

The severe personal and social deteriorations attending the addicted person's overuse of highly refined substances, and related increases in criminal activity in the community and neighborhood, suggest *nothing* of pleasure to the concerned family member or neighbor. But that is a point of view external to the drug user's own awareness; from the "inside," so to speak, the "high" feels good.[66]

The historic response of evangelical Protestants to drug use has been severe disapproval and charges of deficient moral character. Lacking an informed appreciation of drug use as a psycho biological phenomenon with personal and social ramifications, evangelical Protestants, black and white, have traditionally chosen instead to focus on moral abstractions and problematics.[67]

This "moral" overlay and response of the churches, then, more influenced by factors that are culturally determined than ethical, becomes over time a supporting rationale and warrant for the social control of "deviants," their beliefs, attitudes, and behaviors.[68]

The late Kevin Gordon, a theologian who wrote from a critical, lay Catholic perspective, has examined the views on sex of Catholic and Protestant lay people, as they are available without church interposition, in secular polling data. He has argued that there is a huge gap between what the churches' ordained ministers teach about sexuality, and, consequently, about bodily pleasure, and what lay people actually believe and practice. On a wide range of sexuality (and gender-related issues), he concludes, many lay people, with informed good conscience,[69] have come to reject official ecclesiastical authority, and have departed from the churches' received traditions on human sexuality.[70]

Church officials will argue plausibly in rebuttal that the truth value of theological/moral doctrinal propositions does not depend on the number of people who accept them. The African American Christians of antebellum America, progenitors of the churches of black folk, who found moral authority in their own lived experience, were few enough in number relative to the majority population.

They nonetheless rejected chattel slavery as a social institution compatible with their lived experience, their reformed faith in God, *and in their own embodied humanity.* Yet their moral posture toward chattel slavery was contrary — absolutely contrary — to the "orthodox" theological and moral interpretations of self-interested white Christians, drawn "correctly" from scripture and tradition[71] which, over centuries, assumed the rightness of the practice.[72]

This was the fundamental contradiction that Abraham Lincoln, reflecting with prophetic sensitivity on the Civil War, identified in his Second Inaugural Address:

> . . . these slaves constituted a peculiar and powerful interest. All knew that this interest was, somehow, the cause of the war . . . Neither party anticipated that the *cause* of the conflict might cease with, or even before the conflict itself should cease . . . Both read the same Bible, and pray to the same God; and each invokes His aid against the other . . .
>
> . . . fervently do we pray that this mighty scourge . . . may speedily pass away. Yet, if God wills that it continue, until all the wealth piled by the bond-man's two hundred years of unrequited toil shall be sunk, and until every drop of blood drawn with the lash, shall be paid with another drawn with the sword, as was said three thousand years ago, so still it must be said "the judgments of the Lord, are true and righteous altogether.[73]

Abraham Lincoln, who was not religious in the conventional sense represented by church membership, saw clearly enough that if "both sides read the same Bible and pray[ed] to the same God," that is, had access to the same religious traditions and spiritual resources, then the contest reflected in the bloody Civil War had more to do with sociopolitical "interests" than religious concerns. The contest centered on different and opposing conceptions of social justice in a place far distant in time from the setting and circumstances of the biblical writers.

When there is a gap between official religious teaching, regardless of how securely it is warranted by scripture and/or church tradition, and the lived experience of church members, the internal conflict for people under pressure may lead to outright conflict between contending parties, or the disavowal of ecclesiastical authority, or the compartmentalization of religion from other areas of their lives. Or some combination of the three. Both the process and the outcome are called, in common parlance, *demoralization*—a *spiritual* condition and complaint. As the example of Frederick Douglass suggests, it is not necessary to leave the church to "leave" the church.

Reflecting on the interplay of American racial and religious history, and HIV disease, I want to propose for the reader's consideration, a criterion of evaluation of church life offered more than two decades ago by Leon Edward Wright.

Dr. Wright, late Distinguished Professor of New Testament Language and Literature at the Howard University School of Divinity, and a teacher and investigator for more than thirty years of the spiritual dimensions of healing, recognized the problems of credibility raised by strict, uncritical adherence to received Christian doctrine and tradition. With intimations for the present and future credibility of American church life, including the churches of black folk, he wrote:

> The ultimate criterion which tests the effectiveness of such scrupulously guarded conservatism . . . is the difference it makes, or fails to make, in the quality of being and interpersonal response on the part of professing Christians themselves.[74]

By 1998, a cumulative total of 390,692 Americans had died of complications from HIV/AIDS. Of those dead, 132,221 were African Americans; and of that number (though current statistics are unavailable, by the year 1995) 2,913 African American persons with AIDS who lived in Washington, D.C. had died. The rate of new infections in Washington, currently the highest *per capita* in the nation, remains the same today as it was in 1988.

Sad to say, the HIV dis-ease of the Christian churches, black and white, may fairly be cited as a contributing factor in those deaths—many of which could have been prevented. The knowledge and the means were available, but not the will to do the right thing; "morality" forbade it.[75]

Even so, in the face of loss and change (in radical openness and spiritual attunement to "the fulfilling potentialities of the future")[76] — *Jesus wept*. Now finally, may all who suffered unto death from HIV dis-ease rest in peace, and in "that great gittin' up morning," rise in glory.[77] Thanks be to God.

NOTES

1. On the figure of the charismatic prophet/"magician," see John Dominic Crosson, *The Historical Jesus: The Life of a Mediterranean Jewish Peasant*, (San Francisco: Harper SanFrancisco, 1993) 137–167; Morton Smith, *Jesus the Magician* (New York: Harper & Row, Publishers, 1978); and, for example, the Introduction by Marvin Meyer and Richard Smith, eds, *Ancient Christian Magic: Coptic Texts of Ritual Power* (San Francisco, Calif: HarperSanFrancisco, 1994), 1–9.

2. See, for example, Henri Daniel-Rops, *Daily Life in the Time of Jesus* (Ann Arbor: Servant Books, 1980), 115–137; and John E. Stambaugh and David L. Balch, *The New Testament in Its Social Environment* (Philadelphia, Penn.: The Westminster Press, 1986), 84, 123–124. The Reverend Wallace Charles Smith, pastor of Washington's Shiloh Baptist Church, describes the typical African family unit in these terms: "[t]he African family structure, unlike the European structure, tends to form around consanguineal cores of adult siblings." See Wallace Charles Smith, *The Church in the Life of the Black Family* (Valley Forge, Penn.: Judson Press, 1985), 30.

3. See, for example, Kurt Eissler, "Death and the Pleasure Principle," 11–18, and Howard Becker, "The Sorrow of Bereavement," 195–216, in Section 2, "Mourning," 183–286, in *Death: Interpretations edited by Hendrik M. Ruitenbeek* (New York: Delta/Dell Publishing Co., Inc., 1969); Glen W. Davidson, *Living with Dying*; and Ernest Morgan, *Dealing Creatively with Death: A Manual of Death Education and Simple Burial,* edited by Jennifer Morgan (Burnsville, N.C. 28714: Celo Press, 1988).

4. See, for example, Annette Johnson, "The Impact of AIDS on Women and Persons of Color: Ethical and Theological Problems," 67–73, in *AIDS Issues: Confronting the Challenge,* edited by David G. Hallmann; Section 6, "HIV And the Role of the Community," 493–586, in *The AIDS Reader: Social, Political, Ethical Issues*; edited by Nancy F. McKenzie and Daphne C. Wiggins, "African Americans, Gender, and Religiosity," in *Culture and Difference: Critical Perspectives on the Bicultural Experience in the United States, edited by Antonia Darder (Westport, Conn.; Bergin & Garvey, 1995), 169–84. In Washington, New York, Philadelphia, and Boston, lay and ordained women from minority religious traditions have exercised significant leadership roles in the AIDS epidemic, in caregiving and social support (especially among women and their children), health education, outreach, and prevention efforts, and in the founding, development and direction of AIDS service organizations. I am indebted to the Reverend Dr. Cheryl Townsend Gilkes, John D. MacArthur Associate Professor of Sociology and African-American*

Studies, Colby College, Waterville, Maine, for reminding me of the historic, (rela-
tively) independent role and involvement of black churchwomen in congregational
and community health care. Among many studies of ethnicity, religion, gender, and
community leadership, see her exemplary congregational address to the Union Bap-
tist Church, Cambridge, Massachusetts, published as "To Sit and Die or Stand and
Live: Understanding AIDS and Responding Redemptively as Christians to its Vic-
tims," Howard University Journal of Religious Thought, winter–spring, 1990–
1991, 56–63. On the diaconal, health-related ministries of black churchwomen,
see William E. Montgomery, *Under Their Own Vine and Fig Tree: The African-*
American Church in the South, 1865–1900 (Baton Rouge, LA; Louisiana State
University Press, 1993), 95, 114–115, 139; and Susan L. Smith, *Sick and Tired of*
Being Sick and Tired: Black Women's Health Activism in America, 1890–1950
(Philadelphia, Penn.: University of Pennsylvania Press, 1995). The heroic, sacri-
ficial involvement of the African religious community of colonial Philadelphia in
ministering to the sick and dying of both races during the Yellow Fever epidemic
of 1793 is chronicled in Gary B. Nash, *Forging Freedom: The Formation of Phila-*
delphia's Black Community, 1720–1840, 121–25. Also, see the recollections of Richard Allen and Absalom Jones, *A Narrative of the Proceedings of the Black People*
During the Awful Calamity in Philadelphia in the Year 1793 and a Refutation of
Some Censures Thrown Upon Them in Some Late Publications.

5. The story of the early years of the AIDS epidemic has been dramatically told by
the late journalist Randy Shilts, *And the Band Played On: Politics, People and the*
AIDS Epidemic. Timothy F. Murphy has expressed thoughtful reservations about
the dramatic character of Shilts's treatment. See his *Ethics in an Epidemic: AIDS,*
Morality, and Culture, 11–19.

6. For a history of Washington, D.C., and of its early African American population,
see David Levering Lewis, Washington, D.C.: A Bicentennial History (New York:
W.W. Norton and Company, Inc., 1976); and Letitia Woods Brown, *Free Negroes*
in the District of Columbia, 1790–1846 (New York: Oxford University Press,
1972).

7. See Dianne Lynn Brickey (comp.), *A Directory of Churches and Other Religious-*
Related Organizations in the Washington, D. C. Metropolitan Area, edited by
Reginald G. Blaxton (Washington, D.C.: Mayor's Office of Religious Affairs, 1st
edition, 1985).

8. See, for example, Reginald G. Blaxton, "State Church or Community Church?"
The Witness, April 1991.

9. See Gary B. Nash, op. cit., 191–99.

10. For national denominational membership statistics, see Robert Wuthnow, *The*
Restructuring of American Religion: Society and Faith Since World War II, 19; cf.
affiliation estimates for the Washington metropolitan area (which should be approached with caution) compiled by David C. Mitchell, "Where We Worship,"
161, in *The Washingtonian,* vol. 22, no. 3, December 1986, and the cover report by
Howard Means, "God Is Back," in ibid., 151–65.

11. "From the period June 1, 1981–September 8, 1986, there were a total of 24,576
patients with AIDS in the United States. Of these, 6,192 (25%) are Black, and
3,488 (14%) are Hispanic. . . . The proportion of cases by racial/ethnic group
has remained relatively constant over time. However, the number of AIDS cases
among ethnic minorities continues to rise[;]" from "Minorities and AIDS," 86–

87, *AIDS Education and Training of Trainers Manual* (Washington, D.C.: Commission of Public Health, 1987). Also, see Leon Williams and June Hopps, "Acquired Immunodeficiency Syndrome and Minorities: Policy Perspectives," 37–54, in *Decade of the Plague: The Sociopsychological Ramifications of Sexually Transmitted Diseases* edited by Margaret Rodway and Marianne Wright (New York: Harrington Park/The Haworth Press, 1988).

12. See, for example, Ernest Becker, *The Denial of Death*; (New York: Free Press, 1997) Elisabeth Kübler-Ross, *Death: The Final Stage of Growth* (Englewood Cliffs, N.J.: Prentice-Hall, Inc., 1975); John Snow, *Mortal Fear: Meditations on Death and AIDS* (Cambridge: Cowley Publications, 1987); Walt Odets, *In the Shadow of the Epidemic: Being HIV-Negative in the Age of AIDS* (Durham, N.C.: Duke University Press, 1995), especially Section 4, "Life in the Shadow: Loss and Mourning," 63–93; the introductory essay by Edmund Pellegrino, "Ethnicity and Healing," in the anthology, *Trials, Tribulations, and Celebrations: African-American Perspectives on Health, Illness, Aging and Loss*, edited by Marian Gray Secundy, with the literary collaboration of Lois LaCivita Nixon (Yarmouth, Maine: Intercultural Press, 1992); and, for background, Edgar N. Jackson, "The Theological, Psychological, and Philosophical Dimensions of Death in Protestantism," 171–95, in *Explaining Death To Children* edited by Earl A. Grollman (Boston, Mass.: Beacon Press, 1967). Also, see Margaret Washington Creel, "Gullah Attitudes toward Life and Death," 69–97, in *Africanisms in American Culture* edited by Joseph E. Holloway (Bloomington, Ind.: Indiana University Press, 1991), 69–97.

13. For example, men who are socialized to believe that "real" men do not cry will probably have difficulty grieving. The American notion of "stoic" masculinity represented in this belief is a little more than a century old. See E. Anthony Rotundo, *American Manhood: Transformations in Masculinity from the Revolution to the Modern Era*, (New York: Basic Books, 1992) 223–93; and Michael S. Kimmel, "Consuming Manhood: The Feminization of American Culture and the Recreation of the Male Body, 1832–1920," in, *The Male Body: Features, Destinies, Exposures,* edited by Laurence Goldstein (Ann Arbor, Mich.: The University of Michigan Press, 1994), 12–38. Significant, related changes in the gender roles and social responsibilities of women, and of Protestant clergy are examined in Ann Douglas, *The Feminization of American Culture*; (New York: Farrar Straus & Giroux, 1998) and Donald M. Scott, *From Office to Profession: The New England Ministry, 1750–1850* (Philadelphia: University of Pennsylvania Press, 1978).

14. See, for example, Earl E. Shelp, Ronald H. Sunderland, and Peter W.A. Mansell, *AIDS: Personal Stories in Pastoral Perspective* (New York: The Pilgrim Press, 1986); John Fortunato, *AIDS: The Spiritual Dilemma* (San Francisco, Calf.: Harper & Row, Publishers, Inc., 1987); David G. Hallman, ed., *AIDS Issues: Confronting the Challenge* (New York: Pilgrim Press, 1989); Elisabeth Kübler-Ross, *AIDS: The Ultimate Challenge* (New York: Collier Books, 1997); William E. Amos, Jr., *When AIDS Comes to Church* (Philadelphia: Westminsterr Press, 1988); Robert H. Iles, ed., *The Gospel Imperative in the Midst of AIDS: Towards a Prophetic Pastoral Theology* (Wilton, Conn.: Morehouse Publishing, 1989); Letty M. Russell, ed., *The Church with AIDS: Renewal in the Midst of Crisis* (Louisville, Ky: Westminster/John Knox Press, 1990); Harlon L. Dalton, "AIDS in Blackface," in Nancy F. McKenzie ed., op. cit,; 122–39, W. C. Champion, *The Black*

124 — Dangerous Liaisons

Church and AIDS (Dallas: Self published, 1991); B. Michael Hunter ed., Sojourner: Black Gay Voices in the Age of AIDS (New York: Other Countries Press, 1993), vol. 2; the writer's articles: "The Ethics of Moralism: AIDS, Religion and Public Policy," "AIDS Public Health Policy: Will the Church Punish or Heal?," and (commendatory) reviews of William E. Amos, When AIDS Comes to Church, Virginia Seminary Journal (Alexandria, Va.: Virginia Theological Seminary, June 1989), 74 – 75; and of Earl E. Shelp and Ronald H. Sunderland, AIDS and the Church: The Second Decade, Virginia Seminary Journal (Alexandria, Va: Virginia Theological Seminary, December 1993), 87 – 88; and recently, Chip Berlet ed., Eyes Right: Challenging the Right Wing Backlash (Boston, Mass.: Political Research Associates, 1995). In my view, the most thorough, sensitive, and comprehensive text from the early years oriented to religious community interests and concerns is Earl E. Shelp and Ronald H. Sunderland, AIDS and the Church.

15. According to Albert Nolan, "the poor," which translates the Hebrew anawim, refers to (and includes) the following: "the poor, the blind, the lame, the crippled, the lepers, the hungry, the miserable (those who weep), sinners, prostitutes, tax collectors, demoniacs (those possessed by unclean spirits), the persecuted, the downtrodden, the captives, all who labor and are overburdened, the rabble who know nothing of the law, the crowds, the little ones, the least, the last, and the babes or the lost sheep of Israel." See Albert Nolan, Jesus Before Christianity (Mary Knoll, NY: Orbis Books, 1992), 27; and the excellent treatment in Daniel C. Maguire, The Moral Core of Judaism and Christianity: Reclaiming the Revolution (Minneapolis: Fortress Press, 1993). Also, see Arno Karlen, Man and Microbes: Disease and Plagues in History and Modern Times (New York: Simon & Schuster, 1995), 65 – 67, 185 – 4; and William H. McNeill, Plagues and Peoples (Garden City, N.Y.: Anchor Press/Doubleday, 1976), 121 – 23, 136, and, more generally, chapter 3, "Confluence of the Civilized Disease Pools of Eurasia: 500 B.C. to A.D. 1200," 77 – 147. Shelp and Sunderland, op. cit., have argued persuasively that this biblical category also covers persons with HIV/AIDS. Also, see, for example, Bill Kirkpatrick, AIDS: Sharing the Pain: A Guide for Caregivers "Ministers and Other Careers" (New York: The Pilgrim Press, 1990), 73 – 83; Newell J. Wert, "The Biblical and Theological Basis for Risking Compassion and Care for AIDS Patients," 231 – 42; and John Backe, "AIDS: A Serious and Special Opportunity for Ministry," 249 – 61, in AIDS, Ethics & Religion: Embracing a World of Suffering edited by Kenneth R. Overberg, S.J.; and Joseph A. Edelheit, "AIDS: A Transformative Challenge for Clergy," in , AIDS: Crisis in Professional Ethics, edited by Elliot D. Cohen and Michael Davis (Philadelphia, Penn.: Temple University Press, 1994), 197 – 207.

16. See, for example, Reginald G. Blaxton, "The Ethics of Moralism: AIDS, Religion and Public Policy," The Quarterly Review of the AME Zion Church, Spring 1987; Richard Poirier, "AIDS and Traditions of Homophobia," in In the Time of Plague: The History and Social Consequences of Lethal Epidemic Disease, edited by Arien Mack, 139 – 53; Chapter 5, "Black Masculinity and the Sexual Politics of Race," 131 – 70, in Welcome to the Jungle: New Positions in Black Cultural Studies, edited by Kobena Mercer, (New York: Routledge, 1994), especially "AIDS, Racism and Homophobia," 154 – 59; Bruce L. Mills, "Fear & Passion: A Psychological Reflection on the Construction of Homophobia in the Context of AIDS," in Homophobia and the Judaeo-Christian Tradition, edited by Michael L. Stem-

meler and J. Michael Clark, 165-87; J. Michael Clark, *Theologizing Gay: Fragments of Liberation Activity* (Oak Cliff, Tex.: Minuteman Press, 1991), especially "Homophobia & AIDS: Notes on Pastoral Care," 21-34; Gary E. Doupe, "True to Our Tradition," discussing Christianity, 187-204, in *Homophobia: How We All Pay the Price* edited by Warren J. Blumenfeld (Boston, Mass: Beacon Press, 1992); Nicola Field, *Over the Rainbow: Money, Class and Homophobia* (London: Pluto Press, 1995), discussing Christianity, 131-32; George A. Appleby, "AIDS and Homophobia/Heterosexism," 1-24, in *HIV Disease: Lesbians, Gays and the Social Services*, edited by Gary A. Lloyd and Mary Ann Kuszelewicz, (New York: The Haworth Press, Inc., 1995); Keith Boykin, *One More River to Cross: Black and Gay in America* (New York: Anchor Books/Doubleday, 1996), especially "Black Homophobia," 155-211, and "Bearing Witness: Faith in the Lives of Black Lesbians and Gays," 123-54; and William P. Zion, "AIDS, Ethics and Religion," in , *Perspectives on AIDS: Ethica l and Social Issues*, edited by Christine Overall with William P. Zion 43-54. Also see, for example, Terence Huwe, "AIDS, Service, and the Renewal of the Heart: A Personal Reflection," in *Sex and Spirit: Exploring Gay Men's Spirituality* edited by Robert Barzan (San Francisco, Calif.: White Crane Newsletter, 1995) 112-16; E. Michael Gorman, "A Special Window: An Anthropological Perspective on Spirituality in Contemporary U.S. Gay Male Culture," in *Constructing Gay Theology* edited by Michael L. Stemmeler and J. Michael Clark (Las Colinas, Tex.: Monument Press, 1990), 45-61; the pre-HIV-era memoirs by Leonard Patterson, "At Ebenezer Baptist Church," referring to the historic Atlanta congregation, and James S. Tinney, "Struggles of a Black Pentecostal," by the late professor of journalism at Howard University, and founding pastor of the District's Faith Temple, a congregation ministering to black, evangelical lesbians and gay men, in *Black Men/White Men: A Gay Anthology* edited by Michael J. Smith (San Francisco, Calif.: Gay Sunshine Press, 1983), 163-72; discussing these, Charles I. Nero, "Toward a black gay aesthetic: Signifying in contemporary black gay literature," 229-52, in *Brother to Brother: New Writings by Black Gay Men* edited by Essex Hemphill (Boston, MA: Alyson Publications, Inc., 1991), especially "Signifying on the church," 238-43; the theological reflection by Randy Miller (director of the Rafiki Services Project, San Francisco), "On My Journey Now," *Open Hands*, vol. 6, no. 4 (spring, 1991) 8-10; Ronald E. Long and J. Michael Clark, *AIDS, God, and Faith: Continuing the Dialogue on Constructing Gay Theology* (Las Colinas, Tex.: Monument Press, 1992); DeNeen L. Brown, "Citing Spiritual Needs, Black Gays Confront Condemnation From the Church," *The Washington Post*, 1 August 1993, B4; Sidney Brinkley, "San Francisco Mayor Yanks Minister from Rights Panel, *The Washington Blade*, 27 August 1993, discussing the Reverend Eugene Lumpkin, pastor of San Francisco's Ebenezer Baptist Church, erstwhile member of the city's Human Rights Commission; Brian Bouldrey, *Wrestling With the Angel: Faith and Religion in the Lives of Gay Men;* and Gary David Comstock, *Unrepentant, Self-Affirming, Practicing: Lesbian/Bisexual/Gay People within Organized Religion* (New York: The Continuum Publishing Company, 1996), discussing "he Black Church," 189-92.

17. "If the Reagan administration does not put its full weight against what is now a gay plague in this country, I feel that a year from now, President Ronald Reagan, personally, will be blamed for allowing this awful disease to break out among the innocent American public." The Reverend Jerry Falwell, president of the Moral

Majority, cited in Shilts, op. cit., 347. Also, see Richard L. Rubenstein, *Reflections on Religion and Public Policy* (Washington, D.C.: The Washington Institute for Values in Public Policy, Inc., 1984); Bruce Lawrence, *Defenders of God: The Fundamentalist Revolt Against the Modern Age* (San Francisco, Calf.: Harper & Row, Publishers, 1989), especially chapter 7, "American-style Protestant Fundamentalists," 153–88; A. James Reichley, "Pietist Politics," 73–98, and Patrick M. Arnold, S.J., "The Reemergence of Fundamentalism in the Catholic Church," 172–91, in *The Fundamentalist Phenomenon: A View from Within; A Response from Without* edited by Norman J. Cohen (Grand Rapids, Mich.: The Starkoff Institute of Ethics and Contemporary Moral Problems/Wm. B. Eerdmans Publishing Co., 1990); and Paul A. Carter, "The Fundamentalist Defense of the Faith," *Politics, Religion, and Rockets: Essays in Twentieth-Century American History* (Tucson, Ariz.: The University of Arizona Press, 1991), 107–26.

18. "The spread of AIDS is an act of vengeance against the sin of homosexuality." Philadelphia's Archbishop, the late Cardinal John Krol, cited in Robert Goss, *Jesus Acted Up: A Gay and Lesbian Manifesto*, 24. For an elaboration of this perspective, see Orville N. Griese and Eugene F. Diamond, *The AIDS Crisis and the Contraceptive Mentality: Moral, Medical and Social Aspects* (Braintree, Mass.: Pope John XXIII Medical-Moral Research and Education Center, 1988), 40–48. Cf. Edward Norman, "AIDS and the Will of God," in James Woodward, *Embracing the Chaos: Theological Responses to AIDS* (London: SPCK, 1991), 82–89.

19. "AIDS is a lethal judgment of God on America for endorsing this vulgar, perverted and reprobate lifestyle . . . God also says those engaged in such homosexual acts will receive "in their own persons, due penalty of their error." God destroyed Sodom and Gomorrah primarily because of the sin of homosexuality. Today He is again bringing the judgment against this wicked practice through AIDS." The Reverend Jerry Falwell, cited in Goss, op. cit., 24. Cf. Tiemo Rainer Peters, "Orthodoxy in the Dialectic of Theory and Practice," in , Orthodoxy and Heterodoxy, edited by Johannes-Baptist Metz and Edward Schillebeeckx 73–83.

20. R. Jay Wallace, Responsibility and the Moral Sentiments, 54. For a sociological analysis, see Svend Ranulf, *Moral Indignation and Middle Class Psychology* (New York: Schocken Books, 1964). For a (chillingly) clear statement and example, see the article by G. E. Zuriff, "a professor of psychology at Wheaton College (traditionally, a well-regarded redoubt of evangelical thought), and a clinical psychologist . . . of MIT," "Medicalizing Character," 94–99, in *The Public Interest*, Irving Kristol and Nathan Glazer, eds. no. 123, spring 1996, especially "Moral Responsibility," discussing the Americans with Disabilities Act (ADA). ". . . While it may make some sense to protect and accommodate people with schizophrenia who lack control over their illness, the same is not true for people with personality disorders [". . . sexual disorders, drug addictions, and alcoholism can serve as a model"]. Their actions, attitudes, and qualities of character are commonly disapproved of in our society, and they should be held morally responsible for them. They should be encouraged to accommodate to society rather than the reverse. At the same time, we can recognize their suffering and perhaps provide them with the appropriate psychotherapy." Zuriff, 99. Emphasis supplied.

21. According to research conducted in 1986 by the *Los Angeles Times*, one-quarter of the Americans polled believed that AIDS was God's judgment on homosexuals

and drug users for the way they live. See the introductory essay, "The Contemporary Debate in the Churches on the AIDS Crisis," xiii–xxii, by J. Gordon Melton, *The Churches Speak on AIDS: Official Statements from Religious Bodies and Ecumenical Organizations* (Detroit, Mich.: Gale Research Inc., 1989). Also, see Larry Thompson, "AIDS Discrimination On the Rise," *The Washington Post/Health*, 19 June 1990, p. 15; and Robert J. Blendon and Karen Donelan, "AIDS and Discrimination: Public and Professional Perspectives," in , AIDS and the Health Care System edited by Lawrence O. Gostin (New Haven, Conn.: Yale University Press, 1990), 77.

22. See, for example, William F. Fore, *Television and Religion: The Shaping of Faith, Values, and Culture*; Quentin J. Schultze, *Televangelism and American Culture: The Business of Popular Religion* (Grand Rapids, Mich.: Baker Book House, 1991); the prophetic essay by Neil Postman, "Amusing Ourselves to Death: Public Discourse in the Age of Show particularly during times of Business"; Herman Gray, *Watching Race: Television and the Struggle for "Blackness'* (Minneapolis, Minn.: University of Minnesota Press, 1995), especially "Black Bodies and the Reagan Revolution," 26–27; the audience study (financed by Bill and Camille Cosby) of Sut Jhally and Justin Lewis, Enlightened Racism: "The Cosby Show," Audiences, and the Myth of the American Dream (Boulder, Colo.: Westview Press, 1992), especially chapter 4, "Black Experience: Images, Illusions, and Social Class," 57–70; Michelle A. Wolf and Alfred P. Kielwasser, *Gay People, Sex, and the Media* (Binghamton, NY: Harrington Park/The Haworth Press, Inc., 1991), especially "AIDS and the Mass Media," 47–75; and, on "moral panics," Simon Watney, *Policing Desire: Pornography, AIDS and the Media*, 38–57, 123–35.

23. See, for example, Jeffrey Richards, *Sex, Dissidence and Damnation: Minority Groups in the Middle Ages*; cf. the pathfinding study of the late classicist and historian, John Eastburn Boswell, *Christianity, Social Tolerance, and Homosexuality: Gay People in Western Europe from the End of the Christian Era to the Fourteenth Century*. Also, see Donald Tuzin, "Discourse, Intercourse, and the Excluded Middle: Anthropology and the Problem of Sexual Experience," 257–75, in Paul R. Abramson and Steven D. Pinkerton, *Sexual Nature, Sexual Culture* (Chicago, Ill.: The University of Chicago Press, 1995).

24. Barry A. Kosmin and Seymour P. Lachman, *One Nation Under God: Religion in Contemporary Society*, 8–9.

25. "Those who wish to rescue our society's purity rules by designating everyone who deviates from them as 'sick' are merely renaming purity; they are not telling us anything new or illuminating. In many cases they have been uttering falsehoods, and, in the process, they have harmed many generations of the young. . . ." L. William Countryman, *Sex, Greed and Dirt: Sexual Ethics in the New Testament and Their Implications for Today*, 247. Also, see Grace Jantzen, "AIDS, Shame and Suffering," 22–31, in James Woodward, op. cit.

26. The "co-discovery" by French and American researchers of the virus that would be called HIV is the official, "authorized version" of scientific history. In reality, without equivocation, French researchers discovered HIV. For the "revised standard version," on which there is general scholarly agreement, see Elinor Burkett, *The Gravest Show on Earth: America in the Age of AIDS* (Boston, Mass.: Houghton Mifflin Company, 1995), 19–52.

27. On the meaning of "orthodox," "conservative," "liberal," and "progressive," I have followed the analysis of James Davison Hunter. He "us[es] the terms orthodox and progressive as formal properties of a belief system or world view . . . what makes orthodoxy more of a formal property is the commitment on the part of adherents to an external, definable, and transcendent authority . . . what all progressivist world views share in common is the tendency to re-symbolize historic faiths to the prevailing assumptions of contemporary life." See James Davison Hunter, *Culture Wars: The Struggle to Define America*, 44. Also, see, for example, Harvey Cox, (New York: Simon and Schuster, 1984), "Fundamentalism and Postmodern Theology," *Religion in the Secular City: Toward a Postmodern Theology* 72–97; A. James Reichley, *Religion in American Public Life* (Washington, D.C.: The Brookings Institution, 1985), on "liberal" mainline Protestants in crisis, pp. 243–339; Daniel Liechty, *Theology in Postliberal Perspective* (Philadelphia, Penn.: Trinity Press International, 1990), especially "Church Without Dogma," 59–72; and Hugh Montefiore, *Credible Christianity: The Gospel in Contemporary Society* (Grand Rapids, Mich.: Wm. B. Eerdmans Publishing Company, 1993), especially the Introduction, discussing faith and belief, 1–23.

28. See Kosmin and Lachman, op. cit., 130–37; for example, Randall Balmer's fine portrait of contemporary American evangelicalism, *Mine Eyes Have Seen the Glory: A Journey into the Evangelical Subculture in America,* especially 138–53; for background, V. P. Franklin, *Black Self-Determination: A Cultural History of African-American Resistance,* "The Gospel According to Enslaved Afro-Americans," (Brooklyn, N.Y.: Lawrence Hill Books, 1992, 1st pub. 1984), 29–67; and Dewey W. Grantham, *The South in Modern America: A Region at Odds* (New York: HarperCollins Publishers, 1994), 314–18.

29. There is, unfortunately, no consistently used definition of "the black church," which generally describes the historically-black Baptist denominations and the AME, AME Zion, and CME churches. Sometimes the label covers African American members of the United Methodist church, and black Pentecostals. Since African Episcopal and African Presbyterian churches antedate by several years the establishment of the African Methodist Episcopal Church, and the establishment of black Pentecostalism by more than a century, I do not see how these congregations and their clerical leaders can be excluded from the definition. I also know of no historical authority who regards Absalom Jones, John Gloucester, Henry Highland Garnet, Samuel Ringgold Ward, Alexander Crummell, and Edward Wilmot Blyden, for example, as anything other than black churchmen; they were recognized as such by their nineteenth century ministerial contemporaries who were members of historically black denominations. Cf. Peter J. Paris, *The Social Teaching of the Black Churches* (Philadelphia, Penn.: Fortress Press, 1985), xi. This kind of sectarianism has serious implications for the study of the history and experience of 1.2 million black Catholics, who are not generally included in contemporary "black church" studies. Cf. Diana L. Hayes, *And Still We Rise: An Introduction to Black Liberation Theology* (New York: Paulist Press, 1996), discussing "The Black Church," 12–16. Recipient of a pontifical doctorate in theology, from the Catholic University of Louvain, the first to be awarded to an African American woman, Hayes, who is also an attorney, was, in 1985, an accredited representative of the Archdiocese of Washington, where she analyzed District affairs.

30. See, for example, Sara Diamond, *Roads to Dominion: Right-Wing Movements and Political Power in the United States* (New York: The Guilford Press, 1995), 300; Elinor Burkett, op. cit., 169-90; and Clyde Wilcox, *God's Warriors: The Christian Right in Twentieth-Century America* (Baltimore, Md.: The Johns Hopkins University Press, 1992), 55-56, 162-65.

31. See, for example, Stuart Schneiderman, *Saving Face: America and the Politics of Shame* (New York: Alfred A. Knopf, 1995), especially 186-93; and also, Michael A. Milburn and Sheree D. Conrad, *The Politics of Denial* (Cambridge, Mass.: The MIT Press, 1996), especially 73-106. ". . . Our findings raise the possibility that religious beliefs are at the root of a wide range of calls for harshness toward those who would break the rules." Milburn and Conrad, 87. The exception was the Reverend J. Terry Wingate, pastor of the Purity Baptist Church in northeast Washington, and sometime Special Assistant for Religious Affairs to the Mayor of the District of Columbia. For his responsiveness and assistance, then and thereafter, I am very grateful.

32. For a history of the District's (white) gay community, see David K. Johnson, "'Homosexual Citizens': Washington's Gay Community Confronts the Civil Service," in *Washington History: Magazine of The Historical Society of Washington, D.C.*, vol. 6, no. 2, (fall/winter 1994-1995): 45-63, 93-96. Also, see, for background, chapter 4, "AIDS and the 'Homosexual Question': The Gay Sexuality Debates," in Steven Seidman, *Embattled Eros: Sexual Politics and Ethics in Contemporary America* (London: Routledge, 1992), 145-78; Dennis Altman, "Legitimation through Disaster: AIDS and the Gay Movement," in *AIDS and the Burdens of History* edited by Elizabeth Fee and Daniel M. Fee (Berkeley, Calf.: University of California Press, 1988), 301-315; David Román, "Fierce Love and Fierce Response: Intervening in the Cultural Politics of Race, Sexuality, and AIDS," 195-219, in *Critical Essays: Gay and Lesbian Writers of Color*, edited by Emmanuel S. Nelson (Binghamton, N.Y.: Harrington Park/The Haworth Press, Inc., 1993); John L. Peterson, "AIDS-Related Risks and Same-Sex Behaviors Among African American Men," 85-104, in *AIDS, Identity, and Community: The HIV Epidemic and Lesbians and Gay Men* edited by Gregory M. Herek and Beverly Greene (London: Sage Publications, 1995); recently, Chris Bull and John Gallagher, *Perfect Enemies: The Religious Right, the Gay Movement, and the Politics of the 1990s* (New York: Crown Publishers, Inc., 1996); and Larry D. Icard, "Assessing the Psychosocial Well-Being of African American Gays: A Multidimensional Perspective," in *Men of Color: A Context for Service to Homosexually Active Men*, edited by John F. Longres (New York: Harrington Park/The Haworth Press, Inc., 1996), discussing religion, 40-41.

33. See, for example, Laura Sessions Stepp, "AIDS Epidemic Is Slowly Gaining Attention in Local Pulpits," *The Washington Post*, 3 January 1989, D1-2; and Larry Witham, "AIDS Challenges Churches to Keep Teaching, Be Humane," *The Washington Times*, 21 October 1988. Cf., recently, Ted G. Jelen, *The Political World of the Clergy* (Westport, Conn.: Praeger, 1993), discussing evangelical and mainline (white) Protestant clerical attitudes toward people with HIV/AIDS, 39-70. On February 3-4, 1988, the late M. Carl Holman, president of the National Urban Coalition, convened an ecumenical meeting of denominational executives at Shiloh Baptist Church under the name, the National Black Church Consortium on Critical Health Needs in the Black Community. The purpose of the meeting

was to address and develop strategies "to confront the AIDS crisis in the Black community." This ad hoc body, in a resolution, "call[ed] upon all members of Black Churches, nationwide, to mobilize an immediate response to this epidemic which threatens the very existence of our community." Signatories included, among others, the presidents of the National Baptist Convention, USA, Inc., National Baptist Convention of America, National Black Progressive Baptists, and presiding bishops of the AME, AME Zion, CME churches and Church of God in Christ. The Reverend Carl Bean, director of the Los Angeles Minority AIDS Project (later, bishop-founder of the Unity Fellowship Church Movement), and the writer were members of the resolution drafting committee.

34. See, for example, William Gravely, "The Rise of African Churches in America, 1786–1822," Howard University *Journal of Religious Thought*, spring–summer, 1984, 58–73; Edward D. Smith, *Climbing Jacob's Ladder: The Rise of Black Churches in Eastern American Cities*, 1740–1877; and Sidney Kaplan and Emma Nogrady Kaplan, *The Black Presence in the Era of the American Revolution*, rev. ed.(Amherst, Mass.: The University of Massachusetts Press, 1989), "The Black Clergy," 90–130.

35. See, for example, Melva Wilson Costen, *African American Christian Worship*, 91–117; James F. White, *Protestant Worship: Traditions in Transition* (Louisville, Ky: Westminster/John Knox Press, 1989), 150–208; Molefi Kete Asante, "African Elements in African-American English," 19–33, and Portia K. Maultsby, "Africanisms in African-American Music," 185–210, in Joseph E. Holloway, op. cit.; Dewey W. Grantham, op. cit., 323–25; and V. P. Franklin, op. cit., 29–47.

36. See, for example, Emmett D. Carson, "Despite Long History, Black Philanthropy Gets Little Credit as 'Self-Help' Tool," 13–16, in *Philanthropy and the Black Church* edited by Alicia D. Byrd, (Washington, D.C.: Council on Foundations, 1990); and recently, Michael A. Fletcher, "Turning Support into Philanthropy: Schools, Charities Reach Out to Growing Black Middle Class," *The Washington Post*, 10 March 1997, A1.

37. Gary B. Nash, op. cit., 153–54, 164.

38. See, for example, Benjamin Elijah Mays and Joseph William Nicholson, *The Negro's Church*, 281. Self-respect, according to philosopher Bernard Boxill's use, "has . . . to do with how we conceive of ourselves as human beings in our basic moral relations with others." He distinguishes self-respect from self-esteem, which involves "a person's sense of his own value, his secure conviction that his plan of life is worth carrying out." See Bernard Boxill, *Blacks and Social Justice*, rev. ed., 188–204; and also, Howard McGary and Bill E. Lawson, *Between Slavery and Freedom: Philosophy and American Slavery* (Bloomington, Ind.: Indiana University Press, 1992), discussing self-respect, 107–111. My strong conviction is that ecclesiastical HIV dis-ease is profoundly disrespectful, and entails, in Boxill's terms, a failure to act justly in relationship to the two stigmatized groups, male homosexuals and drug users, whose members statistically constitute the vast majority of U.S. AIDS cases. Also, see, for example, Avishai Margalit, The Decent Society, (trans.) Naomi Goldblum (Cambridge, MA: Harvard University Press, 1996), especially "Justifying Respect," discussing religious arguments, 57–75; Richard A. Posner, *Sex and Reason* (Cambridge, Mass.: Harvard University Press, 1992), especially "Moral Theories of Sexuality," 220–40; Richard D. Mohr, *Gays/Justice: A Study of Ethics, Society, and Law* (New York: Columbia

University Press, 1988), especially "But Aren't They Immoral?," 31–33, and "Dignity in America," 144–150; Henry Louis Gates, Jr., "Blacklash?," *The New Yorker*/Reflections, 17 May 1993, 44, and the analysis and assessment of Philip M. Kayal, *Bearing Witness: Gay Men's Health Crisis and the Politics of AIDS* (Boulder, Colo.: Westview Press, 1993), especially chapters 2 and 3, "The Sin Stigma and Gay/AIDS Volunteerism," and "'Morality' and AIDS Issues," 23–50.

39. See Henry Young, *Major Black Religions Leaders, 1755–1940;* Gayraud S. Wilmore, *Black Religion and Blac Radicalism: An Examination of the Black Experience in Religion;* and Mary Frances Berry and John W. Blassingame, *Long Memory: The Black Experience in America* (New York: Oxford University Press, 1982), especially "Family and Church: Enduring Institutions," 70–113.

40. "In the field of social reform, the Negro is the moral hero." Michael Novak, "Christianity: Renewed or Slowly Abandoned?," 396, in *Religion in America* edited by William G. McLoughlin and Robert H. Bellah (Boston, Mass.: Beacon Press, 1968). Also, see Charles P. Henry, *Culture and African American Politics* (Bloomington, Ind: Indiana University Press, 1992), discussing the 1984 presidential campaign of the Reverend Jesse Jackson, "Jackson's Style and the King Legacy," 77.

41. Cornel West, *Prophetic Reflections: Notes on Race and Power in America*, 73–80, and also, bell hooks and Cornel West, *Breaking Bread: Insurgent Black Intellectual Life* (Boston, Mass.: South End Press, 1991), discussing sexuality and spirituality, 81–91, with apposite reference (89) to the 1982 Grammy Award-winning recording "Sexual Healing" (Midnight Love, Columbia; two million albums sold), by Marvin Gaye (Marvin Pentz Gay, Jr., 1939–1984), a native Washingtonian. Gaye's talented, turbulent life, which spans the 1960s and 1970s, as the conflicted son of a strict Pentecostal minister-father, and his tragic death, in 1984, at his alcoholic father's hands, presages for a generation, in many ways, the emotionally complex challenges (and difficulties) of negotiating the swift crosscurrents of deep societal change. Cf. the excellent discussion of spirituality, sexuality, and black popular music (and the mildly censorious treatment of Gaye and other musicians with roots in Afro-Christian traditions) in Martha Bayles, *Hole in Our Soul: The Loss of Beauty and Meaning in American Popular Music* (Chicago, IL.: University of Chicago Press, 1994), 230–32, 270–73.] Generally, see Cain Hope Felder, *Troubling Biblical Waters: Race, Class, and Family* (Maryknoll, N.Y.: Orbis Books, 1989), especially chapter 9, "The Bible and Black Families: A Theological Challenge," 150–66; Beverly Wildung Harrison, *Making the Connections: Essays in Feminist Social Ethics*, edited by Carol S. Robb (Boston, Mass.: Beacon Press, 1985), especially "The Power of Anger in the Work of Love: Christian Ethics for Women and Other Strangers," 3–21, and "Sexuality and Social Policy," 83–114; and Emilie M. Townes, "The Price of the Ticket: Racism, Sexism, Heterosexism, and the Church in Light of the AIDS Crisis," in , *Redefining Sexual Ethics: A Sourcebook of Essays, Stories, and Poems* Susan E. Davies and Eleanor H. Harvey (Cleveland, Ohio: The Pilgrim Press, 1991), 67–73.

42. William S. McFeely, Frederick Douglass, 85. See, for example, Frederick Douglass, "Slaveholding Religion and the Christianity of Christ," 100–9, in *Afro-American Religious History: A Documentary Witness* Milton C. Sernett, (Durham, N.C.: Duke University Press, 1985), and "The Right to Criticize American Institutions," 157–65, in *Forerunners of Black Power* edited by Ernest

G. Bormann, (Englewood Cliffs, N.J.: Prentice-Hall, Inc., 1971). Also, see Wilma King, *Stolen Childhood: Slave Youth in Nineteenth-Century America* (Bloomington, Ind.: University of Indiana Press, 1995), especially "Temporal and Spiritual Education," 67–90; William L. Andrews, "The Politics of African-American Ministerial Autobiography from Reconstruction to the 1920s," 111–133, in *African-American Christianity: Essays in History* edited by Paul E. Johnson, (Berkeley, Calf.: University of California Press, 1994); on Douglass, "dehumanization," and the physicality of domination, Phillip Brian Harper, "Racism and Homophobia as Reflections on Their Perpetrators," in Warren J. Blumenfeld, ed., op. cit., 57–66; George P. Cunningham, "Body Politics: Race, Gender, and the Captive Body," 131–149, in *Representing Black Men* edited by Marcellus Blount and George P. Cunningham, (New York: Routledge, 1996); C. Peter Ripley et al., eds., *Witness for Freedom: African American Voices on Race, Slavery, and Emancipation* (Chapel Hill, N.C.: The University of North Carolina Press, 1993), especially "Black Abolitionism in the Pulpit," 10, 110–117; James Oliver Horton and Lois E. Horton, "Violence, Protest, and Identity: Black Manhood in Antebellum America," in *Free People of Color: Inside the African American Community* edited by James Oliver Horton, (Washington, D.C.: Smithsonian Institution Press, 1993), 80–97; David Brion Davis, ed., *Antebellum American Culture: An Interpretive Anthology* (Lexington, Mass.: D.C. Heath and Company, 1979), especially "The Nonfreedom of 'Free Blacks'," 273–314; "Human Rights and American Religion," 467–97, in Edwin S. Gaustad, ed., *A Documentary History of Religion in America to the Civil War* (Grand Rapids, MI: William B. Eerdmans Publishing Company, 1982), discussing Douglass, 472–74; and the outstanding essays in Eric J. Sunquist, ed., *Frederick Douglass: New Literary and Historical Essays* (New York: Cambridge University Press, 1990).

43. On inquietum (Augustine's term), and activity "in this world," see Peter Ivan Kaufman, *Church, Book, and Bishop: Conflict and Authority in Early Latin Christianity* (Boulder, Colo.: WestviewPress/HarperCollinsPublishers, 1996), chapter 4, "Augustine," 75–78. On Augustine's conversion experience, see Karen Armstrong, *A History of God: The 4,000-Year Quest of Judaism, Christianity and Islam* (New York: Ballantine Books, 1993), 120–25. ". . . [f]rom a hidden depth a profound self-examination had dredged up a heap of all my misery and . . . [t]hat precipitated a vast storm bearing a massive downpour of tears . . . I threw myself down . . . and let my tears flow freely. Rivers streamed from my eyes, a sacrifice acceptable to [You]. . . ." Augustine, Confessions, (trans.) Henry Chadwick, VIII xii (28), cited in Armstrong, 120. On Augustine's pessimistic view of human nature and sexuality, and his crucial, incalculable influence on the subsequent development of Catholic and Protestant doctrines (and practice) concerning sickness and sin, sexuality, suffering, and death, see Elaine Pagels, *Adam, Eve, and the Serpent* (New York: Random House, 1988), 127–150; and Margaret R. Miles, *Practicing Christianity: Critical Perspectives for an Embodied Spirituality* (New York: The Crossroad Publishing Company, 1988), 94–104, 164–175. Generally, see Peter Brown, *The Body and Society: Men, Women, and Sexual Renunciation in Early Christianity* (New York: Columbia University Press, 1988), especially Part 3, "Ambrose to Augustine: The Making of the Latin Tradition," 339–427. Pace Boxill, I can find no historical support for the popular claim that Augustine, a native of Roman north Africa, possibly of Berber stock, "is

a black man." It is more likely, I believe, that later cultural contacts between Europeans and north Africans during the period of the Crusades led to this mistaken impression and identification, which became fixed in medieval legend, and, still later, in the color-conscious, church-naming practices of Catholic and Anglican religious authorities. See, for example, Boxill, op. cit., 177; J.P.V.D. Balsdon, *Romans and Aliens* (Chapel Hill, N.C.: The University of North Carolina Press, 1979), especially "Colour," 217–19; Frank M. Snowden, Jr., *Before Color Prejudice: The Ancient View of Blacks* (Cambridge, Mass.: Harvard University Press, 1991, 1st pub. 1983), 104–5; and the superb study of the "color" black, and "blackness," in European culture, clothing, and consciousness by John Harvey, *Men in Black* (Chicago, Ill.: The University of Chicago Press, 1995), discussing racial attitudes and belief, 101–13.

44. McFeely, op. cit., 83, emphasis supplied.

45. Ibid., 84.

46. H. Richard Niebuhr, *The Social Sources of Denominationalism*, 66. Also, see the insightful study of John Wesley's leadership, and the culture and "sexual politics" of early Wesleyan Methodism by Henry Abelove, *The Evangelist of Desire: John Wesley and the Methodists*; and "Methodism and Sanctification," in the highly original monograph (completed before the advent of HIV) by Peter Gardella, *Innocent Ecstasy: How Christianity Gave America an Ethic of Sexual Pleasure* (New York: Oxford University Press, 1985), 85–94.

47. Douglass's funeral rite, an early example of black Protestant ecumenism, is described by James M[onroe] Gregory, *Frederick Douglass the Orator*, 213–18. During the late nineteenth century, Gregory, a younger contemporary of Douglass's, was tutor in mathematics, instructor in political economy and general history, and Professor of The Latin Language and Literature at Howard University, his alma mater. Cf. Rayford W. Logan, *Howard University: The First Hundred Years, 1867–1967* (New York: Howard University/New York University Press, 1969), on Gregory and Douglass, 36–38, 109–111.

48. See, especially, Donald B. Gibson, "Faith, Doubt, and Apostasy: Evidence of Things Unseen in Frederick Douglass's Narrative," 84–115, in Eric Sunquist, op. cit.; Martin E. Marty, *Varieties of Unbelief* (New York: Holt, Rinehart and Winston, 1964); and Walter E. Houghton, *The Victorian Frame of Mind, 1830–1870* (New Haven, Conn.: Yale University Press, 1985, 1st pub. 1957), especially chapter 4, "The Critical Spirit—And the Will to Believe," 93–109. Cf. Alphonse Ngindu Mushete, "The Notion of Truth in African Theology," in Metz and Schillebeeckx eds., op. cit., 53–63.

49. Gary T. Marx, "Religion: Opiate or Inspiration of Civil Rights Militancy Among Negroes," 220–34, in William M. Newman, eds., *The Social Meanings of Religion: An Integrated Anthology*. See, generally, Michael Corbett, *Political Tolerance in America: Freedom and Equality in Public Attitudes* (New York: Longman Inc., 1982), especially, on "tolerance and religious orientations," 143–49, for a review of studies conducted immediately prior to the beginning of the AIDS epidemic.

50. Ibid., 225. For example, the hostility of the Reverend Joseph H. Jackson, president of the National Baptist Convention/USA (NBC) during the civil rights period, to the goals of activist pastor/members is well known and well attested. The story of the Reverend Gardner C. Taylor's 1961 challenge of the incumbent,

King's ouster from his NBC vice presidency, and the subsequent establishment of a Progressive National Baptist Convention is told by David J. Garrow, *Bearing the Cross: Martin Luther King, Jr. and the Southern Christian Leadership Conference* (New York: Vintage, 1988), 165 – 66, 491; and Taylor Branch, *Parting the Waters: America in the King Years, 1954-63* (New York: Simon and Schuster, 1988), 335 – 40, 372 – 73. Also, see R. Laurence Moore, *Religious Outsiders and the Making of Americans*, 194; and the perceptive comments of the Reverend Frank Madison Reid III, "Deliverance and Development," 51 – 53, in Alicia D. Byrd, ed., op. cit.

51. Ibid., 225.

52. Ibid., 222, n.6.

53. See, however, Ronald L. Johnstone's 1969 study of black clergy in Detroit, which confirms his earlier findings, "Negro Preachers Take Sides," 283 – 92, in Patrick H. McNamara, ed., *Religion American Style*; and the research of Talbert O. Shaw, "A Tentative Profile of the Black Clergy in Chicago," 39 – 51, Howard University *Journal of Religious Thought*, spring-summer, 1973.

54. In remarks delivered in 1962, the Reverend Martin Luther King, Jr. attributed his own militant, nonviolent activism to the influence, during his undergraduate years at Atlanta's Morehouse College, of the nineteenth century writer Henry David Thoreau. This was also the period during which King, age sixteen, "profoundly" influenced by Morehouse president, the Reverend Benjamin E. Mays (a sympathetic critic of "otherworldly" black religion), and other faculty members, rejected fundamentalism as incompatible with social change. See, for example, Martin Luther King, Jr., "A Legacy of Creative Protest," September 7, 1962, in *Black and White in American Culture: An Anthology from the Massachusetts Review* edited by Jules Chametzky and Sidney Kaplan (Amherst, Mass.: The University of Massachusetts Press, 1969), 105; King's earlier, guarded evaluation, in 1956, of the "becoming" militancy of the black church in the South, "The Montgomery Bus Boycott and the Philosophy of Martin Luther King, Jr.," in John H. Bracey, Jr., August Meier, and Elliott Rudwick, *The Afro-Americans: Selected Documents* (Boston, MA: Allyn and Bacon, Inc., 1972), 672 – 80; William D. Watley, *Roots of Resistance: The Nonviolent Ethic of Martin Luther King, Jr.* (Valley Forge, Penn.: Judson Press, 1985), 17 – 46; the outstanding essays in Peter J. Albert and Ronald Hoffman, eds., *Martin Luther King, Jr., and the Black Freedom Struggle* (New York: United States Capitol Historical Society/Pantheon Books, 1990); by Bruce Miroff, "Martin Luther King, Jr.: Dissenting Leadership and Democratic Redemption," *Icons of Democracy: American Leaders as Heroes, Aristocrats, Dissenters, and Democrats* (New York: Basic Books/HarperCollins Publishers, 1993), 305 – 46; Richard Lischer, "What He Received: Units of Tradition," *The Preacher King: Martin Luther King, Jr. and The Word that Moved America* (New York: Oxford University Press, 1995), 93 – 118; Clayborne Carson, "Martin Luther King, Jr., and the African-American Social Gospel," which is arguably definitive, in Paul E. Johnson, ed., op. cit., 159 – 77; and recently, Gerald Early, "Martin Luther King and the Reinvention of Christianity in Modern America," in *Religion & Values in Public Life*, The Center for the Study of Values in Public Life, Harvard Divinity School, vol. 4, no. 4, (September 1996), 1 – 4. But see especially, for example, the title by Coretta Scott King, "The Legacy of Martin Luther King, Jr: The Church in Action," 294 – 97, in Patrick H. McNamara, ed., op. cit; and also the analysis and assessment of Charles M. Payne,

I've Got the Light of Freedom: The Organizing Tradition and the Mississippi Freedom Struggle (Berkeley, Calf.: University of California Press, 1995), 256–63, 272–78. Also, see the "President's Greeting" of the Reverend Joseph E. Lowery to the Southern Christian Leadership Conference (SCLC) National Conference on AIDS and the Black Community, May 29–30, 1987, Howard University, Washington, D.C. According to the conference booklet, the meeting was "sponsored by SCLC/WOMEN, Evelyn G. Lowery, national convener."

55. See, for example, Adolph L. Reed, *The Jesse Jackson Phenomenon: The Crisis of Purpose in African American Politics* (New Haven, Conn.: Yale University Press, 1986), 44, 46, 55, 57, 60; Charles P. Henry, op. cit., "Cultural Politics and the Jackson Campaign," 76–92; and Garry Wills, *Under God: Religion and American Politics*, 237, n. 1, and, recently, Wills' trenchant review essay, "A Tale of Three Leaders," *The New York Review of Books*, vol. XLIII, no. 14, 19 September 1996, discussing Andrew Young, Louis Farrakhan, and Jesse Jackson, 51–74. On image and "celebrity," see studies cited in n. 22, and generally, Daniel J. Boorstin, *The Image: A Guide to Pseudo-Events in America* (New York: Atheneum/Macmillan Publishing Company, 1987, 1st pub. 1961), 45–76; Joshua Gamson, "Postmodern Skepticism and the Pleasures of Deconstruction," *Claims To Fame: Celebrity in Contemporary America* (Berkeley, Calf.: University of California Press, 1994), 155–58; and Philip Cushman, *Constructing The Self, Constructing America: A Cultural History of Psychotherapy* (Reading, Mass.: Addison-Wesley Publishing Company, 1995), on celebrity and "narcissism," 69–73.

56. The Reverend David Weeks, pastor of Shalom Baptist Church, cited in Charles Perrow and Mauro F. Guillén, *The AIDS Disaster: The Failure of Organizations in New York and the Nation*, 99. ". . . It was not until the weekend of June 10, 1989, that leading African-American clergymen in New York City started a campaign to mobilize 600 black congregations to respond to AIDS. Another such call was issued in November 1991. In a sense, the minority community, unlike the gay community, disowned its own." Philip M. Kayal, op. cit., 65–67. Also, see the analysis and assessment by the late anthropologist William G. Hawkeswood, *One of the Children: Gay Black Men in Harlem*, edited by Alex W. Costley (Berkeley, Calf.: University of California Press, 1996), especially chapter 8, " 'This Epidemic Thing': Gay Black Men and AIDS in Harlem," 169–184.

57. In 1994, for example, a 5,000-member black Baptist congregation with a long and distinguished record of community involvement sponsored its first AIDS Awareness Day. A project of the church's AIDS ministry, event organizers proscribed the participation of AIDS service organizations likely to include discussion of safer sex practices and prophylactic condom use as part of their presentations. According to a press report, the stated theme of the event was, A *Clear and Present Danger: The Church Responds*. See Darice Clark and Aras van Hertum, "Churches Condom Ban Angers Gays," *The Washington Blade*, 12 August 1994, 5.

58. On the global characteristics of AIDS, see, for example, Earl E. Shelp and Ronald H. Sunderland, *AIDS and the Church: The Second Decade*, 158–88; "Geography and AIDS: Suffering's Spread," in Kenneth R. Overberg, S.J., ed., op. cit., 12–67, particularly David Sanders and Abdulrahman Sambo, "AIDS in Africa," in ibid., 40–52; the cover report by Philip J. Hilts, "Out of Africa: Dispelling Myths about AIDS: Origins, Sexual Practices, Social Values, Politics," *The Washington Post/*

Health, 24 May 1988; and Simon Watney, *Practices of Freedom: Selected Writings on HIV/AIDS* (Durham, NC: Duke University Press, 1994), "Missionary Positions: AIDS, 'Africa', and race," 103–20. Also, see Jeffrey Goldberg's recent article on disease and development, "Our Africa Problem," *The New York Times Magazine*, 2 March 1997.

59. See H. Richard Niebuhr, *Christ and Culture*.

60. See, for example, James B. Nelson, *Embodiment: An Approach to Sexuality and Christian Theology, and Between Two Gardens: Reflecting on Sexuality and Religious Experience*, 167; Reginald G. Blaxton, art. cit., *The Quarterly Review of the AME Zion Church*, spring 1987; Lionel Tiger, *The Pursuit of Pleasure* (Boston, Mass.: Little, Brown and Company, 1992); Christine E. Gudorf, *Body, Sex and Pleasure: Reconstructing Christian Ethics*; and recently, the highly original, brilliantly realized study of "muscular" Christianity in the New Testament by Stephen D. Moore, *God's Gym: Divine Male Bodies of the Bible* (New York: Routledge, 1996). Also, see Charles Davis, *Body as Spirit: The Nature of Religious Feeling* (New York: The Seabury Press, 1976); George L. Mosse, *Nationalism and Sexuality: Middle-Class Morality and Sexual Norms in Modern Europe* (Madison, Wis.: The University of Wisconsin Press, 1985); and, for psychological perspectives, Alexander Lowen, *The Betrayal of the Body* (New York: Macmillan, 1967); and Wendell W. Watters, *Deadly Doctrine: Health, Illness, and Christian God-Talk* (Buffalo, N.Y.: Prometheus Books, 1993). Cf. Peter Gardella, op. cit.

61. See, for example, Jack Larkin, *The Reshaping of Everyday Life, 1790-1840*, 150–51; and Roger D. Abrahams, *Singing the Master: The Emergence of African-American Culture in the Plantation South* (New York: Penguin Books, 1992), chapter 4, "Festive Spirit in the Development of African American Style," 83–106. "The African and African American organization of the body differs most profoundly in locating the center of gravity at the hips. Movement is initiated from that area and emanates outward to the shoulders, arms, and hands, and the knees and the feet, which play off against the pulse established by the hip movements. The centrality of the hips produces the sense of strong sexuality in African American dance." Abrahams, 98. Also, see Garth Baker-Fletcher, "Black Bodies, Whose Body? African American Men in XODUS," in *Men's Bodies, Men's Gods: Male Identities in a (Post-) Christian Culture*, edited by Björn Krondorfer (New York: New York University Press, 1996), 65–93.

62. On the relationship of body movement and "e-motion," see Elochukwu E. Uzukwu, "Body and Memory in African Liturgy," in *Liturgy and the Body* edited by Louis-Marie Chauvet and François Kabasele Lumbala (London: Concilium 1995/3/SCM Press Ltd. and Orbis Books, Maryknoll, 1995), 71–78. On physicality and consciousness, see the fine essay (1975), with Postscript (1993), by Charles Johnson, "A Phenomenology of the Black Body," in Laurence Goldstein, ed., op. cit., 121–36; Garrett Duncan, "The Zone of Black Bodies: Language, Black Consciousness, and Adolescent Identities," in Antonia Darder, ed., op. cit., 81–101; and by Lewis R. Gordon, "Can Men Worship? Reflections on Male Bodies in Bad Faith and a Theology of Authenticity," in Björn Krondorfer, ed., op. cit, 235–50. Also, see, for example, Charles Joyner, "'Believer I Know': The Emergence of African-American Christianity," in Paul E. Johnson, ed., op. cit., 29–31, 36–37; Anthony S. Parent, Jr. and Susan Brown Wallace, "Childhood and Sexual Identity under Slavery," in John C. Fout and Maura Shaw Tantillo, eds., *American*

Sexual Politics: Sex, Gender, and Race since the Civil War (Chicago, Ill.: The University of Chicago Press, 1993), pp. 19-57; Mechal Sobel, *Travelin' On: The Slave Journey to an Afro-Baptist Faith* (Princeton, NJ: Princeton University Press, 1988), 110, 139–180; "Blacks in Antebellum Boston: The Migrant and the Community," by James Oliver Horton, ed., op. cit., 34–35; David Levering Lewis, *When Harlem Was in Vogue* (New York: Oxford University Press, 1989), 221–24. "Praising the Lord, vibrating with ecstasy, and glowing in a high of momentary deliverance were what a good Harlem Sunday was all about." Lewis, 222; Albert J. Raboteau, *A Fire in the Bones: Reflections on African-American Religious History*, especially chapter 7, "The Chanted Sermon," 145–51; Zora Neale Hurston, *The Sanctified Church* (Berkeley, Calif.: Turtle Island for the Netzahaucoyotl Historical Society, 1981), "Characteristics of Negro Expression," 49–68; Richard Lischer, op. cit., "The Strategies of Style," discussing homiletical "climax," 140–41; Robin D.G. Kelley, *Race Rebels: Culture, Politics, and the Black Working Class*, particularly his insightful discussion, "Building Community in the Dark." ". . . to most of the four million black folk emancipated by civil war, God was real. They knew Him. They had met Him personally in many a wild orgy of religious frenzy, or in the black stillness of the night." Kelley, 43, citing W. E. B. Du Bois, *Black Reconstruction*; and Tom F. Driver, *The Magic of Ritual: Our Need for Liberating Rites that Transform Our Lives and Our Communities* (San Francisco, Calif.: HarperSanFrancisco, 1991), 190, and especially chapter 6, "Ritual's Two Siblings: Performance in the Confessional and Ethical Modes," 107–27.

63. Barry D. Adam, *The Survival of Domination: Inferiorization and Everyday Life*, 45. Also, see "Race and Sexuality: The Role of the Outsider," in George L. Mosse, op. cit., 133–52; and the discussion of antique Roman attitudes toward the sexuality of African peoples in J.P.V.D. Balsdon, op. cit., 69, 218.

64. See, for example, the elegant studies of Samuel Laeuchli, *Power and Sexuality: The Emergence of Canon Law at the Synod of Elvira*, 88–113; Harold J. Berman, *Law and Revolution: The Formation of the Western Legal Tradition*, 68–84, 107–113; and Jean Delumeau, *Sin and Fear: The Emergence of a Western Guilt Culture, 13th-18th Centuries*, trans. Eric Nicholson (New York: St. Martin's Press, 1990), especially, on "Impurity," 436–445. Also, see Kenneth Leech, " 'The Carnality of Grace': Sexuality, Spirituality and Pastoral Ministry," 59–68, and Jeanette Renouf, "Order and Chaos: The Church and Sexuality," 72–79, in James Woodward, ed., op. cit.; and chapter 6, "The Christian Church," in Reay Tannahill, *Sex in History*, rev. ed. (Lanham, Md.: Madison Books/Scarborough House/Publishers, 1992, 1st pub. 1980), 136–61.

65. See, for example, Jeffrey Richards, op. cit., 23–72, 132–63; Abigail Trafford, "AIDS and the Medical Fundamentalists," *The Washington Post*, 17 December 1988; and Dennis Altman, *AIDS in the Mind of America: The Social, Political and Psychological Impact of a New Epidemic* (New York: Anchor/Doubleday, 1987), 10.

66. See, for example, Courtland Milloy, "Heroin and AIDS: Deadly Mix for Blacks," *The Washington Post*, 10 January 1989, D3; John S. Lang, "The Unholy [sic] Triangle: Drugs, Sex and AIDS Hit the Heartland," *The Washington Post*/ Health, 19 June 1990, 10–11; Charles F. Turner, Heather G. Miller, and Lincoln Moses, eds., *AIDS: Sexual Behavior and Intravenous Drug Use*; Avram Goldstein, *Addiction:*

From Biology to Drug Policy; and Andrew Weil and Winifred Rosen, *From Choco-late to Morphine: Everything You Need to Know About Mind-Altering Drugs.*

67. See, for example, Sydney E. Ahlstrom, *A Religious History of the American People* (Garden City, N.Y.: Image Books, 1975), vol. 2, 347–53; Randall Balmer, op. cit., 84, 94, 104, 184, 192–94; recently, Eva Bertram, Morris Blachman, Kenneth Sharpe, Peter Andreas, *Drug War Politics: The Price of Denial* (Berkeley, Calif.: University of California Press, 1996), discussing "The Punitive Paradigm," from 1900–1980, 61–101, and, concerning African American neighborhoods and com-munities, "The Politics of Fear and Intolerance," 42–45. Also, see Peter Bell, *Chemical Dependency and the African-American: Counseling Strategies and Com-munity Issues* (Center City, Minn.: Hazelden, 1990), especially, 32–33.

68. "In Western cultures, at least, as encoded in the Christian tradition, sexual activity has had a special relationship to notions of valid behavior, of truth. A "morality of acts" long enshrined a sexual hierarchy which told us which types of erotic activity were appropriate or inappropriate, right or wrong. These activities in turn de-fined the type of person we were: moral or immoral, innocent or guilty, normal or perverse." Jeffrey Weeks, op. cit., 47. Also, see, for example, Elizabeth Fee, "Sin versus Science: Venereal Disease in Twentieth-Century Baltimore," 121–46, in Fee and Fee, eds., op. cit., especially "Venereal Disease and Racism," 126–28; and "Historiography and context," 3–16, in Rudi C. Bleys, *The Geography of Perversion: Male-to-male Sexual Behaviour outside the West and the Ethnographic Imagination, 1750–1918* (New York: New York University Press, 1995), discuss-ing "Sub-Saharan Africans and African Americans," 32–50, 123–34, 166–74.

69. On the role of conscience, see, for example, Bernard Häring, *A Theology of Pro-test*, 76–94; and John Mahoney, S.J., *The Making of Moral Theology: A Study of the Roman Catholic Tradition* (Oxford: Clarendon Press/Oxford University Press, 1989), especially "Reflections on Authority," 164–74, and "The Witness of Conscience," 289–93. Also, see Edwin S. Gaustad, *Neither King nor Prelate: Religion and the New Nation, 1776-1826* (Grand Rapids, Mich.: William B. Eer-dmans Company, 1993), discussing early American religious establishments, and ecclesial traditions of conscientious dissent, 12–35.

70. See Kevin Gordon, "The Sexual Bankruptcy of the Christian Traditions: A Per-spective of Radical Suspicion and of Fundamental Trust," 169–212, in David G. Hallman, ed., op. cit; and also, Christine E. Gudorf, *Victimization: Examining Christian Complicity* (Philadelphia, Penn.: Trinity Press International, 1992), 90–112. "Bankruptcy does not mean that you have no inheritance, that you are without resources. It means, more precisely, that your resources have been badly managed, poorly used, or possibly even neglected." Gordon, citing Walter Wink, 178. Cf. the analysis and assessment of Joseph Moingt (citing 1 Cor. 11:19), "'Oportet et Haereses Esse'," 64–72, in Metz and Schillebeeckx, eds., op. cit., 71–72.

71. See, for example, the 1850 sermon, *The Rights and Duties of the Masters: A Ser-mon Preached at the Dedication of a Church Erected in Charleston, S.C. for the Benefit and Instruction of the Colored Population* (Charleston, S.C.: Walker and James), by the eminent white Presbyterian divine, the Reverend James Henley Thornwell, revised as "The Christian Doctrine of Slavery," 164–72, in Edwin Scott Gaustad, ed., *Religious Issues in American History* (New York: Harper & Row, Publishers, 1968).

72. See, for example, Winthrop D. Jordan, *White Over Black: American Attitudes Toward the Negro, 1550–1812* (Baltimore, Md.: Penguin Books, 1973), 190–212; David Brion Davis, *The Problem of Slavery In Western Culture* (Ithaca, NY: Cornell University Press, 1966), 165–221, and, recently, his essay, "At the Heart of Slavery, 51–54, in *The New York Review of Books*, vol. XLIII, no. 16, 17 October 1996, discussing slavery as "a fact of life . . . the official view of Christian churches from the late Roman Empire to the eighteenth century," 53; "Slavery, Race, and the Debate on Personality," by J. R. Pole, *Paths to the American Past* (New York: Oxford University Press, 1979), 189–219; and James Oakes, *The Ruling Race: A History of American Slaveholders* (New York: Vintage Books/Random House, 1983), especially "The Convenient Sin," 96–122, and "Masters of Tradition," 192–224. ". . . [T]here is no reasonable doubt that the New Testament, like the Old, not only tolerated chattel slavery (the form prevalent in the Greco-Roman world of Paul's time) but helped to perpetuate it by making the slaves' obedience to their masters a religious duty. This biblical morality was one of the great handicaps that the emancipation movement in the United States had to overcome. The opponents of abolition had clear biblical evidence on their side when they argued." Morton Smith, Slavery," 136–46, in Morton Smith and R. Joseph Hoffman, eds., *What the Bible Really Says* (San Francisco, Calif.: HarperSanFrancisco, 1989); emphasis supplied. Also, see, in ibid., Bernhard Lang, "Segregation and Intolerance," 115–35, especially "Jesus: A More Tolerant Figure," 127–30.

73. See, for example, William John Wolf, Lincoln's Religion, 182–83; the Second Inaugural Address, Washington, D.C., May 4, 1865, in *Abraham Lincoln: The Gettysburg Address and Other Speeches* (New York: Penguin Books, 1995), 84–86; and Lincoln's premonitory "Meditation on the Divine Will," September [30?], 1862, 522, in Edwin S. Gaustad (ed.), *Doc. Hist.*, 518–525. Also, see David Zarefsky, *Lincoln, Douglas and Slavery: In the Crucible of Public Debate* (Chicago, Ill.: The University of Chicago Press, 1990), "The Moral Argument," 166–97; "Toward a Reconsideration of Abolitionists," by David Donald, *Lincoln Reconsidered: Essays on the Civil War Era* (New York: Vintage Books/Random House, Inc., 1989), 19–36; "Blacks and Lincoln," in C. Peter Ripley et al., eds., op. cit., 228–34; "Abraham Lincoln and the American Commitment," in J. R. Pole, op. cit., 146–169; "Lincoln's Black Theology," in Garry Wills, op. cit., 207–21; "Abraham Lincoln: Democratic Leadership and the Tribe of the Eagle," 83–124, in Bruce Miroff, op. cit., especially 102–04; and J. David Greenstone, *The Lincoln Persuasion: Remaking American Liberalism* (Princeton, N.J.: Princeton University Press, 1993), especially "Lincoln's Political Humanitarianism: Moral Reform and the Covenant Tradition," 244–83. For a perceptive analysis of the sociopolitical and economic "interests" of religious conservatives, cf. the review essay by James Epstein, "White Mischief," *The New York Review of Books*, vol. XLIII, no. 16 (17 October 1996): 30–32.

74. Leon Edward Wright, *From Cult to Cosmos: Can Jesus Be Saved?*, p. 67. Also, see his prophetic essay, " 'Black Theology' or Black Experience," Howard University *Journal of Religious Thought*, summer 1969. A past editor of the Journal, the Reverend Leon Edward Wright (AB, Phi Beta Kappa, MA (with distinctions, Boston University), STB (with honor, Harvard Divinity School), Ph.D. (in the history and philosophy of religion, with emphasis upon New Testament language and

literature), Harvard University) was honored over the course of his career with Kent, General Education Board, Rosenwald, and Guggenheim fellowships. His dissertation was selected competitively by the Harvard University Press, in 1951, as *Historical Monograph* No. XXV, *Alterations of the Words of Jesus As Quoted in the Literature of the Second Century*. An ordained minister of the United Church of Christ, Dr. Wright joined the Howard faculty in 1945, where he developed in the 1950s original courses in religion and parapsychology, spiritual dynamics and healing, and on the historical Jesus. He received, in 1963, a certificate (the first to be awarded to an American, according to Logan, op. cit., 552) presented at the Embassy of Burma, to teach Buddhist meditation, following distinguished service as cultural attaché to the U.S. Embassy in Rangoon, and study with Burmese monks. On August 23, 1996, at age eighty-four, Dr. Wright joined Jessie Mae Wyche Wright (Fisk, Radcliffe, Chicago) in death, a fellow educator and master teacher to whom he was married for forty-eight years. He was buried from the Andrew Rankin Memorial Chapel of Howard University.

75. ". . . A thorough review of research evaluating HIV prevention programs found 20 studies that demonstrated long-term behavior change. Skepticism about the effectiveness of HIV programs is not borne out by scientific evidence. . . . [A] comprehensive report prepared for the Centers for Disease Control and Prevention reported 10 studies of needle exchange programs that showed decreases in sharing needles, the . . . route of HIV transmission, as a result of the exchanges." See the Fact Sheet, prepared by Pamela DeCarlo, "Does HIV Prevention Work?," (San Francisco, Calif.: University of California, San Francisco/ Harvard AIDS Institute, February 1995). For the negative comments of two Washington pastors of black Baptist congregations on the moral acceptability of condom use, see Burkett, op. cit., 184. Public health proposals advocating prophylactic use of condoms have also provoked strong negative reactions from the American Catholic hierarchy. See, for example, Michael Warner, *Changing Witness: Catholic Bishops and Public Policy, 1917–1994* (Grand Rapids, Mich.: Ethics and Public Policy Center [D. C.]/ Wm. B. Eerdmans Publishing Co., 1995), 156–58; Richard L. Smith, *AIDS, Gays and the American Catholic Church*; and Mark R. Kowalewski, *All Things to All People: The Catholic Church Confronts the AIDS Crisis*. On the moral response of evangelical Protestant church leaders to HIV/AIDS prevention efforts, see Sara Diamond, *Spiritual Warfare: The Politics of the Christian Right* (Boston, Mass.: South End Press, 1989), 101–4; Philip J. Hilts, "Church Tests Faith of Cleric Touched by AIDS," *New York Times*, 8 September 1992, A1, discussing the Reverend Scott Allen, son of the president, until 1979, of the seventeen-million-member Southern Baptist Convention; and Bill Barol, with Mary Hager and Pat Wingert, "Koop and Bennett Agree to Disagree," in the cover report, "Kids and Contraceptives," *Newsweek*, 16 February 1987, 54–65. Still, there are approximately 2,000 AIDS ministries nationwide, many efficiently organized along interfaith lines. For information on exemplary, effective AIDS ministries/service organizations, and for a model AIDS education curriculum, consult Warren J. Blumenfeld and Scott Alexander, *AIDS and Your Religious Community: A Hands-On Guide for Local Programs* (Boston, Mass.: Unitarian Universalist Association/ AIDS National Interfaith Network, 1991); and Thaddeus Bennett and Gene Robinson, eds., *Being Christian in the Age of AIDS: An Adult Theological Education and Reflection Guide on the HIV/AIDS Pandemic*

(New York: The Domestic and Foreign Missionary Society, 1995). Generally, see Part 3, "The Morality of Making Judgments," in the useful study of quotidian, personal morality by Joshua Halberstam, *Everyday Ethics: Inspired Solutions to Real-Life Dilemmas* (New York: Penguin Books, 1995), 101–164.

76. See H. A. Williams, *True Resurrection* (New York: Holt, Rinehart and Winston, 1972), 115, 177–82. Also, see, for example, L. Gregory Jones, *Embodying Forgiveness: A Theological Analysis* (Grand Rapids, Mich.: Wm. B. Eerdmans Publishing Co., 1995), especially "Prayer and Healing: Living in the Power of God," 197–204; and the discussion of HIV/AIDS in chapter 7, "Undying Erotic Friendship: Foundations for Sexual Ethics," in Carter Heyward, *Touching Our Strength: The Erotic as Power and the Love of God* (San Francisco, Calif.: Harper & Row, Publishers, 1989), 119–55. ". . . In the spirit of forgiveness, the future is always open. This irrepressible blessing draws us into the very essence of that power which is love, which is mutual, which is movement, which is constant, and which is God." Heyward, 148. Cf. Howard McGary, "Is There a Duty to Forgive," in McGary and Lawson, op. cit., "Forgiveness and Slavery," 90–112.

77. The image is traditional in Southern black preaching and public prayer practice. See, for example, the conclusion of "Listen Lord: A Prayer," in James Weldon Johnson, *God's Trombones: Seven Negro Sermons in Verse* (New York: Viking Press, 1969, 1st pub. 1927), 13–15. On the use of eschatological imagery in the prayers of black folk, see the remarks of the Reverend Wyatt Tee Walker, "Lord, We Didn't Come Here to Stay," 251, in the superb collection of James Melvin Washington, ed., *Conversations With God: Two Centuries of Prayers by African Americans* (New York: HarperCollinsPublishers, 1994). Cf., recently, on HIV and eschatology, Amy Harris, "Eden as Metaphor of AIDS' Prehistory," 29–30, in *The Harvard Gay & Lesbian Review*, vol. III, no. 4, (fall, 1996) discussing Homo Spiritualis throughout.

"Whosoever" Is Welcome Here: An Interview with Reverend Edwin C. Sanders II

Gary David Comstock

Reverend Edwin C. Sanders II is the founding pastor of Metropolitan Interdenominational Church, which is located in a working class neighborhood of small houses in Nashville, Tennessee. Reverend Sanders is African American and the congregation is predominantly African American. Lesbian/bisexual/gay/transgendered people are welcome and encouraged to participate in the life of the church. I attended a packed Sunday morning service in June 1998 and interviewed Rev. Sanders in the afternoon.

GARY COMSTOCK: How did the church get started?

REVEREND SANDERS: I had been the Dean of the Chapel at Fisk University. I left in 1980 in a moment of controversy. A new president had come, and we weren't able to mesh. I left and had no where to go. I didn't have a plan. And instantly there were folks who were part of the chapel experience there at Fisk who wanted to organize a new church. I felt no spiritual interest whatsoever in organizing a new church, but about seven months later I felt like I clearly heard the voice saying, "This is something to do." I'm glad it worked out that way, because I think if I had done it directly after Fisk it would have been born out of a reaction and we probably wouldn't have developed the kind of identity, sense of mission, and direction the way we did. There were twelve people who came together and said they wanted to do this.

One of my good friends, Bill Turner, is a sociologist, and we were at Fisk together. Bill has a theory he advanced that institutions—and he built his theory around black institutions—cannot break out of the mold from which they were born. There was something about the way an institution is framed in its beginning, and no matter what you do you don't escape it. I thought that was absurd, but in time I came to think that he had something. The congregation was a mix of white and black men and women from all kinds of denominational backgrounds, and that mix turned out to be significant because from the beginning people identified us as being inclusive at least across racial terms and definitely inclusive and equal in gender terms. The first Sunday we worshiped, one of the reporters from the local newspaper came and covered the service. I felt we went to a lot of effort to have a fairly well structured sophisticated experience that Sunday, but what he chose to focus his entire article on was the fact that women who wore pants served communion, which probably began to say something about who we were going to be. In traditional African-American churches women don't wear pants and the service is male dominated.

In that original group we had also a young man—one of my very dear friends—who was gay. Don was living a bisexual lifestyle at that point, but mainly to keep up appearances for professional purposes. Another one of my dearest friends went through a major mental breakdown at the time we were starting the church. I felt it very important not to abandon him and to include him. So we had a guy going through major psychological problems, somebody who was gay, and we had the racial mix.

We did not have the class mix at the beginning. Most of the folks were associated in some way with the academic community. Nothing like we have now. Today we have an unbelievable mix of people. I mean there are people who are doctors, lawyers, dentists and business people, and we also have a lot of folks who are right off the street, blue collar workers, in treatment for drugs and alcohol, going through a lot of transition. And that mix has evolved. Although we said in the beginning that's what we wanted to be, in actuality the current mix goes beyond that of the original twelve members.

The presence of Don, the one gay black male in the original congregation, had a lot to do with our current mix of people, and it had a lot to do with how we got so involved with HIV/AIDS ministry. The church began in '81 and he died in '84. It's almost hilarious when I think about it because I'm so involved in HIV/AIDS work now, but when he died I remember he was real sick, we didn't know what was going on, and they told us he died of toxicosis. I remember saying what in the world is that? I researched it and found out that it had something to do with cat and bird droppings, but Don didn't have cats. It was AIDS. You'd hear people talking about this strange disease because then it was 1984, but what that meant for us was that we got involved before it became a publicly recognized and discussed issue. Don's presence and death immediately pushed us in ministering to and being responsive to folks with AIDS and in dealing with the issue of homosexuality.

The other thing I was going to tell you which is kind of funny is the name. I will never forget when I told one of my friends we were going to name the church Metropolitan Interdenominational. He said are you sure you want to do that. I said what do you mean, you know, I was pretty naive. He said all the gay churches across the country are called Metropolitan churches. I said that's where I feel the Lord leads me, I feel Metropolitan. In my mind what that meant was that Nashville happens to have been the first metropolitan government in the United States. It's the first place where the county and city combined, so everything in and around Nashville is referred to as metropolitan government. But my friend said to me that everybody is going to instantly say you're the gay church. I said so be it and we went on with it. Like I said, there was a hand bigger than mine at work.

COMSTOCK: Where do you do the needle exchange and HIV/AIDS programs?

REV. SANDERS: We do part of it from here at the church and we do a lot of it as street outreach. We do most of our needle exchange out of vans. We go to where people are, to some of the heavy drug areas. We're blessed in that we've been able to work out some fine relationships with the various powers that be. The health department here in the city actually is a partner with us in doing this. The police department has been cooperative in that they've been willing to acknowledge our identification cards that we give to folk who exchange needles. The cards simply say the person is part of a program designed to curb the spread of HIV/AIDS and please understand that is why he or she has paraphernalia with them. The District Attorney has been very cooperative with us. He's been willing not to prosecute us and hasn't. Nobody will give us that in writing of course. They're unwritten agreements, but they've worked out real well for us.

COMSTOCK: What was the turnaround point for the class mix? How and when did it happen?

REV. SANDERS: It was real clear. Early on what happened was we got involved in prison ministry — actually directed a ministry called the Southern Prison Ministry for a while. Going in and out of the prisons we started to develop relationships that translated to folks coming out of prison and getting involved in the church. After I had done the prison ministry for a while it became crystal clear to me that 80 percent of the people I was dealing with in prison were there for alcohol and drug related issues. I started reassessing this whole issue of drugs and alcohol and decided that's an area we had to begin to focus our ministries. So, I got involved, did the training, and became certified as a counselor. I would venture to say that 25 percent of the people in this church are folks that I first met in treatment. Thirty to 35 plus percent of this congregation are folks who are in treatment from alcohol and drug use. This is a place where a lot of folks know they can come. We've got all these names, you know, the drug church, the AIDS church, we get those labels. But it's all right because that's what we do. We hit those themes a lot.

I've learned some things over the years that I pretty much hold to and this is one of them: we say we don't celebrate anything in this church other than our relationship to Christ, that being the vehicle for liberation in our lives. We don't say we are a black church, we don't say that we are a gay church or a straight church, we don't say that we are anything other than a church that celebrates our oneness in Christ. I'm convinced that has turned out to be the real key to being able to hold this diverse group of folks together. I must admit I'm a person that has a negative thing about the word diversities. I don't use it much. We don't celebrate our differences, we celebrate our oneness. That ends up being an avenue for a lot of folks being attracted and feeling comfortable here. New folks say I got here and I just felt like no one was looking at me strange, no one was treating me different, I was just able to be here.

I think that we probably struggle with not celebrating difference more on racial terms than on any other level. We would not have a racial mix at all if we were not very intentional about it. Our substance abuse initiatives have been the things that have probably helped us to maintain a racial mix more than anything else because my clients come across racial lines. What we've discovered is that for many folks, other than African-Americans to some degree, this is a point of re-entry, a point of folks coming back to discover a spiritual foundation for their lives. I'm thoroughly convinced that churches are as segregated as they are because they are so culturally distinct and completely one dimensional. It's one of those things I think you always need to be resisting. Folks tend not to be as open to cultural experiences other than their own. It's a heavy thing. We did some strange things to avoid it for a long time. For instance, we went twelve years without a choir. I was very intentional about it because I know that choirs do end up taking on a lifestyle of their own and getting locked into an identity. I knew for us it would end up being the contemporary gospel sound. But sometimes I buckle down and fight people's tendency to be celebrate cultural difference and sometimes I give in. With the choir I eventually gave in, but insisted that they do spirituals and anthems as well as the gospel sound.

There are a number of folks who come who are cross dressers, folks who are in the midst of sex changes. People know they are here but just don't pay any attention to it. Folks get to where they say anyone can come here and it's not something that people pay much attention to because those various differences tend not to be a focus.

COMSTOCK: I was impressed by the informality of the service today. People seem to relax and fit in. The choir is not so focused on performance that they're not interacting with the congregation. And your own manner is informal. It's a style that lets people in. You aren't just saying all people are welcomed here, you actually do something that let's them feel at home. I was also struck by the openness of the windows—the plants inside and the view into the park.

REV. SANDERS: The church is 17 years old, and we've been in this building for 11 years. During those first years we were nomads. We tried to stay in this area. There's a community center nearby, but every now and then we'd have a problem with it, and sometimes we'd have nowhere to go. Luckily it was in the summer or spring when it was warm. We discovered a spot down here in the park where there is an old staircase that used to be a part of a development and we would hold our worship services here in the park. The church was less than a hundred people then so it was real easy to do. We got to where we enjoyed worshiping outdoors, and from then on we would have what we called Sunday in the park. Consequently when we got around to designing our own church, there were a lot of folks who said let's try to keep the outdoor effect. Then we discovered this land right next to the park. This piece of property was the eyesore of the community. There was an old abandoned house on it, a bunch of rusted out cars, the property sloped at very sharp angle, but when I saw it I knew that it could be developed. We put a lot into developing the land and when we built the church we wanted an indoor/outdoor effect, a connection with the park, and it's worked well for us. It helps me to worry less about engaging and reaching people when I preach. It's nice to have folks say they felt that they had such a wonderful time in worship and the sermon was great, but what I rely on is that they can always be looking out the windows behind me. The trees, the birds, and the sky take care of it for me, plus you see the seasons so wonderfully.

And another thing is we have the sense of informality. People are arriving from the time we welcome the guests at the beginning until just after the sermon when there's maximum presence in the audience. People come in slow, and we give folks an opportunity to leave early. We even say it in the bulletin, we just say if you need to leave just leave quietly. And we know folks do. There's a lot of folks who want to hear the choir or they want to hear the sermon, but they don't want all the rest of it. So we do it that way. It works out. One of the real hooks for just about everyone at Metropolitan is the fellowship circle at the end. We actually have a few Jews and a couple of Muslims who worship here regularly. The Muslim family does a very interesting thing which helped me to appreciate the significance of the fellowship circle at the end. We offer communion—the Eucharist, the Lord's supper—every Sunday, and they stay until we get to that part of the service. Then they go outside or into the vestibule, but they come back in. I remember when Omar first started attending, I said to him it's interesting to me that you don't leave at that point. He said, "No, no, no, I wouldn't miss the fellowship circle." And it made me realize that the communion of the fellowship circle is more important than the bread and the wine. Probably the real communion is what we do when we stand there at the end and sing "We've Come Too Far to Turn Back Now."[1] We do that every week. It's our theme. That's a very significant moment. I've heard people tell me when they have to be late that they rush to get here just to catch the end of it. One woman said to me it was enough for her if she just got here for the fellowship circle.

A lot of the informality is very intentional. For instance, the only thing at Metropolitan that's elevated is the alter. Nothing else is above ground level. None of the seating is differentiated. In most churches the ministers have different, higher, bigger chairs than everyone else. We don't do that. We sit in the same seats the other folks do. My choir director is always telling me we'd get better sound if we could elevate the back rows. I say no, everybody's got to be on the same level and got to sit in the same seats. We do a lot of symbolic things like that.

COMSTOCK: Do other clergy give you much flack for working with needle exchange, welcoming gay folks, and working on issues that they may see as too progressive.

REV. SANDERS: They do. But let me tell you something. I have been able to have a level of involvement with ministers in this community that probably has brought credibility to what we do. I would like to think that we have maintained our sense of integrity especially as it relates to our consistency in ministry. Folks tend to respect that, so even when they disagree, they also look more seriously and harder at what it is they're questioning. They've come to know over time that we've been a group of folks who try not just to be politically correct but to think and act about where the teachings of Christ will lead us. We just had James Earl Ray's funeral here. He as you know was the convicted assassin of Martin Luther King Jr. Some people, including members of King's family, do not believe he was guilty. Doing his funeral here was one of the more controversial things we've ever done. The one thing that we say all the time about ourselves — it's almost a cliche — is that we are inclusive, we are reconciling, and we are engaged. Those are our three words. We are inclusive of all, constantly involved in issues of reconciliation and engaged in the issues. So that's it. That's who we say we are. What happened was, one pastor who was a leader of the local civil rights movement and a friend of King's seemed symbolically right to do the funeral, but his church said no way. And then there's another congregation here that's very active and in the heart of the African-American community, and it said no. So Metropolitan was the only place that was open to it. It's almost a non-issue for us. To me that's living out who we say we are. We simply say we acknowledge all folks as being children of God and of course the situation with James Earl Ray made it easy, because even though there were all kinds of contradictions in his life, the fact is he was a baptized believer. We have to believe that he had the promise and the guarantee the same way we have it. So we had his funeral service. Obviously folks here were challenged. We had a lot of positive support but we've also had folks asking what are you doing. And I respond that we say that we are a "whosoever" church and James Earl Ray was one of those whosoevers.

COMSTOCK: "Whosoever" is from John 3:16-17: "For God so loved the world that he gave his only Son, that whosoever believes in him should not perish but have eternal life." Has it been an expressed theme from the beginning?

REV. SANDERS: It's been our theme for the last seven or eight years. The theme from the very beginning was Citizens of the World. We've always had a visual focal piece. First it was the Citizens of the World banner. And then for a long time it was the cross that's on the wall in the corner which looks like it's made of kente cloth from Africa, but it's actually cloth made in Guatemala. It's a kind of cloth that people all around the Equator make—in Asia, the Americas, in Africa. That symbolism is important to us. The circle, the cross in the middle of the circle, the cross of cloth made by people circling the world. That was our focal piece for a long time. When we were ready to make a change, I had a vision for it. I said I know the one thing that will work. David, a young artist who does our children's church, did the new theme piece that has the "whosoever" on it.

I think we're growing in this inclusivity all the time. The language issue was big for us. We try to use inclusive language.[2] If somebody else comes into the church that is not into that, it sticks out like a sore thumb. Does our inclusivity also mean that there is a real tolerance for folks who are perhaps not where we think folks should be in terms of issues like inclusive language, issues that relate to sexuality, gay and lesbian issues? I think the answer to that question is yes, you have to make room for those folks too. That's a real struggle. Another one of our little clichés, and we don't have a lot of them, is we say we try to be inclusive of all and alienating to none. Not being alienating is a real trick. It's amazing how easy you can alienate folks without realizing it, in ways that you're just not aware of. Hopefully if someone does come and does not use the language as we use it or is not where we might be in terms of some issues, that doesn't end up being a basis upon which we exclude them. You know, we try to feel for that person and their response. One of my favorite Howard Thurman quotes is the one where he says I'm not only responsible for what I do to you but I'm also responsible for how I respond to what you do to me.[3] And I think there is a way in which we try to get folks to wrestle with that, because even though someone might say something that is out of sync and not where our thinking is, we have a responsibility to respond in a way that isn't alienating to the person, that doesn't create a breach. You need to get beyond difference and engage the person in a way that allows you to have an effect that is transforming for them.

COMSTOCK: What would you do if some new people had trouble with cross dressing, transgendered, lesbian or gay people? How do you get them to stay and deal with it rather than leave?

REV. SANDERS: We tracked that issue a couple of times. Let me tell you what's happened. Most folk are here for a while before some of it settles in, before they start to notice everything. It's amazing to me how people get caught up in Metropolitan. They'll join and get involved and then they'll go through membership class, that's usually when it starts to hit them, that they say to themselves, "Oh oh, I'm seeing some stuff that I'm not sure about here." But what we've discovered is that what seems to help us more than anything else is that folks end up remembering what their initial experience had been when they first came here. We even have one couple, this is my favorite story to tell, who has talked about coming here on one of those Sundays when we were hitting the theme of inclusive hard. And they left here and said what kind of church is that? But then a couple of weeks later they said let's go back over there again. They came back and then they didn't come again for about two or three months. They were visiting other churches. They said when they got down to thinking about all the churches, they had felt warmth and connection here. They said you know that church really did kind of work; and they ended up coming back. When folks are here there's a warmth they feel, there is a connection they feel, there's a comfort zone in which they'll eventually deal with the issues that might be their point of difference. We've seen folks move in their thinking and there's some folks that have not been able to do it. I've got one young man—I really do think he just loves being here—who says, "I just can't fathom this gay thing. Why do you insist on it." I said, "You know, you're the one who's lifting this up."

As I said, we try to make sure that when any issue is brought up, it's in the course of things. It's not like we stop and have gay liberation day, just like we don't celebrate Black History month. We don't focus on or celebrate these identities or difference, but yet if you're around here you can't help but pick up on the church's support for these issues and differences. Today, for instance, we sang "Lift Up Your Voice and Sing," which is known as the black national anthem. But we call it "Our Song of Liberation," and I've tried to help people to understand that. One of the greatest things about that song, which is a little known point, is that song was written by James Weldon Johnson for the competition to establish a national hymn. It was chosen for first place, and then the committee found out that a black person had written it and chose the second place song to win. That's when black people started calling it the Negro national anthem. One of the most telling lines in the song is the last one where it says, "true to our God, true to our native land." Johnson wasn't talking about Africa. He was talking about America. It's such a great song of liberation for all Americans. When you think about the song, you can always make it specific to your own experience. It's a song that was written as an American piece and not as a black piece.

I have a lot of divinity students who serve as my pastoral assistants, and most of them are women. This place has become a real refuge for black women in the ministry. There are not a lot clergy opportunities for them, so I've tried to figure out how to incorporate them into the life and ministry of the church. They actually run a lot of our ministries. And most of them are extremely well prepared academically. They're more prepared than I am to do the work and they do it well. When they started coming we suddenly became a magnet, a place where there was this rush of folks out of divinity school to come and be a part of ministry here. At one level I probably seem like I'm extremely freewheeling and loose, but I'm probably a lot more intentional about how things are going than folks realize, especially as they relate to the focus of ministry here at the church. One of my real concerns was not having the time to orient the young ministers, to bring them into a full awareness of what makes this place click. What I have discovered is that if I get the inclusive piece established in the beginning with them, I don't have to worry about the rest of it as much. If they buy into understanding that inclusivity is at the heart of this church, I don't have to worry about keeping my eye on them all the time.

I think the one thing I do a good job at is getting folks turned on. I'm not necessarily the right person to take them all the way down the road. That's the reason why I don't get upset about folks who come to the church and don't stay because they have struggles with issues. I do find though that if this is the place where they got turned on, it's usually something that continues to be a part of their thought and what they end up wrestling with. At one point it was very clear to me that this church is kind of a conduit. It's a place where a lot of folks come through. We have about 700 members that we see with regularity. And there are another 400-500 folks who claim that they are part of Metropolitan, but we don't see them often. They come when they marry or someone dies. Somebody's got to bury them or their kids need to be blessed or they're in trouble. I guess what I'm saying is I'm all right with the fact that this is a place where folks get engaged sometimes, but the acting or the living out of it occurs elsewhere. But I think it is important that the right seed is planted, and I do think that all the seeds we plant are seeds that have that theme of inclusivity within them. I tell folk all the time, I wish I could say that it was all as well planned as it might seem, but it has evolved. I think that a lot of who we turned out to be was determined by things that we weren't conscious of or didn't see as significant in the beginning. That's kind of how we feel about the needle exchange. Awhile ago I got an invitation from the Harvard Aids Institute to come and speak. Only then as I talked with people outside of our experience did I become aware that there was probably not another church in the U.S. doing needle exchange. I guess what I'm saying is there's a lot of things we do just because we think they're what we ought to be doing, and over time the significance of them probably proves to be something more than I realized.

COMSTOCK: You know that the example here of accepting and welcoming lesbians and gay men is an anomaly in the Church. You provide inspiration and hope, an example of something positive that is actually happening. Most gay people feel alienated from their churches, but I've found that African-American more often than white gay people emphasize the importance of religion in their family, community, and history and say that most of the pain and sadness in their lives centers around the Church. They claim that being rejected by the black church is especially devastating because this institution has been, and continues to be, the only place where they can take real refuge from the racism they experience in the society.[4] Clearly that's not happening here at Metropolitan.

Rev. Sanders: We realized when we started doing our HIV/AIDS ministry that there are organizations that were established by gay white men who had done a good job of developing services, but we kept seeing there was something that was not happening for gay and lesbian African Americans. And we realized it was community. No matter how much they tried to get that in other communities, there is the whole thing of cultural comfort. They were looking for the context where there were people who looked like them, who were extensions of their family supporting them. It became clear to me that what we needed to do was to establish a place where people could literally come and where people had a sense of community. Consequently, what we call the Wellness Center here is more than anything else just a place where you can come and feel at home. It has sofas and tables and chairs. Folks sit around. It's a place where there is a community that is an insulating, supporting place to come to. And although we provide some direct services for those folks, more than anything else I think the greatest service we provide is a safe place, a comfort zone, a community, a way to be connected to community. So I know real clearly what you're talking about, and I've heard it spoken too. It's one of the real issues for African Americans who are gay and lesbian. So our simple response has been to try to create a space where folks will have a certain level of comfort.

The problem I often run into, which speaks to what you were asking about, is that I think the greatest trouble we have sometimes is folks in the gay and lesbian community want to celebrate their sense of life and lifestyle more than Metropolitan lends itself to. In the same way, I have folks who don't understand why we don't do more things that are clearly more defined as being Afrocentric. There's a strong Afrocentric movement now within religious circles, and I end up dealing with them the same way I do with the folks who want to have ways in which they celebrate being gay and lesbian. My greatest struggle ends up being with folks who want to lift that up more, and I say the only thing we lift up is the basis of our oneness. I think the Church has been a place where folks have not been able to find community, where they have been rejected. The African American church is a pretty conservative entity, always has been. It's probably been even better at holding up the conventions of American Christianity than other institutions. Consequently folks can draw some pretty hard lines, and that's what we've been dealing with at Metropolitan. But the other side of the Black church is that it is known as being an institution of compassion. So at the same time you have folks giving voice to some conservative ideas and practices, you can also appeal to a tradition and practice of compassion. That's why in our HIV/AIDS ministry we've been able to bring other churches into the loop. We're trying to get thirty churches to be involved in doing education and intervention on HIV/AIDS. We've been able to engage them on the level of compassion. Once we get them involved at that level then, we see folks open their eyes to other issues. African American churches have been very effective in compassion ministry for years around issues of sickness, death and dying. What we're trying to do is get folks to put as much emphasis on living and not just being there to minister to sickness and dying.

Another thing is the contradictions in the Church. The unspoken message that says it's all right for you to be here, just don't say anything, just play your little role. You can be in the choir, you can sit on the piano bench, but don't say you're gay. We had an experience here in Nashville which I'm sure could be evidenced in other places in the world. You know how a few years ago in the community of male figure skaters there was a series of deaths related to HIV/AIDS. The same thing happened a few years ago with musicians in the black churches. At one point here in Nashville there were six musicians who died of AIDS. In every instance it was treated with a hush. Nobody wanted to deal with the fact that all of these men were gay black men, and yet they'd been there leading the music for them. It's that contradiction where folks say yeah you're here but don't say anything about who you really are, don't be honest and open about yourself. I believe that the way in which you get the

Church to respond is to continue to force the issue in terms of the teachings of Christ, to be forthright in seeing how the issue is understood in relationship to Jesus Christ. One thing I've learned about dealing with inner city African Americans is that you have to bring it home for them in a way that has some biblical basis. I'm always challenged by this, but I'm always challenging them to find a place where Jesus ever rejected anyone. I don't think anyone can find it. I don't think there's anybody that Jesus did not embrace.

NOTES

1. "We've Come Too Far to Turn Back Now," Metro (TM) Theme Song; Robert L. Holmes, *Whosoever: The Voices of Metropolitan* (Nashville: Doorway Music Company, BMI, 1998).

2. "Exclusive language," for example, uses "man" and "mankind" as a generic or universal terms to mean "human being" and "humanity," whereas "woman" means only "female," i.e., "man" is the human race and "woman" is a subgroup under "human." Inclusive language uses "human" and "humankind" as the generic terms and "man" and "woman" when referring to all-male or all- female group. Some religious bodies also attempt to use gender-neutral or gender-inclusive terms for God, e.g., referring to God as Father and Mother or as Parent. See Division of Education and Ministry of the National Council of Churches, *An Inclusive Language Lectionary* (New York: National Council of Churches, 1987); and Beverly Wildung Harrison, "Sexism and the Language of Christian Ethics," *Making the Connections: Essays in Feminist Social Circles*, ed. Carol S. Robb (Boston: Beacon, 1985), 22–41.

3. See, for example, Howard Thurman, *The Search for Common Ground* (Richmond, Ind.: Friends United, 1986) and *The Luminous Darkness: A Personal Interpretation of the Anatomy of Segregation and the Ground of Hope* (Richmond, Ind.: Friends United, 1965, 1989).

4. See my book, *Unrepentant, Self-Affirming, Practicing: Lesbian/Bisexual/Gay People within Organized Religion* (New York: Continuum, 1996), 189–90.

Representation and Its Discontents

Black Lesbians:
Passing, Stereotypes,
and Transformation

Jewelle Gomez

W hen I piece together the snippets of images and ideas that help form the picture of myself that I carry in my head it's as if I'm wrestling with a tornado. Imagine the special effect that experts conjure up in the movies: houses, cars, cows, books, kitchen table conversations all swirl around whole, until, released by the gale, they smash to the ground and I have to reassemble them. It's a cataclysmic process experienced, I think, by many people of color, especially of my generation. Growing up with television news coverage of the civil rights and black power movements, the newly recovered history of black Americans, my father's tales of life as a black man, and the pieces of grandmother's youth on an Indian reservation mingled with all the mainstream books, movies and television shows. These were the competing elements I wrangled into manageable reference points for grounding.

Because I knew, even as an adolescent, that I wanted to be a writer, it's not surprising that I absorbed many aspects of the arts almost as fully as I did personal experience. Released in 1959, *Imitation of Life* raised my first real questions about how we decide who we are — even before I was consciously aware of political movements, analyzing family history or embracing the quest for identity. This remake of an earlier adaptation of the Fannie Hurst novel had a powerful impact on me partly because I was such a media baby and because it featured the young stars who appeared in all the banal teen movies I also watched — Troy Donahue, Sandra Dee, Susan Kohner. But most important was its unexpected emotional impact — it threw me into confusion about race, identity, and loyalty.

The story is of a black girl, Peola, who chooses to pass for white, denying her community and humiliating her dark-skinned mother. For me, as an adolescent child in a mixed-race family (before the term was in vogue), some of whose members were also light-skinned, watching the film evoked dread and sorrow. At the moment when the daughter (played by a black actress in the 1934 film and by a white actress in this later version) denies her heritage my stomach clenched in fear as if I were watching her step out of a twenty story window, a decision that could never be rescinded. The presumed advantages of faux whiteness didn't seem worth the loss of family to me; and the deep shame of disavowing one's heritage shook me to the core. But the allure of masquerading as "the other" was also a compelling mystery.

I didn't know then how common stories about blacks passing as white were, even in my own family. Later, in college, when I read work from the writers of the 1920s I realized that "passing" had a long and complicated history in African American society, and, I imagine in all oppressed communities.

The "passing" novel of the early 1900s was a popular genre written by black writers as well as white. In Nella Larson's classic novel, *Quicksand,* her light-skinned protagonist, Helga, is a schoolteacher who scurries out of the sun to avoid becoming darker. Yet she chafes under the self-hatred of the black middle class which is manifested in their proscriptions: "Dark complected people shouldn't wear yellow, or red or green.[1] She escapes to Chicago where she lives in ambivalence and bitterness. In another novel, *Passing,* Larson's protagonist, Claire, marries a white professional and lives as a white woman and like Helga, cuts herself off from her history and the community that had been her support.

"Passing" novels were thought to help invest white readers in the lives of the light-skinned, educated black protagonists and thereby gain sympathy for the plight of black people in general. That strategy — convincing white people that black people were exactly like them — had some success for the civil rights movement but at the same time its usefulness was limited in an evolving political arena. Its focus on external effects served to short-circuit black exploration of our identities as unique individuals with variations within the group of class, gender, sexual orientation. We formed our own personal mythology of who black people were, which was almost as narrow and misleading as the stereotypes that white people clung to.

During the 1960s, I managed to never mention my sexual desire in any personal conversation with friends. I could feel the expectations pressing in on me. Oblique references made it clear that no contemporary African queen was ever queer. But even a decade earlier, Fanon had written: "If one wants to understand the racial situation psychoanalytically, not from a universal viewpoint but as it is experienced from individual consciousnesses, considerable importance must be given to sexual phenomenon."[2]

Today, the "passing" novel has been gone for more than half a century and the "passing" strategy has lost currency in the black political arena. It is almost that long since Fanon suggested the examination of "sexual phenomenon" within the context of race. Yet African Americans are still walking around the edge of the room, trying to ignore the elephant sitting in the middle. I think many would prefer me to "pass" in the black community. For some African Americans, I can be a lesbian in what they imagine as my "dark, secret world," but when I'm in "the community," the message to me is: don't bring "that mess." Asking me to pass as a heterosexual, to not call myself a dyke is a demand for self-hatred and delusion equal to saying black people shouldn't wear "yellow or red or green." It is a demand for a lie I was able to tell by not telling in my youth. Today, the question of a lie feels more significant. Adrienne Rich wrote some years ago that "Truthfulness has never been considered important for women, as long as we have remained faithful to men, or chaste."[3] I think both women and people of color have been rewarded for lying too long. By pretending to be less than we are we've avoided punitive notice, unfair restrictions, and overt aggression. Girls pretend not to be as smart as boys so they can be dating material; black people pretend not to know "nuthin' 'bout birthing babies." Each pose a lie and a protection; each lie a brick shoring up the status quo, blocking my view to myself. My ongoing engagement with eliminating the layers of illusion and to coalesce the parts that are me is too important to ever concede to such a demand. And each word that some consider a label, I see as a door — a door which opens onto more aspects of me. As Mary Helen Washington says in discussing Nella Larson's classic novel *Quicksand,* "Passing is an obscene form of salvation.[4] Just as a black woman passing for white is required to "deny everything about her past," a black lesbian who passes for heterosexual is required to deny everything about her present.

Recently, I had an experience in a black-owned bookstore in the Bay Area that I'm sure is repeated regularly across the country in all types of establishments. I was browsing the shelves with the comforting camaraderie and laughter of the black cashier and two black patrons in the background. The discussion roamed freely then turned to the topic of the "rights" that gay people were "demanding." The three were united in their disdain for gay peoples' very basic civic concerns. Without thinking, the people I'd thought of as "family" only moments before were repeating the same bigotry I'd heard from radical conservatives. They were refusing to recognize any validity in another's desire to be equal before the law, even though that had been the cornerstone of the civil rights movement. It was as if the previous fifty years had never happened and the idea of struggle for civil recognition was anti-American.

I stood among the shelves, stock-still, feeling like the proverbial deer in headlights. If I moved, or indicated I was listening, they would know I was a lesbian! They would do something ugly. I was the elephant in the room — invisible, passing, lying — until the conversation turned to another topic. Then I reshelved the book I was holding and didn't return to the store for many months. As I slipped out of the store, I understood that I'd missed an opportunity to challenge their misinformation, but there was something disturbing about hearing such callous dismissal from black people in a bookstore who only moments before had felt so close. I wanted to shout at them, words Barbara Smith had written: "The oppression that affects Black gay people, female and male, is pervasive, constant, and not abstract. Some of us die from it."[5]

As I walked away I tried to calm my anger and humiliation. But the reality of how easily they erased who I was kept cutting into me. It was a reminder to me that in my twenty years of writing and presenting my work in the United States, Canada, and Europe, I've only been invited to read in a black-owned bookstore once. If I knew it intellectually before, that day I knew in my heart that it's true: those closest to you can cause the most hurt.

I didn't know what to say to the people in the bookstore, maybe because the work it would have taken to make them see me was more than I could handle in one visit. But the encounter made it clearer still that my image of who I am has no substance without all the elements swirling around inside me. Even if black people would so easily reject me, I would never cast them out of my blood. It is for me alone to decide which face I see in the mirror.

In the mid-1970s, a white woman interviewing me for a job asked me who I would choose to play me if Hollywood was making a movie. She couldn't know how complex a question that was. Finding an image to represent me is a trip back into the maelstrom. Although I'd been an avid fan of popular culture, growing up I knew that I wasn't reflected in the movies or on television. Peola, who'd settled for an "imitation of life," certainly wasn't me. But who could be? The question was both intriguing and frustrating.

I'd always liked Ernestine Wade, the actress who played the much-maligned Sapphire on television's "Amos and Andy." Even then I knew that for a black woman to be independent she would have to risk having her name become synonymous with being a bitch. But I didn't think I'd be mentioning Sapphire to a prospective white employer.

I was a major fan of movie queen Dorothy Dandridge, but the tragedy that remained part of her mystique didn't really fit me. And I never could quite see myself as a sarong-wearing siren.

I finally chose Diana Sands, who'd played the sister in the film version of "Raisin in the Sun." She easily embodied the character's outspoken intelligence and determination, qualities I wanted to believe were mine. Searching for the suitable personality to fit my idea of myself was a great exercise for me but turned out to be useless as an interview tool: my future employer had no idea who Diana Sands was.

Twenty years later if I were asked to make a casting choice I have a wider field to examine, but again who would I pick? Angela Bassett? Too thin and buffed. Vanessa Williams? Too ethereal. Alfre Woodard? Interesting possibility. But I doubted any of them would ever allow themselves to be filmed with their hair natural, not straightened, much less play a lesbian.

In almost every case, when I encountered the images of black women, the subtleties of who we might be were almost completely unexamined—in the media, in the public consciousness, and in the black community. And the particulars of who black lesbians might be are not even a question in the larger world.

Lesbians, usually white in movies and books, are generally presented as a bundle of tics and quirks that reflect the heterosexual world's fear and ambivalence. As a teenager, I looked for myself in all of them. The icy Lakey of Mary McCarthy's novel, *The Group* (produced as a film in 1966), the pathetic Martha of *The Children's Hour* (1962), the predatory Jo in the film version of *Walk on the Wild Side* (1962) were all one dimensional concoctions designed to intrigue and repulse. For years the stereotypical lesbian was the only image I could find with which to identify.

It wasn't until much later that I understood that one way to maintain lesbian invisibility is, paradoxically, to create exaggerations or stereotypes that obliterate the reality. The same had been done with African Americans and most other ethnic Americans over the years: Steppin Fetchit, Aunt Jemima, Charlie Chan, the Frito Bandito helped more than one generation of Americans overlook the real people behind the laugh. When we say that something frightening gives us the "willies" most of us don't remember that the term is derived from the actor Willie Best who perfected a comic character who embodied fear, especially of ghosts. His eye-rolling, stuttering, lazy character was featured in Hollywood movies during the 1930s and in them was often the butt of racial jokes from stars like Bob Hope. But Best's brilliant parody became the stereotype that, lacking solid alternative images, came to stand for all black men. The same can be said for every mammy/maid stock character since *Gone with the Wind.* The reality of who we are as black people is subsumed under the one-dimensional distortions that are standard in mass culture. It has been much the same for lesbians although they haven't been such a standard part of the core consciousness.

In 1968, I saw a film, *The Killing of Sister George,* with which I identified as a lesbian for the first time even though it featured no black women. Unlike the infamous, *The Well of Loneliness,* which I read in the mid-1960s, this was not a romantic plea for acceptance. The Radclyffe Hall novel, published in 1927, was a lesbian "passing" novel of sorts, which issued a call for tolerance because the "invert" supposedly had no choice and so desperately wanted to be just like everyone else. Except for the tragic flaw of desire we might fit into society just fine. *The Killing of Sister George,* based on the British play by Frank Marcus, was no such plea. It featured the first fully developed (not to be confused with saintly) lesbian character I'd ever seen on the screen. Some critics and lesbians condemned it as stereotypical, but it actually worked for me because it took the archetype of a hard-drinking, butch lesbian and gave it dimension, emotion, vulnerability.

In the film, Sister George is the kindly village nurse character of a popular British soap opera. The actress who plays George is her hedonistic opposite. The center of her own dynamic social world, she has an edgy, sexual relationship with a lover, and close supportive friends. George, as she is known off camera too, is successful in her life and her work until her downfall is engineered by a jealous, fashionable television executive who seduces her lover. It's not a pretty picture of lesbians, but it's a gritty, compelling close-up of people.

In the film I found several elements for the first time. First, a real portrayal of the complexity of sexuality between women. George and her girlfriend (who dresses perpetually in baby-doll pajamas) are not the vanilla couple usually depicted, if depicted at all. They are not platonic lesbians or peck-on-the-cheek-lesbians. Their sexual game playing has a guttural quality drawn from a very deep place of desire and need.

The friendship women show each other in the film is also significant to the story, it is as important an element as the lover's betrayal. George's confidant is a sympathetic prostitute who takes their bond seriously. This rendering of a specifically working-class acceptance transcends liberal tolerance.

Additionally, contrasts between the working-class and upper-class women of the story frame the conflicts perfectly. The prostitute, the working-class bit players in the soap opera, and George are clearly at the mercy of the wealthy upper echelons who barely notice the complications of the lives of their "inferiors."

Most importantly for me, I saw lesbians within the context of a community, a possibility that was always being denied by the larger culture. In the passing stories Peola, Helga and Claire sacrifice their family and community connections to achieve their goals. In passing as white they become lonely, isolated women. Literature and media often cast lesbians in the same isolating spotlight. In the other portrayals I'd seen, lesbians were anomalies, the only one of their "kind," doomed because of their desire. George has lesbian friends and places to go. Her best friend is a willing listener; George and her coworkers are regulars in a pub and the gay folk have a club of their own. George is sexually aggressive, with an acerbic wit and a hard-edged, sometimes overwhelming presence; but she's part of a world of people who love and appreciate her. She does not live alone in the woods, she is not the lone one in her class reunion, she is not on the verge of suicide. She's a woman who goes to work every day, drinks in her favorite bar every day, and goes home to a lover every night. Her doom is sealed not by the fact that she's a lesbian but by her stubborn innocence in the face of a wealthy, manipulative rival.

Through much of my twenties, the patching together of ideas about black women and about lesbians became a giant game of hopscotch. I was always balanced precariously on one foot or the other. Shortly after I discovered Sister George, I saw a play which fed into the established stereotypes I'd expected. But, like the encounter in the black bookstore, this experience was more disturbing because the play was by a black playwright. Ed Bullins' short drama *Clara's Ole Man* was originally written and performed in San Francisco in 1965 and I saw it in New York City in 1969. In it, Clara invites a young, educated man home to visit with her while her "ole man" is at work. But her "ole man" is actually a woman called Big Girl, who happens to take the day off. After continuous consumption of cheap wine and much verbal sparring between the two rivals, Big Girl reveals her relationship with Clara to the young man and has him beaten up by friends who are street thugs. Bullins was one of the few black playwrights of the black arts movement of the 1960s to use lesbian or gay characters in his work. It seems his focus was less on queerness itself than it was on exploring "seedy" aspects of the black community, of which homosexuality happened to be one.

Bullins used the very characterizations found in Sister George but to much less effect. Big Girl drinks incessantly, is controlling and rude, she even humiliated her lover, Clara, by revealing an abortion which she aided. Big Girl's bad behavior might be a defensive reaction to an interloper but, as written by Bullins, she has no other side to her character, no tenderness or love. The play leaves you with the impression that Clara could only have stayed with Big Girl because she's grateful for her help with the abortion and so browbeaten she can't make a life on her own. Unwittingly, perhaps, Bullins trotted out the very antilesbian rhetoric that has pervaded middle-class black life.

In the late 1960s, Huey Newton was able to recognize the importance of the gay rights movement and the need for coalition between the Black Panthers and gay activists. It's a recognition that black working-class people have had for generations, always keeping a place for queer people in their communities. When black anthropologist John Langston Gwaltney interviewed a cross-section of black America for a book he was preparing he concluded: "In black culture there is a durable, general tolerance, which is amazingly free of condescension, for the individual's right to follow the truth where it leads."[6] This is the general attitude I'd grown up with living with my great grandmother and with other relatives. My father, Duke, worked in several bars in the South End of Boston in the 1950s and '60s. Wherever he worked it was comfortable ground for straight and gay patrons who crossed class boundaries—railroad workers, prostitutes, and store owners sat side by side.

But as the black middle class grew in the 1960s, class territory became more delineated and the black middle class, who might be said to be "passing" in their emulation of white values and culture, didn't want anyone around who would call attention to difference. Maybe, fearful of the demonization of black sexuality during slavery and the Jim Crow era, sex became a taboo subject. And nothing calls attention to sex more than a black choir queen or a dapper black butch. They both were welcome in Duke's bar but they better not show up in Estelle's Cocktail Lounge. The importance of assimilation for many in the black middle-class made being openly queer increasingly difficult in the black community. As a young woman I was taught to respect the different patrons in my father's bar. Today the black community seems to have only the voice given it by the middle-class or wealthy sports figures and other entertainers who have access to the media which prefers an image of self-righteous rectitude to one of communal inclusivity.

Despite the transcendent nature of the movements of the 1960s, I've come to learn that I cannot depend on the black community to embrace me as long as I refuse to chop off the part of me that's a black lesbian. The narrow focus of both the Million Man March (1997) and the Million Woman March (1998) confirmed that sexuality, gender oppression, and class issues will remain the elephant in the room. But it seemed after I was finally able to find a lesbian community, I couldn't rely on them to embrace me either. My experiences with white lesbians were rarely reflected in the literature. Books with titles such as *Twilight Girl* seemed designed for the titillation of the larger world and served neither black nor white lesbians well.

Through the 1970s most fiction was usually in the same vein featuring hapless, victimized white lesbians and victimizing black lesbians. Their characteristics and behavior (haughty, disturbed, unstable, hysterical, violent, greedy, manipulative, to name a few from several books) seem attributable to their being black. No further social context was ever provided. So in the end, as with Willie Best, the reader experiences a pathology not a person.

Ann Allen Shockley broadened that universe in 1974 with *Loving Her,* the first novel by a black woman about black lesbians. It tells the story of a young black singer who finds the courage to escape an abusive husband and accept the love of a white woman. Written in the wake of the wave of pulp fiction, it relies on some of the same conventions and drew some criticism because of the interracial relationship. But Shockley continued to write best-selling stories featuring black lesbians, many of which had something every other story had failed to include: a sense of humor. Her hysterically funny novel *Say Jesus and Come to Me* (1982) has some issues and ideas I have examined more critically in other essays. But the most engaging aspect of the work is its ability to capture the cultural substance of black women—the language, physicality, and the humor. The story of a black lesbian minister who ends her slippery seductive ways when she falls in love with a singer allowed black lesbians to recognize ourselves within a black context for the first time on the page.

Although purely popular literature, Shockley's books raise more ideas about black lesbians than any fiction written before it. They introduce the issue of the isolation of the black professional woman in her own community, racism within the recording industry and in the women's movement, and the layers of fear of black lesbians in and out of the closet. Shockley also places her black lesbian characters within the realms of many economic classes of the black community. The black lesbians Shockley presents are workers, mothers, ministers, and all the possibilities one should expect. They, like Sister George, are part of a large community that recognizes their existence.

Published in the same year as Shockley's novel, Alice Walker's *The Color Purple* and Audre Lorde's *Zami* were for the first time literature in which I saw credible and indelible images of black lesbians that related to me. By then I was no longer scanning pages and screens looking for the idea of a lesbian. I had made my own life working in New York, and had developed a circle of friends, many of them black lesbians and gays. The distorted images offered by pulp novels and B movies no longer meant much to me except as historical markers. But I understood that they formed the basis for many others' ideas about who I was.

In the black community I was/am still a peculiar individual; a black lesbian is more often seen through than seen. I understood the need to not speak of sexuality in the black community. The enduring effects of the distortion and exploitation of black sexuality during slavery were still like solid chains around our thoughts. We dared not draw attention to our desire.

But Walker's and Lorde's books smashed that enforced black silence in ways that no other work had done and few books have done since. The effect of these books was felt so strongly, to some extent, because they both were set in our historical past. The idea that lesbianism was a white, modern thing was challenged when we read about the loving between Shug and Celie in the era of juke joints and moonshine. Shug Avery's reputation as a lively lusty woman gives her choice of Celie considerable weight. It implies the power and validity of black women's desire as no heterosexual love story has ever done. Reading about Audre Lorde making her way through the lesbian life of New York's West Village in the 1950s makes that sexual self-determination a heroic goal akin to the other struggles for human rights she's experienced. And just as had been true with the recovery of black history in the 1960s, it was no longer easy to dismiss black lesbians once we were identified as part of black history.

Audre Lorde's *Zami* was the first autobiographically based, full-length work from the perspective of a black lesbian. Previous to that only individual articles by Anita Cornwell in *The Ladder* and some pieces in the short-lived black lesbian publication *Azalea* were available. Audre's development of the term "biomythography" helped her to create the cultural context that previous writers either didn't know, didn't care about, or didn't understand were crucial. When she wrote about the magical yet ordinary event of a party of black lesbians in Queens, New York, she's offering a recognizable setting that allows for the complexity of black lesbian life. The party revealed the possibility of fulfilled working-class and middle-class black lesbians—there is the implication that the world is larger than simply their rejection from mainstream society.

Today, in an era in which the white gay sidekick has become *de riguer* in films and on television; in a decade when the publishing arms of corporations have invested millions in writers of queer fiction, autobiography, and queer studies; the black lesbian is still rarely represented on film or in print. And if she is, it is never as fully realized as the characters created by Alice Walker or Audre Lorde. When a black lesbian does make an appearance, she's still tragic (television adaptation *The Women of Brewster Place*), peripheral (the teacher, Blue, in the main-

stream novel *Push)*, or a caricature (Cleo, played by Queen Latifah in the film *Set It Off)*.

There is a surface similarity to Sister George in the Queen
Latifah's Cleo in *Set It Off* that almost engaged me. She's loud,
overbearing, sexually aggressive, intriguing breaks from the traditional passive roles, even though it represents a simplistic heterosexual reading of lesbian. The script's focus on only those
characteristics leaves Cleo with little else to define her. The film
portrayal is also something of an artifact—in the alternative
meaning of that word—that is something observed in a scientific
experiment, something that doesn't exist naturally. Other than
Cleo's lover, the lesbian community is completely invisible.
Once again the lesbian is alone in an island of heterosexuality.
Cleo is dropped down into the working-class black life of Los
Angeles with no history or antecedents, either socially or in cinema.

To see Queen Latifah's posturing, violent, immature character in 1998, one would never imagine the previous existence of
any film portrayal of black lesbians. Although there may be no
mainstream, popular culture reference points, two films from
the mid-1980s had already opened up the territory with more
insight and complexity. Sheila McLaughlin's *She Must Be Seeing Things* and Lizzie Borden's *Born in Flames* each featured
black lesbian characters in central roles. In one case the black
woman is a jealous lover, comically obsessed with her fantasies
of betrayal, and in the other the black character leads a contemporary lesbian feminist revolution. More recently, other film-
makers have created better realized black lesbian characters.
Julie Dash's film *Daughters of the Dust* subtly presents two
women in the early part of the century who are clearly partners.
In Cheryl Dunye's comedy, *Watermelon Woman,* a young lesbian researches the life of a fictionalized black character actress
who was a lesbian in order to help find herself. These depictions
are spread widely along the spectrum of lesbian representation
and postulate the possibilities of so much in between, it's difficult to accept the single dimension offered by *Set it Off*.

In Cleo I hear echoes of Willie Best and Butterfly McQueen—character actors whose marvelous eccentricities (parodied so sweetly in *Watermelon Woman*) came to stand for being black in the general culture and ultimately obscured the possibility of taking them seriously as actors or as black people.

When the three people in that black bookstore dismissed equal rights for gays, they didn't picture me or any of the characters created by Audre Lorde or Cheryl Dunye. They imagined the caricature of lesbians that is repeatedly reinforced by popular culture in films like *Set It Off*. I wouldn't argue against the artistic freedom that results in such archaic portrayals. I can only be grateful that there are alternative places for young lesbians of color to now look for their reflection and at the same time feel very sad that mainstream culture—black and white—still needs the comfort of such distorted information.

In retrospect, what made me flee from my brothers and sisters in that store was more than anger and humiliation, it was exhaustion. After a lifetime commitment to human rights, I feel almost the same about educating black people about their heterosexism as I do about educating white people about their racism. It's time for them to check themselves.

In an essay written by Cheryl Clarke in 1983, she says: "It is ironic that the Black Power movement could transform the consciousness of an entire generation of black people regarding black self-determination and, at the same time, fail so miserably in understanding the sexual politics of the movement and of black people across the board." The underlying tone of Clarke's essay reveals a similar weariness with confronting the lagging black community that I feel continually. It is also a sentiment sadly echoed more than a decade later by the editors of *Afrekete*, the first anthology with the words "black lesbian" on its cover. Published in 1995, it takes its name from a mythic character in Audre Lorde's Zami. In the introduction, the editors comment: "We did not contemplate too long the specter of political debate that the writing would meet. We take on these debates every day in everything we do. It is tiring. It mutes our passion."[7] There always comes a turning point in a struggle, when the focus shifts, the power dynamic changes. I feel that happening in my pursuit of approval from the black community. The energy I've put into recognizing myself as a whole person has come to mean more than my disappointment at their failure to transform themselves.

For years I had hoped for growth and change in the black community so that the one-dimensional, male-dominated mythology of who we are did not continue to represent all that we could be. But the discourse of black politics and culture flows through the generations with the same male voice — from Baraka and Bullins to Gates, Lee and Als. Even when it is queer or queer friendly, it's a voice comfortable with leaving black women in the background or speaking for black women and letting black lesbians remain invisible.

Maybe in moving from the East to the West Coast in mid-life I got to see things from a different perspective. Unlike in New York, African Americans are not the primary voice for progressive social change in California. The larger Asian American and Spanish-speaking communities have varying strategies and philosophies they employ — not to mention thier different histories. Because we are a part of the Pacific Rim, there is a more global orientation to the activism. Discussions about ethnic concerns are presumed to be connected to the environment, gender parity, and economic class.

But, whatever the reasons, in the struggle for social change it is I, in fact, who have been transformed. I see a larger picture of human rights than the civil rights or black power movements showed me. Those movements were only the first door I walked through. Learning the extent and complexity of oppression on a global as well as local level has necessitated walking through many more doors than I ever would have suspected in the 1960s.

When I work with my writing students or relate to my young cousins and nieces and nephews, I insist that they see these doors, I could be the "unmarried aunt" but I prefer to be "the dyke aunt" — much more interesting and more accurate. And if it causes a storm, better the maelstrom I know than the one caused by unspoken secrets. One of my greatest joys was telling my ten-year-old niece that I was a lesbian and seeing the understanding fill her eyes. Whatever she'd heard in her school or with her friends was forever changed by my ability to be that image she had been unable to find for herself. Her affection for me and my partner, because my family made room for that experience, is the radical social change I've been looking for. She is the community I need for my context, my support.

When I talk to her and other young people I want them to be willing to go out into the storm, no matter how uncertain the outcome. I pass on to them Audre Lorde's words: "I speak without concern for the accusations/that I am too much or too little woman/that I am too black or too white/or too much myself . . ."[8]

NOTES

1. Nella Larson, *Quicksand*, (New York: A.A. Knopf, 1928), 191.
2. Frantz Fanon, *Black Skin, White Masks* (New York: Grove Press, 1967), 160.
3. Adrienne Rich, *On Lies, Secrets, and Silence* (New York: W.W. Norton, 1979), 188.
4. Mary Helen Washington, ed., *Invented Lives* (New York: Doubleday, 1987), 164.
5. Barbara Smith, ed., *Home Girls* (New York: Kitchen Table Women of Color Press, 1983), xlvii.
6. John Langston Gwaltney, *Drylongso*, (New York: Random House, 1980), xxvii.
7. Audre Lorde, *Zami: A New Spelling of My Name* (Watsonville, Calif.: The Crossing Press, 1982), xi.
8. Audre Lorde, *Undersong: Chosen Poems Old and New* (New York: W.W. Norton & Co., 1992), 110.

Writing Robeson

Martin Duberman

S oon after my biography of Paul Robeson had been published in February 1989, I was in San Francisco on the
final leg of the book tour. Between the usual signings and
readings, I made time to pay a return visit to Lee and Revels
Cayton. Both had been helpful during the seven years I spent on
the biography and Revels, a radical veteran of the trade union
wars and one of Robeson's closet friends, had at several points
given me crucial information and advice.

I had sent the Caytons an early copy of the book, and Revels
greeted me with a bear hug, effusive with congratulations for
having "gotten it right." Later, over coffee, he made a comment
that startled me: "You know, I've been thinking about it and I
believe that *only* a gay man could have understood Paul's sex
life."

I had been thinking about it too—far a long time—and
thought I knew what Revels meant: most heterosexual scholars,
a conservative breed not known for their erotic capers, would be
likely to share the mainstream view that lifetime, monogamous
pair-bonding is the optimal path to human happiness—not to
say moral decency. That assumption, in turn, would incline
them, when confronted with the unorthodox erotic history of
someone like Robeson, to evade, minimize, condemn, or apolo-
gize for this unconventional, robust sexuality.

A legion of heterosexual scholars strenuously believe in their
hearts, not merely in their public pronouncements, that sexual
"restraint" is one of the admirable moral cornerstones of our
national character. (It took DNA, remember, finally to break
down their adamant denial of a sexual liaison between Jefferson
and Sally Hemings).

Confronted with Robeson's many sexual adventures, such
scholars would most likely characterize them as "womanizing"

or "Don Juanism." Additionally, they would probably "explain" the fact that Robeson's most intense, long-lasting affairs were nearly all with white women by regurgitating hoary, simplistic formulas about his need to probe himself to the white world, or to work out his anger toward it.

By the time I visited the Caytons, Revel's view that most heterosexual scholars would react uneasily to Robeson's sexuality had already been borne out in some of the early reviews. The critic in the *San Francisco Chronicle* had referred to Robeson's "compulsive womanizing," *The Village Voice* reviewer had wondered about "the unquenchable need that lay behind his behavior," and Ishmael Reed, while praising my "fine" biography, had taken me to task for the book's "excessive and voyeuristic detail" about Robeson's romantic and sexual encounters. And Paul Robeson, Jr., would soon issue a formal statement, printed in *The Amsterdam News*, characterizing my biography as "prurient." When I later told Revels about *that*, he shook his head in disbelief, chuckling over what he called my *restrained*" account of Robeson's erotic activities.

It was Paul Robeson, Jr., who had invited me, back in 1981, to be his father's biographer. He had offered me exclusive access for seven years to the vast family archives long closed to scholars, and had stressed at our very first meeting that he wasn't looking for a "Saint Robeson" but rather a tell-it-like-it-was account that would make his father an accessible human being rather than a pedestalized god.

Impressed, flattered, and eager as I was to accept Paul, Jr.'s offer, it also puzzled me. "You can see that I'm white," I said to him during that first meeting, "but do you also know that I'm gay, and that I've been actively involved in the gay political movement for years?" He casually replied that he did, that he had had me "thoroughly checked out." He had become convinced that I was the right biographer for his father because (as I recorded his words in my diary) of my "nuanced prose," my "complex understanding of personality," my leftwing politics and my experience in the theater.

Since I was not the only historian with leftwing views who wrote "nuanced" prose, I remained skeptical that Paul, Jr.'s stated reasons for inviting a white gay activist to become his father's biographer exhausted the range of his motives. But wanting to believe him, I kept my skepticism to myself and accepted his invitation.

But I did set one condition. I told him that I could comfortably undertake the biography only if he drew up a legal agreement in which he formally gave up all control over what I might ultimately choose to write. No self-respecting scholar, I explained, could work with someone looking over his shoulder — and especially not a son, deeply invested emotionally, and his own pronounced views and agenda. Paul, Jr. said he had expected me to set those conditions, and was willing to sign such an agreement. "As we move ahead," he added with a sly grin," "I'll doubtless backslide." (Oh, Lord, would he backslide!)

And so we were launched. Paul Robeson, Jr., had given me the necessary assurances, had insisted he wanted a wholly truthful — not a plastercast — portrait, and was soon, moreover, introducing me to some of his father's closest friends. But as I set to work on the mountainous source materials, a sense of unease lingered. *Was* this, I asked myself, a case of bizarre miscasting, a grotesque mismatch of author and subject — as some were quick to charge as soon as the project was publicly announced.

To quiet my discomfort, I tried putting the issue in a larger context: What, after all, *are* the essential qualities in a given biographer that heighten the chances for understanding life? Who is best qualified to write about whom — and why? Are there certain unbreachable guidelines that must be followed, certain fundamental boundaries that must not be crossed? Do we want to argue, for example, that no man should attempt to write about a woman, a younger person about an older, an adult about a child, a straight person about a gay one, a white person about a person of color (or vice versa)?

Even the most committed essentials, I feel sure, would balk at strictures this severe: We have become too aware of how reductive the standard identity categories of gender, class, race, and ethnicity are when trying to capture the actual complexities of a given personality. (Paul Robeson cannot simply be summarized as "a black man." Nor Martin Duberman as "a gay one.") Besides, many people have overlapping identities that compete for attention; over time, moreover, how we rank their importance in shaping our personalities can shift, which in turn leads to a reallocation of political commitments.

But why is the assumption so widespread in the first place that a match-up between author and subject in regard to standard identity categories *is* the best guarantor of understanding? Indeed, who do we lazily assume that these categories are, in every case, the critical ones, while ignoring any number of other commonalties between biographer and subject that might provide critical insights—matters such as having been raised in comparable family or regional cultures, sharing similar psychologies of self, professional experience, religious affiliations, political ideologies.

Which of the affiliative links, standard or otherwise, between biographer and subject are likely to prove the most trenchant pathways to understanding? Perhaps—heresy!—the answer is *none*, or none that can be presumed in advance to guarantee access into the furthest recesses of personality. Perhaps what will turn out to matter most is that which is least visible and hardest to define: something to do with an elusive empathy of the spirit between biographer and subject, a shared if shadowy sense of how one should try to navigate through life, to treat other people, to leave a mark and make a contribution without succumbing to grandiosity—or obliteration. How one positions oneself will always reflect to some degree the seminal experiences and indoctrinations of class, race or gender, but may also, perhaps even to a greater degree, float above them, wondrously unanchored in categorical imperatives, mysteriously untraceable in derivation.

The simplifications currently at work are easily enumerated. Whether, for example, one defines "working-class" in terms of income, job status or educational level, it should be obvious that not all working-class people have had an interchangeable set of experiences; being on an assembly line cannot be equated with cooking hamburgers at McDonald's, nor illiteracy with a high school education, nor life in a trailer park with life in a slum. An historian with a "working-class" background cannot assume that that fact alone will open the gates of understanding to his or her working-class subject.

Turning to race, surely whites now realize that there is no homogeneity of lifestyle or opinion among members of a minority group. African Americans, for example, vary widely in their views on everything from parenting to education to politics to white people. As for gender, the mere fact of being a woman would not in itself prepare a university-trained PhD doing the biography, say, of Grandma Moses, to understand a rudimentary rural life, the techniques of primitive painting, the process of aging, or the morass of celebrityhood.

To take as a given that no white person is able (or morally entitled) to write about someone black can itself be seen as a form of racism—a particularly simplistic form, for it is based on the insidious assumption that fellow-feeling hinges on the color of one's skin and that an individual's character can be accurately prejudged on the basis of his or her membership in a particular group.

Because no biographer can duplicate in his or her person the full range of their subject's experience—or exactly duplicate any of it—every biographer will be found wanting in some areas. And, yes, the disability *can* sometimes be directly linked to racial (or class or gender) dissonance. I do not doubt, for example, that *as a white person* I failed to capture some of the nuances of what it meant for Robeson to grow up in the black church (his father was a minister). Yet, oppositely, my own second career in the theatre gave me a background few if any scholars could bring to bear in evaluating Robeson's stage experience.

Which brings us back to the "gay issue." Was Revels Cayton

right in seeing my homosexuality as an *asset* in writing Robeson's biography, or was it—as many more have asserted—an offensive disability. Lloyd L. Brown, who collaborated with Robeson in the 1950s on his autobiographical manifesto, *Here I Stand*, has been among the more publicly outraged. When my editor at Knopf sent Brown an early copy of the biography in 1989, he wrote back that I was "a sick writer" whose "homosexual values" were asserted throughout the book. Down to the present day, Brown continues to denounce my "preoccupation with the bedroom aspects of Robeson's life."

One of the ironies in all this is that my biography is, if anything, a rather truncated—one might even say, chaste— rendering of Robeson's highly charged erotic life. Only Robeson's half-dozen significant romantic attachments are discussed in any detail, and his many short-term encounters are barely mentioned. Nor do I ever describe, let alone itemize, his actual sexual behavior—his preferences and performances in bed.

Moreover, as I made clear in the biography, Robeson's wife Essie had early on understood that her husband was not cut out for monogamy and domesticity; wanting to remain Mrs. Robeson, she had made her peace with his extramarital pleasures. That Essie was knowledgeable about Paul's sexual adventures would not, of course, make them more palatable to traditional moralists—including many church-going African American adherents of mainstream sexual mores.

White conservatives, long since enraged at Robeson's political militancy, gleefully latch on to his erotic history as an additional weapon in portraying him as a "moral transgressor." For white racists, moreover, Robeson's exhuberent sexuality can usefully be made to play into the longstanding, vicious stereotype of the black man as a "rampaging lustful beast." That almost all of Robeson's major affairs were with white women, finally, can be used to diminish his stature even among those who otherwise deeply admire his unyielding struggle against racism and colonialism. (After my biography was published,

Paul Robeson, Jr. claimed that I had deliberately omitted a "list" he had given me of his father's black female lovers. If there is such a list, I was never shown it. Besides, the evidence of Paul Sr.'s preference for white lovers is overwhelming and incontestable.)

The biographer's job is to tell the truth—to the extent that inevitable gaps in the evidence and subjective distortion will allow for it. The biographer is not responsible for how others manipulate that truth to serve agendas of their own. Those who despise Robeson's socialism will always manage to find grounds for justifying their hostility; neither the inclusion nor omission of evidence about his sexual life will dislodge their underlying animus to his politics.

Yet even some who feel deeply sympathetic to Robeson's politics experience discomfort over his troubled marriage and his frequent extramarital affairs—and especially traditional socialists of the older generation, for whom economic, not sexual or gender, liberation remains the one legitimate issue of abiding importance.

This discomfort needs to be directly addressed, along with the underlying assumption that feeds it: namely, that monogamous, lifetime pair-bonding is, for everyone, the only defensible, natural, moral path. But how much sex *is* too much sex? Does the answer hinge on the number of different partners involved, the number of encounters with the same partner, particular configurations (three-way or group sex, say) or particular sexual acts (anal intercourse, say, or sadomasochism)? The answers will hinge on individual assumptions about what is "normal," "healthy" or "moral." In this country numbers alone are likely to settle the argument: the higher the figure, the more brows start to furrow—even when we are talking about consenting adults.

We need to take a closer look as well at what most people in our culture mean when using the designation "womanizer"— the charge Robeson's detractors most often level at him (that is, when they are not denouncing his "Stalinism"). Three definitions currently predominate: a "womanizer" is someone whose self-regard hinges on multiple conquests; is someone incapable of love and, to disguise that fact (not least from himself), pursues multiple sexual encounters; and, finally, is someone who treats his partners as exploitable objects, to be used disdainfully and discarded cavalierly.

None of these definitions, I would submit, apply to Paul Robeson. That is the overwhelming testimony both of his lovers and his psychiatrists. Every woman I spoke to who had been involved with Robeson for an extended period of time emphasized that he treated her as an equal, not a mere convenience or appendage. He could be difficult, neglectful and secretive, but was much more often tender, considerate and loving. As if in confirmation, one of Robeson's psychiatrists described him to me as a man whose "motivational spring was compassion, not ego."

And so when I hear Robeson described as a "womanizer," I've learned to take it as a rule of thumb that I'm listening to someone who despises the man politically and wishes to discredit him—as nothing can do more powerfully in our sexnegative culture than the accusation of "philanderer."

Unless it be, of course, to spread rumors that he was to some degree erotically involved with men. Such rumors, as I learned to my astonishment, were already in circulation when I began Robeson's biography. In a 1981 issue of the leftwing magazine *WIN* (now defunct), an article on Robeson had referred to his bisexuality as if it was a well-established fact. Some years later *The Advocate* (a national gay magazine) printed the claim that Robeson had "recently [been] revealed to have been gay." At the time I protested both pieces, and later, in the biography, wrote that I had "found absolutely no evidence of Robeson's erotic interest in men."

The candidate most often urged on me as Robeson's male lover was the Russian filmmaker Sergei Eisenstein. When I discussed that possibility with, among others, Zina Voynow, Eisenstein's sister-in-law, she scoffed at the notion of such an affair—though she did not, as some of his biographers have, deny Eisenstein's homosexuality.

Nevertheless, even after my biography was published, the rumor surfaced yet a third time (in a 1990 article by a Hugh Murray) that insisted—at length, and based on a fatuous twisting of suspect scraps of "evidence"—that the matter of Robeson's bisexuality remained "an open question." It does not. Baring the (almost unimaginable) surfacing of new evidence to the contrary, Robeson was—as I wrote in the biography and as I have repeatedly said in response to ongoing queries—singularly, rigorously, contentedly heterosexual.

For merely insisting on scholarly standards of evidence, I didn't expect a medal for Meritorious Resistance to Political Correctness. But I *was* surprised that among the several critics who denounced Robeson as "oversexed" and my biography of him as "prurient," only one—in *Commentary* magazine, no less—so much as mentioned that my book had put to rest the long-standing rumors of Robeson's bisexuality. Not even the *Commentary* reviewer thought to mention that I had done so as a gay man who might have been expected to maximize every remote innuendo or shard of evidence that could have left open the opportunity to claim Robeson for Our Side.

When non-gays credit anything valuable about the gay perspective—and only a few leftists ever do—they usually cite its iconoclasm, its insistent challenge to "regimes of the normal"—especially in regard to gender and sexuality. In writing Robeson's biography, iconoclasm stood me in good stead. Yet, ultimately, I came to feel that it was less important in helping me get beneath the layers of his personality than what I would call our shared status as outsiders—outsiders who to a significant degree had been "let in," had been treated by the mainstream as acceptable representatives of our otherwise despised groups.

Years into researching the book, I was still mulling over the question of whether or not I was an appropriate biographer for Robeson. I finally came to the conclusion that a strong argument

could be made—just as Revels Cayton would later suggest—
that far from disqualifying me as an effective interpreter of Robeson's life, my being gay had in fact given me some important
advantages. Here is how I ultimately summed it up in a diary
entry:

> Like Robeson, I know about the double-bind of being accepted and
> not accepted.
>
> I know about the outsider's need to role-play (the uses of theatre
> off-stage).
>
> I know about the double vision of the outsider who is let inside;
> about being a "spy" in the culture.
>
> I know some of the strategies of concealing pain, including from
> oneself.
>
> I know about the exuberant investment of hope in a "liberation"
> movement—and the attendant despair when it falls short.
>
> I know about the seductive double-talk employed, when consid-
> ered serviceable, by the white male power structure.
>
> I know about the tensions of trying to be a "good" role model.
>
> I know about the conflict between the yearnings of lust and the de-
> mands of a public image.
>
> I know about the tug-of-war between the attractions of career and of
> doing "good works."
>
> I know about the disjunction between the desire to be liked (and
> knowing one has the necessary social skills to accomplish that) and
> feeling disgust at the neediness or grandiosity of the desire.
>
> I know about stubbornness—and about the need to sometimes
> play the supplicant.
>
> I know about the counter pulls of feeling gregarious *and* longing
> for—requiring—solitude.
>
> I know about concealment.
>
> I know about buried anger.
>
> I know about politeness substituting for anger, about anger eating
> up one's vitals, distorting one's judgment.
>
> I know about loneliness.

Once the biography was published, it came as an enormous
relief to me that many of the leading African American intellectuals who reviewed the book—including Herb Boyd, Nathan
Huggins, David Levering Lewis, Nell Irvin Painter and Arnold
Rampersad—praised it highly.

The review that perhaps pleased me most was Nell Irvin Painter's. Some years earlier, she had rather sharply attacked me and other white historians (during an American Historical Society panel on "Black Biography") for "wrong-headedly" undertaking biographies of African Americans. Yet when she came to review my biography of Robeson in *The Boston Globe*, she reversed fields, writing that the book especially "rates high marks for having seen much that white biographers of African-American subjects frequently disregard, notably anger and strategies for its management . . ."

Nell Painter did not suggest that my being gay might have been importantly connected to my ability to see "much that white biographers . . . frequently disregard." But I myself, after years of anguished inner debate, *have* come to hold that view. To whatever extend my biography of Robeson does represent an "empathy of the spirit," I believe the sensitizing factor of critical importance was precisely my homosexuality.

Transferences and Confluences: The Impact of the Black Arts Movement on the Literacies of Black Lesbian Feminism

Cheryl Clarke

> *The history of participation by poets in American social and political movements of this country has been important to the feminist poetry movement. . . . [I]t has provided examples of women poets, some of them early feminists, to whom we have been able to look for inspiration and encouragement. The Harlem Renaissance, a chapter of the Black struggle that was a social as well as a cultural movement, was led by poets. . . . Gwendolyn Brooks, Nikki Giovanni, and Sonia Sanchez were closely identified with the Black Power movement.*
> —Jan Clausen, *A Movement of Poets*

> *The fact of music was the black poet's basis for creation. And those of us in the Black Arts movement were drenched in black music and wanted our poetry to be black music. Not only that, we wanted that poetry to be armed with the spirit of black revolution. An art that could not commit itself to black revolution was not relevant to us. And if the poet that created such art was colored we mocked him and his inspiration as brainwashed artifacts to please our beast oppressors!*
> —Amiri Baraka, *The Autobiography of LeRoi Jones*

In 1968, the assassinations of Martin Luther King and Robert Kennedy within two months of one another are only two of the weighty and salient deaths on the North American landscape since the 1953 *Brown v. Board of Education*, Topeka, Kansas decision. Media spectacles of violence against black citizens in the African American freedom struggle became major signifiers of oppression and liberation. State-sanctioned police violence was inscribed over every major urban center, from L.A. to Detroit to New York City. And the urban rebellions that punctuated the decade from 1965 to 1968 were only the most expressive gestures of despair and rage. African Americans — from integrationists to nationalists — were intensely alienated from white people, American institutions, and American so-called values. The black arts movement articulated the alienation. The black arts movement interpreted the varied longings for community among African Americans. Poetry became a discursive repository for the black power movement — as spirituals and gospel music were to the earlier Black Civil Rights Movement.

In his 1969 antimodernist tour de force "Black Art," Amiri Baraka radically redefines poetry as visceral life, "Poems are bullshit unless they are/teeth or trees . . ."[1] This redefinition of poetry is also a redefinition of blackness in which the death of whiteness is explicit. Baraka theorizes further:

> . . . We want poems that kill. Assassin poems. Poems that shoot guns. Poems that wrestle cops into alleys and take their weapons leaving them dead with tongues pulled out and sent to Ireland.[2]

Baraka here exemplifies a critical piece of black arts literacy: the enunciation of a violent rhetoric.

Audre Lorde's 1977 essay, "Poetry Is Not a Luxury," meditates on poetry as the language of women's deepest emotion, power, and creativity. Written in the same vein as her later essay, "The Uses of the Erotic" (1978), this essay reifies poetry (and women) as the source of "true knowledge" and "lasting action." Baraka's less essentialist work externalizes the potential of poetry as a force of destruction and regeneration. Lorde sees poetry as a "dark" and "hidden" resource — much like the erotic — women carry within themselves that will ultimately enable them to take action:

> For women, then, poetry is not a luxury. It is a vital necessity of our existence. It forms the quality of light within which we predicate our hopes and dreams toward survival and change, first made into language, then into idea, then into more tangible action.[3]

Similar to developments in jazz and black theater, black poetry of the late 60s became instrumental to advancing black nationalism, a radical revisioning of the place of black people in the mind and body politic of "wite America." The work of black arts poets and black lesbian feminist poets signified a decided rupture with the "West/a grey hideous space."[4] Both paid homage to black consciousness and black culture. Black arts deferred to the new music, exemplified in the work of John Coltrane, Eric Dolphy, and Sun Ra, to name a very few. Black lesbian feminists—as many black feminists—reclaimed past black women writers such as Zora Neale Hurston, Nella Larsen, Alice Dunbar Nelson, and exalted contemporary black women writers, especially Alice Walker and Toni Morrison. According to Larry Neal, in his crucial article of the same name, "The Black Arts Movement is the aesthetic and spiritual sister of the Black Power concept," and called for a "cultural revolution in art and ideas" opposed to the "Western aesthetic . . . which must either be radicalized or destroyed."[5] The ritual of rejection of all manner of white patriarchal narratives was as crucial to black lesbian feminists as rejection of the "Western [white] aesthetic" was crucial to black arts literacy. Such rejections made a counter narrative, that is, change, imperative.

Black lesbian feminists struggled with white lesbian feminists for reallocations of resources within their communities; and—along with other women of color—opened spaces within lesbian-feminist organizations for more diverse representation and participation. By the time black lesbian feminists became visible and active, the black power phase of the African American freedom struggle had waned; and J. Edgar Hoover's Counter Intelligence Program[6] had destroyed or disabled most black nationalist and revolutionary nationalist organizations. Black lesbian feminists, while critical of racism and class oppression within the lesbian feminist movement, rejected black nationalism and lesbian separatism, and warily participated in multiracial enterprises and alliances that included white lesbians.

INSTRUMENTALITY OF POETRY

Longings for a militant literacy, sexual autonomy, and a poetics uncircumscribed by whiteness and maleness fomented black lesbian feminist production circa 1973–1979. By the early seventies lesbian feminists — mostly white, some black — were forming and joining autonomous women's organizations, institutions, businesses, and communities — some as separatists. They shared a desire for "women-identified-women's" culture and politics. U.S. black, Latina, Native American, and Asian lesbians embraced feminism more visibly in the seventies.

> San Francisco was inundated with women poets, women's readings, & a multilingual woman presence, new to all of us & desperately appreciated. . . . During the same period, Shameless Hussy Press & The Oakland Women's Press Collective were also reading anywhere & everywhere they could. In a single season, Susan Griffin, Judy Grahn, Barbara Gravelle, & Alta, were promoting the poetry & presence of women in a legendary male-poet's environment. This is the energy & part of the style that nurtured *for colored girls*. . . .
>   *In the summer of 1974 I had begun a series of seven poems, modeled on Judy Grahn's* The Common Woman . . .[7]

In the passage above, Ntozake Shange describes her witness of the ways women's literary culture changed women's lives in the 1970s. That Shange cites the work of lesbian feminist poet Judy Grahn and the West Coast women's independent press movement as having enabled and influenced *for colored girls who have considered suicide when the rainbow is enuff*, is striking. In 1976, citing an allegiance to feminism and lesbianism was still risky for ostensibly straight black women writers. Even more striking is the poet's omission of her debt to the black arts movement. Shange was deeply influenced by the movement's vernacular poetics and politics, its theater, and its reverence for the new music. Like her older black lesbian poet sisters, Pat Parker and Audre Lorde, Shange had lived through the black power movement and carried its lessons to the nascent feminist projects in which she became involved. The lessons of the black arts movement internalized by black lesbian feminists were internalized by white lesbian feminists. Perhaps in citing Grahn as an influence, Shange pays tribute to her black arts influence. (Rather like knowing that behind every Jerry Lee Lewis there's a Little Richard.)

This article focuses primarily on how black arts strategies were deployed by black lesbian feminist writers to advance a "cultural revolution of art and ideas" about women. The texts of black women writers, mostly poets, will be used to read the "racial" and cultural strategies applied by proponents of Black Arts and black lesbian feminism. It will illuminate tensions, ruptures, erasures, elisions, and intertextualities. It is hoped that there will be some illumination of the theory that "Black Aesthetic theorizing [which] opened up exciting new possibilities of artistic experimentation . . . and sought to redefine the relationship between writer and audience" created spaces for lesbian feminists to do the same thing.[8]

Despite its antifeminism, homophobia, and heterosexism, the uncompromising assertion of identity politics practiced by Black Arts exponents served black lesbian-feminist writers well—as it did much of the multicultural lesbian feminist movement. The counter-historical narrative, the rejection of the "West," the reverence for same ("race" and/or sex), the embrace of revolution, the taking of public space, the establishment of alternative institutions and venues were the literacies many lesbian feminists appropriated and reappropriated from the black arts movement. This paper will privilege black lesbian feminist appropriations.

BLACK ARTS, SEXISM, HETEROSEXISM, AND HOMOPHOBIA

I am not a lesbian but I would like to have a real experience with a girl who is. What should I do?
—June Jordan, *The Talking Back of Miss Valentine Jones*

From Montgomery, Alabama in 1955 to the San Francisco Bay Area in 1970,[9] black women were key organizers, theorists, revolutionists, and artists and coexisted with subtle and overt forms of sexism, male chauvinism, and male dominance in the black freedom struggle. According to Paula Giddings, "when the [civil rights] movement began to deteriorate after 1964, the intensity of that chauvinism increased."[10] In her 1974 autobiography, Angela Davis speaks of her firsthand experiences with male domination. Giddings uses this example in *When and Where I enter*. As Davis tells it, she was organizing speakers for a political rally in San Diego in coalition with several other groups, among them Ron Karenga's U.S. organization, when she "ran headlong into a situation . . . to become a constant in my political life," that is, the dread male jealousy of competent women:

> . . . I was criticized very heavily, especially by male members of Karenga's organization, for doing "a man's job." Women should not play leadership roles, they insisted. A woman was supposed to "inspire" her man and educate his children.[11]

From 1975 to 1979, Ntozake Shange and Michele Wallace were censured soundly by the black intellectual community for their unsparing critiques of black male-female relationships in *for colored girls who have considered suicide when the rainbow is enuff* and *Black Macho and the Myth of the Superwoman* (1977). Robert Staples' long opinion piece in then-influential journal, *The Black Scholar*, captures the curious defensiveness of black men over black women writing about the funky sexual politics in the black community. Staples, also an editor of *The Black Scholar*, stops short of calling black feminists an instrument in a white women's conspiracy to destroy black men:

> Since white feminists could not marshal an all out attack on black males, and well-known black female activists such as Joyce Ladner and Angela Davis would not, how could they be put in their place? Enter Ntozake Shange and Michele Wallace. While other black writers have trouble finding a forum to discuss the persistence of racist conditions,

> Ms. Shange's play, 'For Colored Girls Who Have Considered Suicide When the Rainbow Is Enuff' [sic] is on Broadway and road shows have drawn sell-out audiences throughout the United States. . . . Michele Wallace's new book, *Black Macho and the Myth of the Superwoman,* has been heralded as the most publicized book since *Roots.* . . . Watching a performance [of *for colored girls* . . .] one sees a collective appetite for black male blood.[12]

Whither sexism goes, heterosexism does not lag far behind, if lag at all. In the passage quoted at the beginning of this section, June Jordan's questioner is seeking advice from Miss Valentine Jones regarding her desire to "sleep with a girl who is" a lesbian.[13] Talking back, Miss Jones counsels, "Jesus is the answer. Join the church. The Lord will keep you busy on weekends." Jordan's poem exposes the hazards of lesbian desire "within the circle" of blackness.[14]

Some, however, braved the hazards. Using as guide Alice Walker's singular 1974 essay, "In Search of Our Mother's Gardens," black lesbian feminist critic Barbara Smith visited the gardens of black literary foremothers and ushered in the watershed era of contemporary black feminist writing with her provocative essay, "Towards a Black Feminist Criticism."[15] Her theory of reading black women's texts generated unparalleled conversations that more than twenty years later enrich the soil of black feminist thinking.[16] Smith asserted that lesbianism was a broad intellectual bed: "[Toni] Morrison's work poses both lesbian and feminist questions about black women's autonomy and their impact upon each other's lives."[17] Not content to keep herself busy on weekends with "the Lord," Smith proposed the same theory at a Black Writers Conference at Howard University in 1978. Smith thought herself on the solid ground of a beloved black text when she made her claim that Morrison's "*Sula* is an exceedingly lesbian novel in the emotions expressed," hastening to add not that she meant Morrison is a lesbian and "[n]ot because the women are 'lovers,' but because they are the central figures, are positively portrayed and have pivotal relationships with one another." Interestingly, June Jordan was the moderator of the panel in which Smith participated, which also included Acklyn Lynch and Sonia Sanchez. Jordan had gone out on her own limb when she introduced the panel by telling the audience that she had been raped the fall before and, on a very primal level, understood why she needed feminism. Howard's Cramton Auditorium, which at that time held approximately 500 people, was filled to capacity. Audre Lorde was in the audience, along with twelve or thirteen other black lesbian feminists, including this writer, who had come to see and support Smith (and Jordan). A visceral collective groan resonated throughout the room when Smith said the words "lesbian novel." We witnessed extreme reactions from a number of well-known figures of the black cultural world—nationalists and nonnationalists—in response to Smith's lesbian reading. The emphatic hostility astounded both Smith and Jordan. In the midst of the contention both Lynch and Sanchez fled the stage to be other places, leaving Jordan and Smith to field all the questions, comments, sermons, and ravings. Jordan held the stage and Smith held her position. The audience was finally subdued enough for Stephen Henderson, Howard professor, literary critic, and conference organizer, to come onto the stage to close the session. Many people stayed to talk through and argue through the vexed questions of sexuality—lesbianism at that—with Smith, Jordan, and many of Smith's lesbian supporters. Why was this racial confluence disrupted? Smith's article deploys signal traits of Black Arts signifyin(g): critique of white cultural dominance and affirmation of black cultural traditions. However, their deployment in the interest of a lesbian reading, albeit black, did not make for a happy nexus with the black literary public, hell-bent on having its literature be heterosexual.

In 1979, Smith and Lorraine Bethel coedited *Conditions: Five, the Black Women's Issue*.[18] *Conditions: Five* featured for the first time in the history of African American literary strivings the work of self-identified black lesbian writers. However, Toni Cade Bambara's 1970 work *The Black Woman: An Anthology*, the first collection of writings by black women with feminist leanings, gave impetus to *Conditions: Five*. In their introduction to the issue the coeditors cite the perils of writing as a feminist or a lesbian "within the circle:"

> In choosing from the work that was submitted we placed a priority on writing concerning itself with the issues of feminism and lesbianism as they related to Black women. Our major reason for this standard comes from the belief that anti-feminism and homophobia in the Black community make it difficult, if not impossible, for Black women to publish lesbian/feminist writing in the traditional Black media.[19]

Newspapers, journals, anthologies, presses, and bookstores were established in the 1970s primarily by white women. Jan Clausen, in her little-known monograph, *A Movement of Poets*, discusses the enabling power of these independent ventures.

> By the mid-1970s, Diana Press and Daughters, Inc. had emerged as relatively powerful, well-organized lesbian controlled publishing efforts. Out & Out Books issued its first titles in 1975, among them *Amazon Poetry: An Anthology*, the largest collection of lesbian poetry then available, and the most comprehensive through the end of the decade. . . . Audre Lorde subsequently became poetry editor of *Chrysalis*, begun in 1976 — as was the more explicitly lesbian-focused *Sinister Wisdom. Azalea*, a magazine by and for Third World Lesbians, and *Conditions*, a magazine of women's writing with an emphasis on writing by lesbians, began publication in 1977. Throughout the mid-1970s, most feminist presses and periodicals published substantial amounts of poetry . . . [and were] extremely important to lesbian poets because of their role in the development of a specifically lesbian-feminist literary culture and community.[20]

Despite the fact that most of the lesbian-run publications, bookstores, and presses were established by white women, women of color, including African descent women, were integral to this "lesbian- feminist literary culture and community."

PARALLEL LONGINGS

If "I am a woman" had been the central proposition focusing the poetic explorations of early-'70's feminists, then "I am a lesbian" was by mid-decade the resounding theme . . . interpreted not merely in a sexual sense but as self-affirmation, proclamation of independence from patriarchy, and assertion of the primacy of emotional bonding among women, was indeed at the heart of their work.

—Clausen, *A Movement of Poets*

Much lesbian feminist poetry rejected heterosexual conventions just as the black arts poems rejected any sexuality but heterosexuality. Black Arts women poets proclaimed, "I am a black woman," privileging race as precedent and the primary category of struggle. Open heterosexuality was also the only sexual option for women (and men) in the circle of the black arts movement, as Sonia Sanchez's 1966 poem "to all sisters" proclaims:

> there ain't
> no MAN like a
> black man.
> he puts it where it is
> and makes u
> turn in/side out.[21]

Gender, because of the entire uppercasing of "man," seems to take precedence over race in this poem. Or perhaps it is heterosexuality that is primary in this early Sanchez poem, as she signifies sexual intercourse?

In Nikki Giovanni's "Seduction,"[22] the speaker announces a step-by-step process of how she will seduce/objectify her correct revolutionary brother. All the while she imagines him more intent on making revolution than on her *making* him: "I'll be taking your dashiki off . . . licking your arm . . . and unbuckling your . . . pants."[23] Cleverly Giovanni inserts herself into the narrative, heralding her heterosexuality—at least in the context of the poem. She imagines the object of her desire will question the revolutionary appropriateness of her move. "Nikki/isn't this counter-revolutionary . . . ?" One wonders if it is the sexual desire that the lover challenges or "Nikki's" initiative.

On a more somber note, Chicago poet Carolyn Rodgers is

concerned with self-knowledge—as a black person and as a poet, but more ambivalent about her desire for artistic autonomy. Her 1969 poem "Breakthrough" hardly acknowledges gender except in the speaker's relationship to "littl [sic] bruthah" and "my man"[24] though the speaker's "partial pain" comes from her silence about being a woman writer. She best exposes her dilemma in the lines:

> u see, the changes are so many
> there are several of me and
>   all of us fight to show up at the same time[25]

Are the "changes" producing "the several of me" or are the changes already produced by the losses of certain kinds of possibilities? Is there a resistance to the "dialectics of [black] women's lives," that is, the contradictory and complex affiliations that vie for black women's commitments?[26] Audre Lorde once longed for a place she could go where all of who she was would be accepted—that is, those female selves, namely mother, lesbian, feminist. Does Rodgers' anxiety about the "several of me" mask her anxiety about self-assertion, particularly if that self-assertion is as a woman? And as Lorde says "within the confines of Black society . . . the punishment for any female self assertion is still to be called a lesbian and therefore unworthy of the attention or support of the scarce black male."[27]

The speaker's pain is primarily related to the all-consuming requirements of blackness, which she quite poignantly laments:

> I am very tired of trying
> and want Blackness which is my life, want this to be
> easier on me, want it not to suck me in and
> out so much leavin me a balloon with no air, want it
> not to puff me up so much sometimes
> that I git puffed up and sucked in to the
> raunchy kind of love Black orgy I go through.[28]

"Breakthrough" is the poet's longing to be understood for who she is by the people for whom she is writing.

> I really hope that
> if u read this u
> will dig where I'm at
> and feel what i mean/that/where
> i am
> and could very possibly
> be
> real
> at this lopsided crystal sweet moment . . .[29]

Untypically, Rodgers uppercases her first person pronoun, "I," throughout the poem until the sixth and seventh lines from the end. This shift to a lowercase first person, "i," could possibly be a typographical error or the poet's subversion of her self-assertion.

The insistence on heterosexuality causes one of the great tensions between the poems of the black arts and lesbian feminist movements. Audre Lorde's 1971 "Love Poem"[30] a metaphoric tour de force about oral and digital penetration, counters the obligatory nods to heterosexuality. Though a bold post-Black Arts movement move, the speaker's identity is still coded.

> fingers whispering sound
> honey flowed
> from the split cups
> impaled on a lance of tongues[31]

Using as a model Black Arts' poets' critiques of white people and white institutions, Pat Parker's 1978 poem, "Exodus (To my husbands and lovers)," quietly refuses marriage, the cornerstone of heterosexual culture:

> i will serve you no more
> in the name of wifely love
> i'll not masturbate your pride
> in the name of wifely loyalty[32]

Movement In Black, a collection of Pat Parker's poetry originally published by Diana Press in 1978, is constructed as a black woman's emotional and political journey. Sometimes the poems are autobiographical. "Exodus" appears in the first section, "Married," and marks the speaker's refusal to be bound within an institution she likens to slavery: "Hidden within folds of cloth/a desperate slave."[32]

Kay Lindsey, one of the contributors to Toni Cade Bambara's anthology, *The Black Woman*,[34] *rejected the black nationalist assertion that women should be the custodians of the revolution*:

> I'm not one of those who believes
> That an act of valor, for a woman
> Need take place inside her.
>
> *My womb is packed with mothballs*
> And I hear that winter will be mild.[35]

The black arts movement demanded that black men *and* the "race" become men, as evidenced in Nikki Giovanni's popular 1968 poem, "The True Import of the Present Dialogue, Black vs. Negro."[36] Whether read by Giovanni or any other reader *schooled* in the word, during its heyday "Present Dialogue" left audiences breathless with its incantatory query, "Nigger/Can you kill/Can you kill." Black arts poets, such as the black preacher, allowed audiences to engage in what Lawrence Levine calls "ritualistic hypnosis."[37] The shifts in address from "you" to "we" signify the dissensions in the movement over the instrumentality of violence. Obviously being "a nigger" is inconsistent with manhood and revolutionary behavior. One wonders if the speaker is including women in the invocations of "you" and "we." Perhaps women fall into the "nigger" category, as "nigger" is only instrumental to the understanding of what a man (or a revolutionary) is not? Thus, I agree with Phillip Bryan Harper's argument in *Are We Not Men: Masculine Anxiety and the Problem of African-American Identity* that the "insistent use of the second person pronoun" in much of black arts poetry by men and women, and particularly in "True Import," represents "the implication of intraracial division within the black Aesthetic poetic strategy . . ."[38]

Giovanni chooses not to evoke gender until the poem's last line, when the "we" is masculinized through the "killing" of the "white" and the "nigger."

> Can we learn to kill WHITE for BLACK
> Learn to kill niggers
> Learn to be Black men[39]

Perhaps Giovanni is projecting an urgency for unity, for everybody to be "one nation in a groove," not to focus on any identities that might rend one from pursuit of blackness *cum* manhood. The "race" must be masculinized, and women are erased in the race's race to manhood.

In her poem "Of Liberation" the irrepressible Giovanni, exploiting the stereotypes of lesbians and gays as weak and cowardly, tries to shame the indecisive subject, "black people," into organizing:

> Dykes of the world are united
> Faggots got their thing together
> (Everyone is organized)
> Black people these are facts
> Where's your power?[40]

The volume in which this poem appears, *Black Judge/Ment*, was published in 1968, a year before the Stonewall rebellion in New York City, which ushered in the gay liberation movement. Perhaps we can credit Giovanni with prefiguring the new demands for homosexual rights. This poem is striking for its appropriation of what would become the reclaimed terms of lesbian and gay liberation to advance timeworn stereotypes of black people as unorganized, trifling, "3/5 of a man/100% whore."[41] Giovanni, whose poetry is a running critique of the unreadiness of black people for liberation, became one of the chief female enunciators of the new black consciousness, the "princess of black poetry," according to the acerbic Michele Wallace in *Black Macho and the Myth of the Superwoman.*[42]

Audre Lorde's poem, "Who Said It Was Simple"[43] theorizes on the complexity of privilege and oppression. It opens with the cautionary words about the dangers of repressed anger:

> There are so many roots to the tree of anger
> that sometimes the branches shatter
> before they bear.

The narrative tells of an "almost white counterman" who passes a "waiting brother" to serve first a group of white "ladies [who] neither notice nor reject/the slighter pleasures of their slavery." Conflicts and contradictions will destroy revolutionary possibility as long as privilege is unexamined. Issues of color, class, sex, and gender collide as never before in this terse and packed eighteen-line lyric. "Simple" is one of the earliest black feminist testaments of the simultaneity of oppression, and one of Lorde's many critiques of a core Black Art tenet, to "be black first."[44]

By 1973, Lorde had allied with the lesbian feminist movement, though she always maintained contacts with other progressive and radical movements. Like many political poets of the era, Lorde, writer, teacher, librarian, lent her strong voice to many progressive causes. *From a Land Where Other People Live* was nominated for a National Book Award, along with Adrienne Rich for *Diving into the Wreck* and Alice Walker for *Revolutionary Petunias*. Rich won and insisted on sharing the award with her sister feminists, Walker and Lorde. All three books cross the restricted borders of race, sexuality, gender, and class. All three texts critique heterosexual, white, and/or male projects, for example, motherhood, marriage, work, state, and nation.

From a Land Where Other People Live exemplifies these critiques. Most of the poems were written between 1969 and 1971 and signal black feminists' break with black nationalist politics and mainstream white feminism

Lorde's 1973 poem "Now" signifies on black power by rejecting its primacy:

Woman power
is
Black power
is
Human power[45]

Refuting the black nationalist charge that feminism ("Woman power") and blackness are binary opposites, Lorde makes them equivocally human. The title of the poem implies there is no time like the present, that is, "Now," to accept the multiplicity of who one is.

Compulsory manhood and heterosexuality marred and limited the accomplishments of the black arts movement. However, the assertive and militant literacy, assumed provocatively by the black women poets, enabled black lesbians to open a space within the circle of lesbian feminism for themselves and other women of color. Now, the essay will move forward to discuss black lesbian feminist applications of black arts literacies.

Nikki Giovanni's "True Import" finds its parallel in Lorraine Bethel's poem, "What Chou Mean *We*, White Girl," with its fantasy of an autonomous black lesbian feminist community suggested in its expansive subtitle, ". . . Or, The Cullud Lesbian Feminist Declaration of Independence/(Dedicated to the Proposition That All Women Are Not Equal, i.e. Identical/ly Oppressed)." This poem critiques the tokenism within the lesbian feminist movement and utters very bitter commentary on the material privilege of white lesbian feminists and their institutions, ". . . Volvos, country houses, town apartments, health centers, stores, magazines, universities' compared to the virtual lack of resources which often limited black women's participation in movement culture.

I am so tired of talking to . . .
the "I really want to know what your life is like without/
giving up
    any of my privileges
to live it" white women
    . . . while we [black women]wonder where the next meal, job,

payment on/
  our college loans
  and other bills,
the *first* car, Black woman-identified bookstore, health/center,
magazine, archives, bar, record company, newspaper, press,
forty/acres and a mule,

  or national conference
  are going to come from.[46]

Though white lesbians are demonized for their acquisitive-
ness by the speaker, she longs for many of the same acquisitions
for black lesbians. Black women "who won't deal with *real* sista
love"[47] that is, whose lovers are white women, come in for several rounds of vilification. Like the black nationalist claim on the
sexual loyalty of black people to one another, Bethel's vision of a
black lesbian nation won't include the ones

  who've accepted and glorify in myth roles
  Black bull dyke stud or Black
  lesbianfeministgoddesstokenstar
  of the white women's community
  modern day political and apolitical minstrels in colored girl
  face
  The radical Black ones who insist that "the personal is/
  political"
    applies to everything
  except their succession of white woman lovers or their/
  lifetime one
  We will leave them[48]

The poem's chanting enjambment, its black vernacular ease, its
spillage of depredations of the enemies of "Black people Black
women Black lesbian feminists"[49] pay homage to the black arts
poets and are indicative of the speaker's desire to see a tradition
of black culture.

  They will come
  from us loving/speaking *to* our Black/Third World/
  sisters not *at* white women
  They will come

> from us taking Black woman energy presently being used
> to legitimize your [white women's] movement[50]

The poem's yearnings for a black lesbian nation are every bit as serious as, say, Sonia Sanchez's call for a revolutionary black culture in many of her black arts era poems. Harper very astutely sees Sanchez's "Blk/rhetoric,"[51] as "writing beyond the end" of Baraka's poem, "SOS," in which "all black people" are called presumably to join the "nation," but the poem never says. Harper continues with his intertextual interpretation of Sanchez's poem as a "calling into question what will ensue among the black collectivity after it has heeded the general call."[52] She asks: "who's gonna give our young/blk/people new heroes. . . ."[53] As in "True Import" and the Bethel poem, we see the concern for correct behavior, as the speaker catalogues activities in which young black people should not be engaging: "wite whores," "drugs," "new dances," eating "chitterlings," drinking "a 35 cents bottle of wine," "quick/fucks in the hall/way/of wite/america's mind." These latter references, especially "white whores" and "quick fucks in the hall/way," offer a critique of male behavior cleverly concealed in the category "young blk people." The elision allows for the critique to be heard by those who need to hear it without endangering the poet's status within the circle of blackness. This is rather different from Harper's theory of the speaker inside the circle of blackness defining intraracial distinctions, so that "Black Arts poetry . . . achieves its maximum impact in a context in which it is understood as being *heard* directly by whites, and overheard by blacks."[54] Both the white people who hear the signifying directly and the blacks who overhear it are "without the circle." However, Bethel's speaker defies both theories, for she situates her speaker outside the space of privileged white lesbian feminists and "Black/lesbianfeministgoddesstokenstar[s]," and whoever white or black hears or overhears her signifying will not endanger her status.

NATIONALIST NOSTALGIA AND
REVISIONIST MOTHERHOOD

The important "A Black Feminist Statement," written in 1977 by The Combahee River Collective, is a manifesto that posited black feminism as radical praxis and ideology.[55] It opposed the "bourgeois feminist stance" of the National Black Feminist Organization (NBFO), founded in 1973; The Combahee River Collective had been the NBFO's Boston chapter in 1974–1975. The Combahee statement helped stimulate the development of black lesbian feminist organizing, but although it emphasizes racism, sexism, and classism as the political "province" of black feminist struggle, homophobia and heterosexism are not referenced at all, even though the writers refer to themselves as "feminists and lesbians." The submersion of the lesbian into the feminist identity functions in a way similar to Sanchez's elision of any direct critique of black male behavior discussed above in the poem, "blk/rhetoric." Because the Combahee statement accuses black men and black people of being "notoriously negative" toward and "threatened" by feminism,[56] the manifesto writers might have worried that a strong statement about the antigay and antilesbian attitudes of the black community would risk driving another wedge between black (lesbian) feminists and the rest of the black community. The manifesto also erases all but negative history of work with white feminists. While it says black feminists "must struggle together with black men against racism" and "struggle with black men about sexism,"[57] "[e]liminating racism in the white women's movement is by definition work for white women to do."[58] In the Combahee statement, as in "What Chou Mean *We*, White Girl," a nostalgia for a black nationalism is expressed, even though both lesbian separatism and black nationalism are rejected by The Combahee River Collective.

Black feminists were not the only black people who posited a nationalist longing. In *how i got ovah*, Carolyn Rodgers' fourth book of poetry since 1968, she critically reexamines her contributions to the black cultural revolution, her relationship to blackness, and, in many of the poems, expresses concerns about her heterosexuality. Five of the poems, were published previously in her 1969 volume, *Songs of a Black Bird*. A singularly stunning poem in this collection is "I Have Been Hungry," which the author tells us in a preface that it

> was written because I was asked to contribute to an anthology of black and white women, and the title of the anthology was *I Had Been Hungry All My Years*[59]

Though published three years before Lorraine Bethel's "What Chou Mean *We*, White Girl," it expresses some of the same tensions, though from a decidedly antifeminist and antilesbian perspective. The poem is a good example of how feminism had permeated the poetry of nonfeminist black women. "I Have Been Hungry" expresses the same anger at black women's instrumentality to white women. While Bethel's poem expresses anger at being a token, Rodgers' poem is suspicious of sisterhood with white women because

> there is still the belief that
> i am
> a road
> you would travel
> to my man.[60]

Despite the loneliness, always a recurring theme in her poetry, Rodgers rejects sisterhood because of her fantasy of women's liberation as sterile lesbianism:

> do not tell me
> liberated tales of woman/woeman
> who seek only to *satisfy them selves*
> with them selves, all, by them selves
> I will not believe you
> I will call you a dry canyon
> them, a wilderness
> of wearying failures . . .[61]

"Hungry" talks about relationships with men as a "puffing out," without which a woman is deflated, hungry, insubstantial. Of course by 1975 artistic cross-fertilization had taken hold, despite sacred and secular nationalisms and strident separatisms. Feminist ideas, though not often identified as such, began to influence contemporary black women's writing, if only in terms of hostile responses. "Hungry" seems to chide feminists for stating the obvious, the always already fact that women are women:

> ah, here i am
> and
> here have i been
> i say.[62]

Conventional motherhood came under heavy examination during the '70s both by white and black feminists and lesbian feminists. Yet, at the same time, leading poets such as Adrienne Rich, a mother of three sons and a lesbian, and Audre Lorde, a self-defined black lesbian feminist mother of two, were busy reinventing and renegotiating motherhood. Rich, during this time, had published a major feminist statement, *Of Woman Born*.[63] Lorde's references to children in her poems are myriad; children are future, regeneration, and liberation from the old paradigms. And her treatment of motherhood sometimes borders on essentialism. At the base of lesbian-feminist critiques of motherhood is the struggle to separate sex from procreation. Rich and Lorde, however, gave voice to the sensual and sexual feelings involved in mothering. Lorde, particularly, believed that women, feminists, lesbians should not give up mothering and constantly challenged women not to limit mothering to the biological and to "Speak proudly to your children/wherever you may find them . . .".[64]

Regeneration had been a key theme in the poetry of women and men of the black arts movement. Regeneration for women not only meant childbearing capacities, but also strength, indestructibility, infinite powers. Mari Evans' poem, "I Am a Black Woman," epitomized, in unimpressive, spare enunciations, the provincial black arts perception of black womanhood: "I/am a black woman . . . strong beyond all definition."[65] Nikki Giovanni's humorous and hyperbolic "ego tripping" continues this trend: "My strength flows ever onward."[66] The relentless reified "I" of "ego-tripping" finds itself lowercased in Sonia Sanchez's "for blk/wooomen: the only queens of this universe," an encomium of black women's "blk" omnipotence; and like Evans' black woman, she can cause the world to be "shaken" and "reborn."[67] Perhaps influenced by the black arts movement, white poets also celebrated birth—a birth of new consciousness—despite lesbian feminist rejection of conventional motherhood. Using imagery of the birth process, Jan Clausen's poem, "A Christmas Letter"[68] manifests this interest, as the speaker warns her mother of her own impending breach with the old ways: "we can't sit around talking/in the womb anymore/for i already have/begun to be born"[69]

BLACK WOMEN POETS AND THE PUBLIC

The African American freedom struggle of the 1960s sought to redefine Africans in North America and in so doing to transform the African American psyche. Black writers and other artists were integral to the transmission of this new black consciousness. The sixties revolution in black arts, that is, the writing, theatre, music, and rhetoric of African American people, cleared a large space—almost two hundred years' worth—for poetry's complex tutelage; and poetry became a deep resource for the 1960s' black revolution in letters.

The dialogic relationships of black nationalist poetries and black lesbian feminist and lesbian feminist poetries continued throughout the 70s. Black arts women reified heterosexuality and nation, black and white lesbian feminist poets reified lesbian sexuality and lesbian "ways of knowing." But as we have seen, feminism was not lost on black arts women poets nor was black autonomy lost on black lesbian feminists. Even those nonfeminist women who remained for a time within the circle of the black arts movement offered coded critiques of the sexism of black male poets as in Sanchez's "blk/rhetoric" and Giovanni's "Seduction" and "True Import."

The literacy gained from black movement poetry became a large house of resistance to patriarchal culture—black and white. Audre Lorde's 1978 collection of poetry, *The Black Unicorn*, is an amazing statement of a black lesbian "cosmology and mythology,"[70] rooted in Dahomey, West Africa, which is the place where Lorde traces her own lineage of woman-centered consciousness. Black lesbian feminism continued its expressivity throughout the 1980s, into the era of Reaganism and bourgeois narcissism. Black dyke pasts were recovered and invented by writers and critics like Jewelle Gomez, Gloria Hull, Ann Allen Shockley, and this writer—from within and without the accepted traditions of poetry and history. In "for muh dear," Carolyn Rodgers celebrates the black self's permeability to blackness, that is, "black lay backin and rootin."[71] Black arts poetics "lay backin and rootin" in the vernacular and written culture of black lesbian feminists. Black lesbian feminist literacy of sexuality exposes the sexist and heterosexist (homophobic) commitments of black arts practitioners, and simultaneously pays homage to black arts revolutionary literacy.

NOTES

1. Amiri Baraka, *Transbluesency: Selected Poems, 1961–1995* (New York: Marsilio Publishers, 1995), 142.
2. Ibid.
3. Audre Lorde, *Sister Outsider* (Freedom, Calif.: Crossing Press, 1984), 37.
4. LeRoi Jones, "Black Dada Nihilismus," *The Dead Lecturer* (New York: Grove Press, 1964), 62.
5. Larry Neal and Michael Schwartz, *Visions of a Liberated Future: Black Arts Movement Writings* (New York: Thunder's Mouth Press, 1989), 184, 186.
6. COINTELPRO was the FBI's secret and well-known war against "black nationalist, hate-type groups . . . to expose, disrupt, misdirect, discredit, or otherwise neutralize" them. J. Edgar Hoover, "1967 Memorandum to Special Agent in Charge, Albany, New York," in *Modern Black Nationalism: From Marcus Garvey to Louis Farrakham*, edited by Van Deburg (New York: NYU Press, 1997), 134.

7. Ntozake Shange, *for colored girls who have considered suicide when the rainbow is enuff* (New York: Collier-MacMillan,1977).

8. David Lionel Smith, "The Black Arts Movement and Its Critics," *American Literary History*, vol. 3, no. 1 (Spring 1991), 93–110.

9. The Montgomery (Alabama) Bus boycott was spearheaded by several black constituents in Montgomery: NAACP president E. D. Nixon, Joanne Robinson, head of the Women's Political Council, and later the young minister, Martin Luther King, Jr., who was asked by Nixon to head the Montgomery Improvement Association. The bus company observed a segregated seating policy, of course. Giddings reports in *When and Where I Enter: The Impact of Black Women on Race and Sex in America* (New York: William Morrow & Co., Inc., 1984) that a fifteen-year-old girl was jailed for refusing to move to the back of the bus just weeks before the famous incident with Rosa Parks. However, "[t]he girl's mother forbade her to appear in court, for her daughter was visibly pregnant — and unmarried" (263). Nixon believed that Parks'" case would be the better case to test the law. The time that she was arrested was not Parks' first transgression of the city's transportation segregation codes. "Parks . . . was previously evicted from a bus and sometimes drivers refused to pick her up . . ." (262). According to Branch in *Parting the Waters*, "All thirty-six seats of the bus she [Parks] boarded were soon filled, with twenty-two Negroes seated from the rear and fourteen whites from the front. Driver . . . seeing a white man standing in the front of the bus . . . called out for the four passengers on the row just behind the whites to stand up and move to the back" ([New York: Touchstone, 1988], 129). Rosa Parks, the only one of the four black riders, was arrested for refusing to give up her seat to the white man. Parks, secretary of the Montgomery NAACP, seamstress, and community activist, chose and was chosen to be "the symbol of the challenge to southern segregation" (Giddings, 265). After a year of organized boycotting of the bus system, black citizens won their right to sit where they wanted. Montgomery was a major victory in the struggle against segregation in the South and ushered in a whole new phase of the African American freedom struggle. The Free the Soledad Brothers Movement in California had been organized to defend the rights of three black prisoners, George Jackson, John Cluchette, and Fleeta Drumgo, who had been accused of killing a prison guard. This prison guard, O. G. Miller, had just been acquitted on grounds of justifiable homicide, of killing three black prisoners in a prison-instigated melee. Angela Davis became one of the chief activists involved in their political defense activities. In 1970, also, Jackson's younger brother, Jonathan, along with three others, was killed in a shoot-out in the parking lot of the Marin County courthouse after trying to free two San Quentin prisoners in court on assault charges. In 1971, George Jackson was murdered in the prison yard of San Quentin Prison, where he and his codefendants had been transferred. Angela Davis, at the time of George Jackson's death, was in jail in Marin County preparing for her trial on charges of murder and kidnapping in connection with the Marin County shoot-out. Davis emerged victorious in 1972. Angela Davis, *Angela Davis: An Autobiography* (New York: Random House, 1974).

10. In *When and Where I Enter*, Giddings provides a rich feminist narrative of black women's historical leadership in the freedom struggles of Afro-Americans, particularly in her telling of the race and gender collisions at the height of the civil rights/black power movements, 1955–1965. See Mary King, *Freedom Song: A Per-*

sonal Story of the 1960's Civil Rights Movement (New York: William Morrow, 1987), and Sara Evans, *Personal Politics*, for white women's accounts of their experiences as members of SNCC. Anne Moody's *Coming of Age in Mississippi*, (New York: Dell, 1968) remains a vivid story of a black woman's account of her SNCC experiences during the voting rights struggle in Mississippi. *A Circle of Trust: Remembering SNCC*, (Cheryl Greenberg, ed. New Brunswick, N.J.: Rutgers University Press, 1998) is published from the taped sessions of the 1987 SNCC conference and reunion. Black and white women, such as Diane Nash, Mary King, Joann Grant, Bernice Johnson Reagon, Casey Hayden, and others share memories of their experiences as SNCC staffers and volunteers. The notorious 1964 position paper on women in the organization is contentiously discussed in the chapter, "SNCC Women and the Stirrings of Feminism." Joan Nestle, lesbian feminist writer whose lesbianism predates Stonewall, writes compellingly about her experience of the 1965 Selma to Montgomery march in "This Huge Light of Mine" from her book of essays, *A Restricted Country* (Ithaca, N.Y.: Firebrand Books, 1988): "I did not put the word *Lesbian* my [white index] card. I put Jewish and feminist. . . . I did not talk about the bars I went to and the knowledge about bigotry I had gained from being a queer" (61).

11. Angela Davis, *Angela Davis: An Autobiography* (New York: Random House, 1974), 161.

12. *The Black Scholar* (May/June, 1975), 24–26.

13. June Jordan, "From the Talking Back of Miss Valentine Jones, No. 2," *Things I Hate to Do in the Dark* (New York: Random House, 1977), 152.

14. In his 1845 *Narrative of a Slave*, Frederick Douglass meditates on how he, as a slave, "did not understand the deep meanings of those rude, and apparently incoherent songs" which enveloped his childhood. Being "within the circle" of slavery necessitated a kind of self-protection from understanding the depth of the songs' expressions that once he was "without" the circle, that is, escaped from slavery, he could take in. Thus, being within the circle of blackness necessitates a self-protectiveness of the feeling/knowledge that, if known, would cause ostracism.

15. Barbara Smith, "Towards a Black Feminist Criticism," *Conditions: Two* (October 1977).

16. Black feminist critics and theorists have contributed mightily to the study of black women writers in the last twenty years. The late 1970s and 1980s was a watershed period of black feminist critical production. Truly, sometimes the criticism is as daring as the literary works themselves. Articles, anthologies, and books that have pushed me are: Akasha (Gloria) Hull, "'Under the Days': The Buried Life and Poetry of Angelina Weld Grimke," *Conditions: Five, the Black Women's Issue* (1979), 17–47; Jewelle L. Gomez, "A Cultural Legacy Denied and Discovered: Black Lesbians in Fiction by Women"; Hull, "What It Is I Think She's Doing Anyhow: A Reading of Toni Cade Bambara's *The Salt Eaters*"; Linda C. Powell, "Black Macho and Black Feminism," all in *Home Girls,* (1983) Smith, ed.; Hortense Spillers, "Interstices: A Small Drama of Words," *Pleasure and Danger, Exploring Female Sexuality*, edited by Carol Vance (San Francisco: Thorsons Publishing, 1991) June Jordan, *On Call: Political Essays.* (Boston: South End Press, 1985); Marjorie Pryse and H. Spillers, *Conjuring: Black Women, Fiction, and Literary Tradition.* (Bloomington, Ind.: Indiana University Press, 1985);

Hazel Carby, *Reconstructing Womanhood: The Emergence of the Afro-American Woman Novelist* (New York: Oxford University Press, 1987); Mary Helen Washington, "The Darkened Eye Restored: Notes Toward a Literary History of Black Women." *Invented Lives: Narratives of Black Women, 1860–1960. (New York: Doubleday, 1987); Cheryl A. Wall, ed., Changing Our Own Words: Essays on Criticism, Theory, and Writing by Black Women* (New Brunswick, N.J.: Rutgers University Press, 1989), esp. Hull's and Henderson's articles.

17. Smith, "Towards a Black Feminist Criticism," 33.
18. Elly Bulkin, Irena Klepfisz, Rima Shore, Jan Clausen founded *Conditions* as "a magazine of writing by women with an emphasis on writing by lesbians" in 1976 and published the first issue in 1977. *Conditions* closed its pages in 1990 because of flagging resources and editorial energy. During its years of publication, it became a repository of the multicultural lesbian literary culture. Its contributors included Paula Gunn Allen, Dorothy Allison, Gloria Anzalda, Jewelle Gomez, Judy Grahn, Joy Harjo, Audre Lorde, Cherrie Moraga, Minnie Bruce Pratt, Adrienne Rich, Sapphire, Shay Youngblood as well as Barbara Smith and this writer. *Conditions: Five*, however, caused the editors to rethink their commitments to lesbian communities. Not only must black women and other women of color see themselves on the pages of so-called lesbian publications, but they must also be involved in the decisions that produce those publications. In 1981, the editors recruited an eight-person collective, which included three African American women, one white working-class woman, one Latina, two Jewish women, and one white Anglo-Saxon Protestant lesbian. Successive collectives remained committed to this model as well as to each member's requisite lesbianism. This writer was a member of the collective from1981 to 1990.
19. *Conditions: Five, The Black Women's Issue*, 12.
20. Jan Clausen, *A Movement of Poets* (Brooklyn: Long Haul Press, 1982), 17.
21. Leroi Jones and L. Neal, eds. *Black Fire*: An Anthology of Afro-American Writing (New York: William Morrow & Co, 1968), 255
22. Nikki Giovanni, *Black Feeling, Black Talk, Judgment* (Detroit: Broadside, 1970).
23. Ibid, 38.
24. Carolyn Rodgers, "Breakthrough," *how i got ovah* (Garden City, N.Y.: Anchor Press, 1976), 36.
25. Ibid, 35.
26. Deborah K. King, "Multiple Jeopardy" (1995), 300.
27. Audre Lorde, "Age, Race, Class, and Sex," *Sister Outsider: Essays and Speeches* (Freedom, Calif.: Crossing Press, 1984), 121.
28. Rodgers, *how i got ovah* 36.
29. Ibid.
30. Audre Lorde, "Love Poem," *Undersong: Chosen Poems, Old and New, Revised* (New York: W.W. Norton, 1992).
31. Ibid., 141.
32. Pat Parker, *Movement in Black* (Ithaca, N.Y.: Firebrand Books, 1985).
33. Ibid., (37).
34. Toni Cade Bambara, *The Black Woman* (New York: New American Library, 1970).
35. Ibid., 17. Emphasis added.

36. Giovanni, *Black Feeling, Black Talk, Black Judgment (New York: William Morrow & Co., 1970)*, 20.

37. Lawrence Levine, *Black Culture and Black Consciousness: Afro-American Folk Thought from Slavery to Freedom* (New York: Oxford University Press, 1977). Levine pays close attention to the impact of black music on the physical and psychic survival of African Americans: "Secular work songs resembled spirituals in that their endless rhythmic and verbal repetitions could transport the singers beyond time, make them oblivious of their immediate surroundings, and create a state of what Wilfrid Mellers has referred to as 'ritualistic hypnosis' . . ." (213).

38. Phillip Brian Harper, *Are We Not Men: Masculine Anxiety and the Problem of African-American Identity* (New York: Oxford University Press, 1996), 47.

39. Giovanni, *Black Feeling, Black Talk, Judgment,* 20.

40. Giovanni, *Black Judge/Ment* (Detroit: Broadside Press, 1968), 2.

41. Ibid.

42. Michelle Wallace, *Black Macho and the Myth of the Superwoman* (New York: Dial Press, 1978), 166.

43. Audre Lorde, "Who Said it Was Simple?" *From a Land Where Other People Live* (Detroit: Broadside Press, 1974).

44. Don L. Lee, "Introduction: Louder but Sofdter" *We Walk the Way of the New World Black Fire* (Detroit: Broadside Press, 1970)m 180.

45. Audre Lorde, *Chosen Poems: Old and New* (New York: W.W. Norton, 1982), 88.

46. Lorraine Bethel, "What Chou Mean *We,* White Girl," *Conditions: Five, the Black Women's Issue* (1979), 87–88.

47. Ibid., 89. Emphasis added.

48. Ibid, 90.

49. Ibid, 91.

50. Ibid, brackets mine.

51. Sonia Sanchez, "Blk/rhetoric," *We a BadddDDD People* (Detroit: Broadside Press, 1967).

52. Harper, *Are We Not Men?,* 43.

53. Sanchez, "Blk/rhetoric,"15.

54. Harper, *Are WE Not Men,* 46.

55. Combahee River Collective, "A Black Feminist Statement," first published in *Capitalist Patriarchy and the Case for Socialist Feminism,* edited by Zillah R. Eisenstein (New York: Monthly Review Press, 1979).

56. Combahee River Collective, "Beyond the Margins: Black Women Claiming Feminism" *Words of Fire,* edited by Beverly Guy-Sheftall (New York: The New Press, 1995), 237.

57. Ibid., 235.

58. Ibid., 239.

59. Rodgers, *how i got ovah,* 49.

60. Carolyn Rodgers, "I Have Been Hungry," *how i got ovah.*

61. Ibid., 51. Emphases added.

62. Ibid., 52.

63. Adrienne Rich, *Of Woman Born* (New York: W.W. Norton, 1973).

64. Audre Lorde, "For Each of You," *Chosen Poems* (New York: Norton, 1982), 43.

65. Mari Evans, *I Am a Black Woman* (New York: William Morrow Publishers, 1970), 12.

66. Nikki Giovanni, *The Women and the Men* (New York: William Morrow, 1975), 20.

67. Sonia Sanchez, "Blk/rhetoric," *We A BaddDDD People*, 6.

68. Jan Clausen, "A Christmas Letter," in *Amazon Poetry2 ed. Elly Bulkin and Joan Larkin (New York: Out & Out Books, 1975), 52.*

69. Ibid.

70. Shariat (1979). Fahmaisha Shariat, "The Black Unicorn" *Conditions: Five, the Black Women's Issue* (1979), 173–176.

71. Rodgers, *how i got ovah*, 1.

More Man Than You'll Ever Be: Antonio Fargas, Eldridge Cleaver, and Toni Morrison's *Beloved*[1]

Darieck Scott

I

The 1976 movie comedy *Car Wash*, a late entrant of the blax-ploitation era, tended to deemphasize the cookie-cutter mili-tancy of its harder-edged contemporaries such as *Foxy Brown* in favoring instead the inspired buffoonery always latent in the genre. The movie offers little more than slight pleasures, being rather disheveled in structure and flush with caricatured types only partly redeemed by the enthusiasm and skill of the actors portraying them (including Richard Pryor).[2] But there is one scene I recall from my first viewing as an adolescent that gave my friends and me fodder for many a laugh. We repeated the scene in the school hallways between classes and on our various play-ing fields for many a day after; and indeed, everyone I know who ever reminisces about the film today mentions it. It is the scene where the cookie-cutter militant Abdullah squares off against his putative opposite, campy lipstick-lacquered queen Lindy, perhaps the most inspired of *Car Wash*'s many buffoons.

Abdullah, played by a glowering and sometimes intensely sweaty Bill Duke, has had enough of the girly antics of Antonio Fargas's Lindy, who preens the frosted locks of his straightened 'do ("It's supposed to be mango, honey, but it didn't come out right," he says) and twists and contorts the corners of his large mouth with such boldly gleeful contempt for Abdullah's politi-cal pedantry that one has little doubt of the film's allegiances. Fed up, Abdullah calls Lindy a "sorry-looking faggot" and lec-tures the assembled car-washers whose amusement at Lindy he finds offensive. "Can't ya'll see that *she* ain't funny? She's just another poor example of how the system has of destroying our men." Lindy cocks his head, slightly jiggles the hand on his hip, and replies, "Honey, I am more man than you'll ever be, and more woman than you'll ever get!" He snaps his fingers in the air and pirouettes for a grand exit. The other car-washers—and the audience—howl.

Lindy's "win" in this confrontation of types is on its most basic level merely a triumph of verbal dexterity—the most celebrated skill of the black queen figure. Of course, it goes no further—the game of dozens is a game of ebbs and flows, peaks and valleys. Lindy could be expected to lose the same battle when the men gather at work the next day. But the scene perhaps does reflect or signal a change in the winds of popular tastes. Abdullah is "out of touch"; he *cannot* continue the game of dozens, because he is no longer in step with the people he would liberate. Lindy's quip might also read: *Après le deluge* (the Black Power revolution), *c'est moi* (a silky slide into the disco years).

Looking back on this little scene played for laughs and reflecting on its resonance with my friends both then and now, I want to read still more significance into it. I want to think, wishful though the thought may be, that Lindy not only demonstrated the slyer wit but got the better of the argument, in the sense that the *figure* of the black male over which he and Abdullah are wrestling is in fact—as Lindy suggests—both "man" and "woman." Also, Lilndy helps us laugh at opposition that too many of us who partake in or sympathize with a version of Abdullah's politics like to draw: that between the strong black male and the effete white or white-identified faggot.

It is in the Black Power and Black Arts movements—represented ineptly in *Car Wash* by Abdullah, that this opposition got its trial run, so to speak; homophobia, observes Henry Louis Gates, Jr., "is an almost obsessive motif that runs through the major authors of the Black Aesthetic and Black Power Movements."[3] Amongst these authors I find myself returning again and again to Eldridge Cleaver's rather puzzling essay, "Notes on a Native Son," in which the soon-to-be legendary Minister of Information of the Black Panther Party has the threat of homosexuality very much on his mind.

The issue at hand in "Notes on a Native Son" is a critique of James Baldwin, who by the time that Cleaver's essay was published in the collection *Soul on Ice* in 1968 was an influential and provocative advocate of black liberation. However, Baldwin was primarilily associated with the civil rights movement rather than the Black Power, movement); and he was also known to be homosexual. Cleaver castigates Baldwin for failing to take a sufficiently oppositional stance against white racism—though you tend to wonder just how Cleaver was apt to define such a stance when you realize that the essay is written as a defense of Norman Mailer's *The White Negro*—and Cleaver takes this failure to be a result of Baldwin's sexuality. The meat of Cleaver's argument is that homosexuality among black men is often the symptom of self-hatred. Black self-hatred, he says, frequently takes the form of "a racial death- wish."[4] Immediately, Cleaver relates this analysis to African American practices of breeding, for want of a better term (I'm afraid the word captures the tenor of the analysis all too closely): Self-hating blacks don't want to have their children marry other Negroes who are too black, and no one, Cleaver says, wants to see very dark people together. Thus, the "blood and genes" are corrupted by the perverse will of black self-haters; this weakness, moreover, is a legacy transmitted by white men's "access" to black women. Baldwin and black gay men of his white-loving ilk somehow exemplify this cancer in African American communities.

> [M]any black homosexuals . . . are outraged and frustrated because in their sickness they are unable to have a baby by a white man. The cross they have to bear is that, already bending over and touching their toes for the white man, the fruit of their miscegenation is not the little half-white offspring of their dreams but an increase in the unwinding of their nerves—though they redouble their efforts and intake of the white man's sperm. (Cleaver, 102)

Cleaver's fantasy-Baldwin, this creature of wound-up "nerves" (read: hysteria) greedily gobbling "white" sperm as though it were the elixir of the gods, is engaging in an "underground guerilla war, waged on paper, against black masculinity" (Cleaver, 109). Baldwin's literary works present "a grave danger," Cleaver gravely warns, because they give aid and succor to the white men Baldwin so adores, the white men who threaten "the very continued existence of human life on this planet" (Cleaver, 110).

What is all this nonsense? The figuration of the homosexual as a threat to the survival of humankind and as race-traitor, for all its patent hyperbole, unhappily has a well-entrenched history.[5] But why should Cleaver select gay men as a target at all, when his most obvious enemy is the White Man whom he certainly ought to have seen as having been reasonably successful at both ideologically and biologically reproducing progeny to carry on his racial ruling class? Why should homophobia be an obsessive motif for Cleaver and other intellectuals of the 1960s/70s Black Power movement and its contemporary heirs?

A certain school of progressively slanted pop psychology would have you believe that the men who get exercised about homosexuality are themselves "really" gay, for anyone who is obsessively, deathly afraid or hateful of something has an intimate investment in the thing feared and hated. The progressive, nonhomophobic man's boast is that he is "secure" in his heterosexuality, and thus need not trouble himself with the niggling questions over which the homophobe endlessly frets. Yet the he-really-wants-it formulation at its simplest presupposes that *he* is in a position to believe that what he *wants* is fully attainable. The pop psychology critique of homophobia is, like almost any pop psychology notion, a cutting from the tree of Freudian theory; as such it is premised on the centrality of Freud's patriarchal father, that lusty fellow whose drives are redistributed and canalized by the Oedipus complex and the incest taboo, so that the fulfillment of his "true" desire—to have sexual access to everyone in his household—is stymied. This omnivorous desire, Freud postulates, stems at least in part from the "natural" hydraulic drives of the insatiate libido, but arguably it seems also to be an effect of patriarchal authority itself, a desire gestated in the glowing penumbra of wielding power over other human beings.

Such power was not of course the domain of most black men in the past, and the recognition of this historical fact still lingers in the recurring anxiety about the strength of the strong black male figure, long after the patriarchal nuclear family of which Freud wrote has become more or less economically feasible in significant portions of African American communities. The corresponding historical fact that white men in the antebellum South *did* in fact wield such power, and as masters of slaves had the privilege of casting the little matter of the incest taboo aside at will, suggests something of the particularity of black male homophobia against gay men. For in the realm of this recurring anxiety lies the unpleasant suspicion that the very claim of being secure in one's heterosexuality is no more than that: a claim—and claims can be contested. Cleaver and his cohort fear and hate the queer that lurks in the figure of the strong black male, that "more woman than you'll ever get" that Lindy embraces with a mocking smile.

I I

One of the things that most draws me to psychoanalysis as a way of reading the operation of "blackness" in American culture is the dependence of psychoanalytic theory upon the imagination of a *scene*, its propensity for inventing a creation myth in which all the various pressures of language, economics, culture—and history, at least potentially—are collapsed into a single symbolic and theatrical *play* that describes the crucible of the self: the Oedipal triangle, the Mirror Stage, the totem meal. By this same token, of course—but by no means as a diminution of its usefulness, in my view—psychoanalysis, in tending toward a final product that in important respects seems to eschew narrative, always teeters on the brink of being ahistorical.

Indeed, this is one of the most damning criticisms levied against psychoanalytic theory by critics of many persuasions: That in propounding supposedly universal scenarios which are claimed to found the individual human subject, the interlocutors of psychoanalytic theory fail to take into account the specific historical and cultural context in which psychoanalysis was born and in which it continues to be refined; they miss the very crucial fact that the subject that the theory describes is highly particular rather than general—white, male, bourgeois, and heterosexual, a person whose occupation of "universal" status is predicated on his membership in a group of societies significantly defined by their political, economic, and military history as imperial and colonial powers.[6]

Yet such criticisms need not be entirely fatal; the terms and perhaps the methods of psychoanalytic theory, it seems to me, may prove useful nonetheless. Striking a balance between history and the individual, between history and myth, is precisely the challenge (and the pleasure) of deriving the psychoanalytic *scene* in which the subject is born; with the scene as an analytic tool we may glean knowledge which we might not otherwise obtain.

In his keynote address to the 1996 Ford Foundation Fellows conference, Cornel West lamented his inability to purge himself of his internalized racism, his sexism and homophobia, and cited this inability as a compelling reason to interrogate the self as an important part of antiracist struggle. To look keenly at the wilderness within us, he said, is to unearth the ugly and complex histories of American culture. It is possible, then, that in the *scene*, in the imagined, created mini-narrative that supposedly founds the individual subject, we can draw close to representing and understanding those relationships between race, gender, and sexuality which cannot be understood by analogy; we can map some of the dynamics that operate between these categories of being by both defying and assimilating the linear narratives of history.[7]

I would like, then, to read a scene from African American literature as a psychoanalytic scene illustrating an aspect of blackness — or, more properly, black(male)ness.

The psychoanalytic paradigm indicates that at the heart of any such scene lies its symbolic coding of memories repressed by the psyche. Freud's theory about the so-called hysteria of his female patients was that the women's suffering arose from the repression of a memory experienced as so horrible that the patients were unable to speak it in language. In essence, the repressed memory was expressed by the unconscious, where the otherwise unacknowledged memory continued to reside, and the unconscious, bereft of spoken language, in excess of language, spoke this memory through the hysterical symptoms of the body.

This memory was frequently one of the patient having been sexually seduced by her father. According to Freud, it was not necessary to ascertain the "truth" of this memory. The historical relation of the patient to her father was not important; it was rather the patient's relationship to a father figure or to the paternal metaphor that was salient, the Father as culture, society, regulation, law, and the gender role these various structures forced her to live out. This relationship was embedded in the symbolic scene that the patient held as memory and in which she was emotionally invested, and it is this scene which gave rise to the psychic and physical manifestations of sickness or unrest.

Arthur Flannigan Saint-Aubin, in an essay on black male sexuality, makes productive use of the terms of psychoanalytic theory.[8] Following the logic of Freud's theory of hysteria, Flannigan Saint-Aubin posits the existence of what he calls "testeria," neatly substituting the male testes for the female uterus as the metaphoric site of psychic disturbance. Testeria, he argues, can be understood as the response of black males to the position in which we are called into being in white supremacist patriarchy in the United States, where the sole subject, the sole being who is synonymous with human and whose experience counts axiomatically *as* experience, is the white male. "[I]nhabiting the untenable space of identification with yet dislocation from the Symbolic Order of the Father," feminized and other in relation to the White Father at the same time as he feminizes black women in particular and women in general, the black male is "simultaneously complicitous yet dissonant with and occluded by" the patriarchal power of the white Father (Saint-Aubin, 1069). In Saint-Aubin's formulation, the black male, in his history as African slave, is/was the object of control or desire for the White Father; the subjectivity imposed on him is as object—a position analogous to that occupied by women. He resists this imposition in various ways, while nevertheless being simultaneously drawn into a vexed and emotionally invested identification with white male power.[9] This resistance and identification must be understood as coextensive with, and at times indistinguishable from, forms of desire: the urge to recover a lost (and ultimately fantastic) sense of wholeness. As Leo Bersani elegantly puts it, desire "combines and confuses impulses to appropriate and identify with the object of desire."[10] The rather provocative conclusion, then, of Flannigan Saint-Aubin's argument is that at bottom the crucible of black male subjectivity is the development of the black man's relationship to white men and/or to white male power and privilege; this relationship is characterized by hidden desire and the struggle for control—indeed, desire and a struggle for control which possibly incorporate sexual elements in some form—and moreover, this desire replicates, mirrors, the white male's desire for the black male.[11] The repressed memory which is at the heart of testeria is thus the record or imagination of this complicated relationship of control and desire.

What, then, might we choose as a scene that brings together history with myth, that encodes and reveals the unspeakable memories that underlie "blackmaleness"? Following the trend of both psychoanalytic theory and historical analysis, we go looking for something which can credibly serve as an originary moment—and for African Americans, it makes sense to locate this moment in the experience and history of slavery.[12]

Kobena Mercer and Isaac Julien note,

> the historical violation of black bodies in social formations structured by slavery gives rise to a discourse . . . which has . . . the countervailing force to rival the problematic of castration rhetorically placed at the centre of psychoanalytic theory by the grand Oedipal narrative.[13]

For one possible scene, then, I turn to Toni Morrison's novel of slavery, *Beloved*, and the character Paul D.

III

As Barbara Christian has argued, Toni Morrison in *Beloved* aims to create a kind of literary "fixing ceremony," both for the unremembered, unmemorialized African dead who perished in the Middle Passage and for those who survived it—and, by extension, for us as well, as Americans and African Americans who are the inheritors of the largely unspoken but nonetheless persistently powerful experiences of the Africans who survived.[14] The novel's project is the recovery of painful and traumatic memory, of "what is not spoken and what is not seen."[15] In the development of the narrative, the strategies which the characters Sethe, Paul D, and Denver pursue of living only for the present or future, of holding the past at bay, constantly fail, and impede the characters' full attainment of a primal freedom and integrity of self that yearns to be realized despite their conscious desires to maintain safe and truncated lives.

Morrison's narrative drives the characters to claim themselves in a way which perhaps seems at odds with the many contemporary appropriations of the psychoanalytic approach, which emphasize the observation that identity is always a failure, always threatening to collapse against the pressure of what it has walled out. But in fact the "identity," if we can name it as such, to which the characters are driven to establish claim in the novel, is rarely anything but divided and fractured from within, even when Sethe at last glimpses that undisturbed center in her spirit and psyche that is herself, her "best thing."[16] In that final moment of Sethe's development, her realization is incomplete, her journey unfinished. So, too, the "wholeness" which Morrison's novel offers to American readers as it performs its fixing ceremony: Rather than providing an end, a complete satisfaction, a successful exorcism of the ghosts of the Middle Passage and slavery, the novel re-opens wounds, to begin a healing that can only be understood as an ongoing process—a healing that *is* that process rather than the end of process, because Morrison's aim is above all to prevent forgetting.[17]

Morrison vigorously engages in trope work—the reworking and reconfiguration of metaphor to create figures by which new knowledge can be transmitted. The novel's operative term is, to use Sethe's word, "*re*memory." *Beloved* does not seek to give an "accurate" account of Margaret Garner's history (the woman on whom the character Sethe is based), but to mine that history for possible meanings that, heretofore largely hidden from histories and absent from popular consciousness, seem available only in metaphor. The difficulty of this undertaking is evidenced in Morrison's handling of the Middle Passage. The Middle Passage experience is not, in Morrison's novel, actually figured: It is instead enunciated as fragment, as nonfigure, a collection of unpunctuated and seemingly hallucinatory words that do not cohere. The difficulty in transmitting knowledge of the Middle Passage is in part one of its virtual absence in language as an easily available trope. Therefore, Morrison does not offer us a figure that is easy to assimilate, but instead tries to force us to confront the outrage that is the erasure of that history, by figuring the Middle Passage as a point of resistance to *being read* in the text itself.

We can discern elsewhere in the text the difficulty of asking the questions that are not asked, of figuring what has not been figured, of representing those histories, those traumas, that have been erased and forgotten. This problem is provocatively evident in what Christian has said has proven to be one of the most controversial parts of the novel: the sexual exploitation of Paul D and other black men on the chain gang in Alfred, Georgia (see Morroson 106–113).

The sexual exploitation of black women under slavery in the United States is to some degree acknowledged, however inadequately. Indeed, the "rape of black women" has become the trope around which questions of "black feminism" and "black female sexuality" arise without great controversy in discussions among sometimes contentious feminists, African Americanists and Afrocentrists. More prevalent still is the idea of the "emasculation" of the black male, another primary trope for various kinds of discussions about both "blackness" (because the masculine becomes conflated with the race as a whole) and "black manhood." The emasculation trope is, in effect, one of the most popular readings of the founding *scene* of African American male subjectivity, the reading which animates most discussions of men's experience of slavery. The emasculation trope has as its corollary the figure of castration, an image which does not remain only as a shadowy fear in the male mind as it does in Freudian theory, but becomes a practice in the long and ugly history of the lynching of black men.

Thus, these two tropes, "rape of black women" and "emasculation/castration of black men," are almost never placed in any but parallel relation: The rape is like the emasculation, the emasculation what they did to men instead of rape, etc.—formulations which leave untouched the question of whether this "emasculation" of black men might have occurred *because of or through* rape *of men by other men*. That is, might this emasculation have been enacted, on a systemic level, not only by the physical (nonsexual) and psychological subordination of black men (that is, they had to watch their wives being raped by the white master, etc.), but by sexual subordination as well, *to* white male masters *for* white male masters' sexual gratification or experience of dominance? And even if this were not true, might the imagination of such a scene, the revelation of such a secret however resistant it may be to verification, illuminate matters that resonate in African American male subjectivity?[18]

Morrison's *Beloved* has an answer to these questions, in the incident on the chain gang in Alfred, Georgia.

> All forty-six men woke to rifle shot . . . Three whitemen walked along the trench unlocking the doors one by one. No one stepped through. When the last lock was opened, the three returned and lifted the bars, one by one . . . When all forty-six were standing in a line in the trench, another rifle shot signaled the climb out and up to the ground above, where one thousand feet of the best hand-forged chain in Georgia stretched. Each man bent and waited . . .
>
> Chain-up completed, they knelt down . . . Kneeling in the mist they waited for the whim of a guard, or two, or three. Or maybe all of them wanted it. Wanted it from one prisoner in particular or none — or all.
>
> "Breakfast? Want some breakfast, nigger?"
>
> "Yes, sir."
>
> "Hungry, nigger?"
>
> "Yes, sir."
>
> "Here you go."
>
> Occasionally a kneeling man chose gunshot in his head as the price, maybe, of taking a bit of foreskin with him to Jesus. Paul D did not know that then. He was looking at his palsied hands, smelling the guard, listening to his soft grunts so like the doves' . . .
>
> (Morrison, 108–109).

Here, the forgotten possibility, the thing not said, is the tale of the sexual exploitation of black men by white men, under the system of total control which whites enjoyed over black bodies. It may be useful to recall in this context the well-worn bromide that makes homosexuality the unspeakable, the crime or love which dare not speak its name. What I wish to suggest is that the horror of the repressed memory—acted out among black men, if Flannigan Saint-Aubin is on the right track, in the unspoken language of testeria—might not only be the horror of sexual exploitation as such (that is, one could always make the argument that black men were sexually exploited in that they were used as stud animals to produce slave progeny at their masters' whim). The repressed memory might also be of the horror of homo-erotic domination and desire enacted by and engendered in sexual exploitation.[19]

We might also consider here the findings of researchers who studied early twentieth century interviews with African Americans who had been slaves as children. The study found that despite the relative frequency of sexual exploitation of slaves, slave children were generally quite insulated from direct knowledge of sexuality—perhaps because their elders wished to shield them as long as possible from this most invasive aspect of chattel slavery, or because their elders did not trust them to keep quiet the various private activities in the slave quarters (sexual relationships not sanctioned by the master, and other infractions, such as thefts of livestock or harboring fugitives). This silence as to sexual matters—likely shared by masters as well as slaves—in a context accented by forced sex, the researchers suggest, was a suppression of knowledge which, predictably enough, generated a range of psychological conflicts and crises for the ex-slaves.[20] Morrison attempts—almost in passing but as an inextricable part of the novel's larger project of excavation—to figure this heretofore unacknowledged possibility. That the excavation of this buried past is itself a kind of trauma, not unlike the traumas Sethe and Paul D undergo in what constitutes the novel's narrative conflict, is evidenced by Christian's reports of audience response to the novel's account of black males as victims of sexual exploitation in the novel—an angry and disbelieving response that seems quite out of proportion to the event's abbreviated appearance in the novel.

What is at stake in the intense reactions to *Beloved*'s chain gang episode, I think—reactions both convergent with and divergent from the homophobia and heterosexism of the dominant culture in the United States—is the very manliness of black men as a matter of fact and history: What is in jeopardy is African Americans' own investments in the "truth" of black manhood. African American critiques have long argued that any ascription of a kind of "superior masculinity" to black men is rooted in racist conceptions of the inherent savagery, the supposed authenticity and rapacious sexuality of black(male)ness. But that supposed authenticity, the vitality which racist discourse often projects onto the black male body, has also been used as a source of political strength, as a strategic essentialism of sorts. This was especially true in the late 1960s brand of Black Power and its cultural arm, the Black Arts movement (from which Morrison cannot be completely separated), and is arguably true of 1980s and 1990s Afrocentrism and hip-hop-flavored black nationalism.[21]

In a sense, Morrison's story threatens the stability of a history which has itself had to be painfully excavated—that of the heroic black male, who has been cast in white histories as a crafty, grinning coward at best. The figure of the black male has been recovered, in a long tradition of black historical scholarship, as a hero—on Civil War battlefields, in slave revolts, and even as scholar/writer-warriors, such as Frederick Douglass or W. E. B. Du Bois. It is this painfully wrought history that exists almost as an affirming mantra in Paul D's head as he ponders "where manhood lay" (Morrison, 125):

> [H]e was a man and a man could do what he would; be still for six hours in a dry well while night dropped; fight raccoon with his hands and win; watch another man, whom he loved better than his brothers, roast without a tear just so the roasters would know what a man was like. (Morrison, 126)

Here, the black man is, in effect, more of a man than the men who enslaved him. Yet the desperate coherence of this image, of this series of man-in-the-wilderness tropes which might do any mythical Euroamerican frontiersman proud, cannot ultimately provide Paul D—or American readers of all races with a stake, political, erotic, or otherwise, in the authentic masculinity of the black male—with a satisfying answer to the question of where manhood lies. History, acknowledged or unacknowledged, remembered or forgotten, returns. In the narrative, Paul D is first compelled to ask where manhood lies in order to resist being controlled by Beloved — to resist being controlled by the unspoken past. Though Beloved embodies Sethe's past, a haunting, maliciously active ghost plagues Paul D as well, for the traumas he has experienced continue to affect his life, forcing him to withhold himself from life and love. Morrison figures Paul D's response to his past with the image of his heart encased in a rusty tobacco tin.

Morrison is unyielding in her conviction that the wounds of the past, however heartbreaking, must be confronted; Paul D is free from the chains of the Georgia work gang, but the rusty tobacco tin that encases his heart, though of his own making, is another, and perhaps more deadly kind of restraint. By playing out the trope of emasculation in a sexual *scene* that seems almost to be its logical conclusion, Morrison disturbs the stable meanings which congregate around the idea of the emasculation of black men, with results that are both painful and, Morrison insists, potentially healing.

The particular horrors of the chain gang experience and its challenge to black manhood are hinted at in the novel long before readers learn what occurred: Paul D does not pursue the subject of Sethe's jail tenure with her because "jail talk put him back in Alfred, Georgia" (Morrison, 42); Alfred, we learn on the previous page, is the place that left him "shut down" (Morrison, 41). Other, more oblique references point to a specificity to the experience of black *men* in the slavery and postslavery U.S. that sometimes dovetail depressingly well with the contemporary discourse that describes black men as an endangered species. Paul D, we learn, first accepts Beloved's status as drifter because of his own hard-won knowledge of the bands of mostly old and mostly female ex-slaves who wander the backcountry, "configurations and blends of families of women and children, *while elsewhere, solitary, hunted and hunting for, were men, men, men*" (Morrison, 52, my emphasis). In a similar vein, Paul painfully relates to Sethe a moment in his captivity in which he watched a rooster who was freer than he was — the rooster being already, of course, a figure for a kind of strutting masculinity, and here doubly so, for the rooster's name is Mister.

In recounting Paul D's life with the chain gang in Alfred, Morrison begins by describing Paul D's uncontrollable trembling—a "flutter," a "rippling—gentle at first and then wild," a "swirl" and "eddy" within, that Paul felt powerless to control (Morrison, 106). This feeling is, of course, fear, but we would not go too far to suggest that, in a world in which the endlessly circulating trope of emasculation invites black men to be hyperconscious of a manhood which is always under attack or erasure, the language here of "roiling blood" and of a "trembling" that migrates through the body is a form of hysteria—that bodily expression of a repressed memory held in the unconscious, a hidden knowledge of what has been done to you to compel you to fit a subordinate position.

That hysteria is in popular if somewhat inaccurate interpretations of Freud a feminine disorder[22]—and that one might as easily claim this fluttering, rippling blood to have a relationship to familiar representations of female orgasm—suggests the precariousness of Paul D's "manhood" and the depth of his shame. The incapacity of Paul D's hands as a result of this trembling is first evidenced in the text by the fact that he cannot hold his penis to urinate. The trembling is elsewhere related to a "womanish need" (Morrison, 117).

The chain gang, in some ways like the emasculation trope, is itself an image which works to confirm the tale of the heroic black male. As Frantz Fanon argues, the black (male) body, in the various racist discourses which make the notion of "blackness" intelligible, is first and always corporeality itself: The black man *is* his body, is *the* body, is the excess of meaning associated with the body, above all the sexuality of the body.[23] The chain gang as figure situates this body within the folklore that makes the black male body most palatable: He is powerful but restrained; he sings even though he is forced to perform body-breaking labor; he endures heroically but there hangs about him the lingering question of criminality. He is thus a body invested, saturated, with pathos, with the nonintellectual, the emotive, which is also the province of "blackness" in the black/white binary.

Into this familiar scenario, this well-worn page in what Morrison calls "the glossary of racial tropes,"[24] Morrison places an incendiary device: the "breakfast." That is, we are prepared for beatings, yes, and murder and mutilation and atrocity, because that is what one expects of these tales. The notion of breakfast, then, offered though it is by the hand of one who uses the word "nigger," seems merely diversionary. Except for the inclusion of that one statement — "Occasionally a kneeling man chose gunshot in his head as the price, maybe, of taking a bit of foreskin with him to Jesus" (Morrison, 108) — which, along with the guards' "soft grunts," tells us that the black men are being forced to perform fellatio. The utter lack of spectacle, of sensation, with which Morrison communicates this fact seems to suggest that it, like so many other tales of sexual exploitation in the novel, is what passes for "normal" under the circumstances; for example, the ex-slave Ella's year-long capture and rape by a white father and son is mentioned almost parenthetically.

Here the blackness = corporeality equation is transformed, its elements given different valences. We are accustomed to reading the emasculation of black men under slavery in the following fashion: To recur to Fanon, "In relation to the Negro, everything takes place on the genital level" (Fanon, 157). Fanon is of course performing his usual conflation — that is, the person of African descent is a man. The "genital level" of which he speaks, then, concerns the penis, and the penis, in its relation to the Phallus — which in the psychoanalytic theory of Lacan is the symbol of power — is associated with kinds of sexuality, kinds of behavior, which are ascribed the relatively positive value of "active." The penis penetrates; it acts on; as the stand-in for the Phallus and vice versa, it has and is power, dominance. The black genitalia in this schema is a focal point whose power radiates outward over the black (male) body, and however savage, frightening, and overwhelming that body becomes in this schema, it nevertheless carries the value of being associated with the Phallus. Even—or most especially—when the black (male) body is castrated, literally emasculated, its corporeal associations are with a certain kind of male power.

In Morrison's "breakfast" tale this corporeality is rendered "passive." The black man is *kneeling*; he is a *repository* for the white man's seed; he is a *mouth*, at best ("best" judged in terms of "action" and "power") he is merely *teeth*, an orifice dentata. His penis—so overwhelmingly present when black men are viewed through the lens of the racial-epidermal schema Fanon outlines—disappears. In this dismembering, his corporeality is divested of that which was perhaps its chief claim to power, to value: "active," penetrative sexuality. Where the black (male) body in its Fanonian incarnation is a surface on which white psychic needs and desires are projected, here that body satisfies the white male body directly and physically, as sexual plaything; it is the white guard's corporeality which now is the focus of interaction between white and black.

In this context, a rereading of Paul D's earlier (and somewhat odd) thought that, "Certainly women could tell, as men could, when one of their number was aroused" (Morrison, 64), suggests a kind of intimate knowledge not only of female sexuality (which Paul D, as a man, might boastingly profess to have), but of a white male master's sexuality as well. It is this knowledge, which in discussions of slavery is always exclusively imputed to black women, and the humiliation by which such a knowledge is acquired—again always said to be the province of black women—which has not been said, which remains hidden, and which the novel unflinchingly uncovers.[25]

Paul D, predictably, perhaps, for a character obsessed with a rooster, regains his sense of manhood on the chain gang when he has a hammer in his hand. Wielding his hammer, he stills the trembling within. But ultimately the hammer is not enough. Indeed, manhood, as such, is not enough. As Paul D himself remarks,

A man ain't a goddam ax. Chopping, hacking, busting every goddam minute of the day. Things get to him. Things he can't chop down because they're inside." (Morrison, 69).

The "inside," figured by the red heart in the rusty tin, the "roiling blood" and trembling interior of his body, the softness which the world says must be hidden behind the strain which is masculinity—must also, somehow, be acknowledged, grieved for, and reclaimed. The process by which this reclamation might be said to occur is, in both the novel and in reader reception of it, far from complete or satisfying, far from an "identity" already achieved or a "wholeness" that heals without pain. At the novel's end, Paul D is grateful that Sethe, by *not mentioning* a part of their past together in which he was tortured, has "left him his manhood" (Morrison, 273)—which suggests that though he knows that manhood to be something of a fiction, he also feels still, and will likely always feel, the pull of manhood, the seduction of the acts of denial, disavowal and forgetting which constitute it. This pull and seduction, and the conflict-ridden and unsatisfying nature of the seduction's goal, are the ancestral legacy, the knowledge, with which Paul D as figure, as bearer of an ambiguous trope, has endowed us.

Part of what *Beloved* implies is that for black people to attain wholeness, the black body must be recovered, revalued (as we see in Baby Suggs's sermon, when she exhorts her congregation to love each part of their bodies). This black body is a part of and a stand-in for the black self. The dismembered parts of the black self torn apart in slavery must be healed and reintegrated by the self-love of unflinching memory. This is a responsive strategy consistent with the logic embedded in the emasculation trope, which by focusing on what has been taken away urges us to take it back.

The emasculation trope—the emasculation reading of the founding *scene* of "blackness" and African American male subjectivity—supposes that there is a natural, real, untainted, uncompromised black maleness which can be recovered if the effects of its emasculation are reversed; the trope emphasizes memory, but only to a degree. The trope places manhood at the center of its reading of the scene; it makes manhood, lost or recovered, the *meaning* of the scene, the answer to the riddle of black male subjectivity. In so doing, it recognizes the history of the exploitation of black bodies to the extent that it subsumes that history under the sign of a threatened manhood which can be recovered and defended. The emasculation trope's account of black male subjectivity tends toward a denial or erasure of part of the history of slavery: the sexual exploitation of enslaved black men by white men, the horror of male rape and of homosexuality—all these memories are bundled together, each made equal to and synonymous with one another, and all are hidden behind the more abstract notion of lost or stolen manhood, and most readily figured by the castration which was so much a part of the practice of lynching.

This move secures black male identity by a denial which parallels and mirrors the denial that stands at the heart of white bourgeois heterosexual identity. I think here of Judith Butler's reading of the psychoanalytic notion that any process of identification always involves a disavowal, a disidentification with something deemed to be opposite, something rendered abject: Butch can't be butch unless she throws out everything femme about herself, white can't be white unless it throws out everything it considers black and projects it outward, man can't be a man unless he abjects the feminine. Yet this disavowal holds the very thing being repudiated in intimate relationship to the identity; unresolved, the attempted abjection results in a kind of melancholy, a repressed but constantly returning wish for what has been repudiated.[26] Paul D's story in *Beloved* brings us a step further in the process of addressing that melancholy, by avowing what the emasculation trope disavows.

In Morrison's fiction, the heart must be liberated from its tin tomb: What is intimated in *Beloved* might be said to be a spiritual rather than a strictly psychoanalytic developmental trajectory, where some measure of wholeness is possible, is a necessary and worthy goal, and is not a fantasy. But this wholeness must be understood as a necessity in the context of an ongoing political struggle for black liberation, and moreover, as a *process* always ongoing, never quite complete. It must also be understood as a historical trajectory. In the text, past experiences produce "blackness" and "black(male)ness" and whatever distinctiveness these categories of identity might be said to possess; it is the history and the practices that respond to that history that found subjectivity; it is the encoding of that wider history in personal tales of loss and love, in *scenes* of memory whose importance lies less in their factual nature than in the knowledge they force us to reclaim, that founds subjectivity. Thus, the ascension to a liberated black male identity must not only involve the recovery of the memory of the black male body's violation, but also the recovery of the painfully acquired knowledge of other modes of being male than the model of phallocentric mastery.

The "other mode" figured in this *scene* encodes important aspects of African American history. As Hortense Spillers has argued, under slavery both the law (in its sense as legislation) and the Law (the rules and regulations unwritten, circulating as culture) erase paternity and render virtually oxymoronic the position of the black father as holder of the Phallus. Correspondingly, Paul D is absent in the role of father in the novel. His presence is in relationship not to children, but as a lover to Sethe and a brother of sorts to his fellow male slaves; moreover, his knowledge of himself is mediated by his memory of a particular relationship to white male power and white men, and thus to his own internal, idealized masculine image.[27]

Psychoanalytic theory tells the story that white male subjectivity comes into being through the workings of the Oedipal triangle between son, father, and mother, and in the Mirror Stage between son, mother and the son's idealized image of himself. These give rise to the abjections, repressions and taboos that structure heterosexuality and traditional gender roles. Yet the founding story of black male subjectivity in slavery is one in which the family as such does not or cannot form the crucible of identity. As W. E. B. Du Bois observed, the black church preceded the black family, and here in this originary *scene* as elsewhere in accounts of African American history, the position which a black male identity occupies is not necessarily defined by a nuclear family structure, and it is not solely or primarily in the nuclear family that the black male forms the basis of his sexuality. Instead, his identity is formed in other kinds of relationships, other forms of connectedness, that vary from his partnership with black women, to his brotherhood with other black men, to his complex relationship to white men wielding near absolute power.

There is a reading of this scene from *Beloved* that emphasizes its loss, its deprivation, its degradation, the outrage of it—and this reading we know in part because the emasculation trope has taught it to us. Another reading of this scene, not exclusive of the first and yet equally valid, is that in the horror which shattered African kinship groups on these shores, and in the convoluted and ridiculous and ugly ideology which justified and continually reproduces that shattering, we may nevertheless glimpse through this other mode of being male the model of another world, another form of connection between people. If we look more closely at the scene despite the inescapable hideousness of its context, it perhaps provides a glimpse of a kind of identity in which we might vault over the high walls that mark the limits of traditional family and gender roles, in which we could recover what we have abjected; it is a vision that moves beyond the merely parochial and constrained bonds of paterfamilia and everything that we build in imitation of paterfamilia, to begin to see connections that force us to embrace a wider community, because to do so is the only way we can embrace and empower ourselves. It is a vision predicated on, the translucent prism of blackness.

Of course, what we glimpse, illuminated and created as it is by the depredations of rape and slavery, is far from a utopia. Though in this brief flash, the queer lurking within the figure of the strong black male is illuminated, and though in that haunting vision the simple oppositions between "black" and "gay" males crumble, no simple unity or harmony necessarily follows.[28] Psychoanalytic theory tells us that the workings of identity and the unconscious will never settle or shelter us in a place of security, but will always propel us toward the edge of a precipice, where the mere whisper of something not yet acknowledged in the light of day threatens to hurl us into the abyss—only then to force us to ground in a new place of continued struggle.

This, I would like to believe, is the import of Lindy's words, as he strokes the mango-frosted strands of his hair and pirouettes to give Abdullah a teasing taste of what he's been missing.

NOTES

1. I would like to thank Barbara Christian, whose talk on *Beloved* at a seminar at Stanford in 1993 and our subsequent conversation provided the spark for this essay.

2. This is essentially what film historian Donald Bogle argues. See Donald Bogle, *Blacks in American Films and Television: An Illustrated Encyclopedia* (1988; New York: Fireside, 1989), 45–49. But Richard Dyer makes an interesting case for approaching the repetitious structure and constantly changing musical backdrop of *Car Wash* as the defining elements of a paradigmatically "black" musical. See Richard Dyer, "Is *Car Wash* a Musical?" *Black American Cinema*, edited by Manthia Diawara (New York: Routledge, 1993), 93–106.

3. Henry Louis Gates, Jr., "Looking for Modernism," *Black American Cinema*, edited by Manthia Diawara (New York: Routledge, 1993), 203.

4. Eldridge Cleaver, "Notes on a Native Son," *Soul on Ice* (New York: McGraw-Hill, 1968, 101.

5. Nationalist movements of any stripe can surrender to anxiety about the "threat within" posed by homosexuality. Stuart Marshall writes that easy comparisons between the mass murder of Jews in Nazi Germany and the incarceration of male homosexuals in concentration camps inadvertently blurs the justifications for these actually rather disparate policies. "The extermination of Jews was conceived by the Nazis precisely as the extermination of a 'race,' which unless sterilized and gassed would continue to propagate its putative racial characteristics. The problem with homosexuals, as far as the Third Reich was concerned, was the fact that they supposedly did *not* reproduce . . . they did not propagate themselves or their 'race.'" Stuart Marshall, "The Contemporary Political Use of Gay History: The Third Reich," *How Do I Look? Queer Film and Video*, edited by Bad-object Choices (Seattle: Bay Press, 1991), 78.

   Reading black nationalists through Nazi German history runs the risk of sounding hysterical or manipulative, but I do find the resonance between Cleaver's arguments and those of the Nazis interesting and instructive, not least because Cleaver and his fellows' frequent invocation of the homosexual monster strikes me as bizarre and by no means transparent, and I want to find ways of making sense of this peculiar phenomenon. The Nazis of course are a kind of free-floating and at times almost ahistorical symbol in American culture for absolute evil, and while I myself may engage in this usage and concur in its implicit judgment, I do not think that drawing comparisons between Nazi ideology and activities and the ideologies and activities of Black Power movement/Black Nationalism intellectuals such as Cleaver means that they are in any way equivalent to Nazis, even if they might share some characteristics. My interest, rather, is in locating points in the etiology of a particular ideological stance toward sexuality in political-cultureal movements in the twentieth century.

6. Observing Marx's coinage of the term "commodity fetishism" and Freud's use of the term "fetish" to describe aspects of sexuality, Anne McClintock writes, "The 'sciences of man'—philosophy, Marxism and psychoanalysis—took shape around the invention of the primitive fetish. Religion (the ordering of time and the transcendent), money (the ordering of the economy) and sexuality (the ordering of the body) were arranged around the social idea of racial fetishism, displacing what modern imagination could not incorporate onto the *invented domain of the primitive*." Anne McClintock, *Imperial Leather: Race, Gender and Sexuality in the Colonial Contest* (New York: Routledge, 1995), 181–82. Emphasis added.

7. Kobena Mercer warns, "Analogies between race and gender in representation reveal similar ideological patterns of objectification, exclusion and othering. But while they facilitate important cognitive connections, there is also a risk that such analogies repress and flatten out the messy intermediate steps in-between." Kobena Mercer, *Welcome to the Jungle: New Positions in Black Cultural Studies* (New York: Routledge, 1994), 191.

8. Arthur Flannigan Saint-Aubin, "Testeria: The Dis-ease of Black Men in White Supremacist, Patriarchal Culture," *Callaloo* 17 (1994): 1054–73. Quotations in the text are referred to by Saint-Aubin.

9. Flannigan Saint-Aubin maintains that this identification takes many forms: It leads black men to mock and exaggerate the pose of white masculinity, to attempt to occupy the white male's space by opposition or by imitation (flattery), to "appropriate . . . the white male body and therefore white male privilege" (Saint-Aubin, 1067). Frantz Fanon, making an observation informed by sociology and philosophy as much as by psychology, writes of the colonial situation: "The look that the native turns on the settler's town is a look of lust, of envy; it expresses his dreams of possession—all manner of possession: to sit at the settler's table, to sleep in the settler's bed, with his wife if possible for there is no native who does not dream at least once a day of setting himself up in the settler's place." Frantz Fanon, *The Wretched of the Earth*, (New York: Grove Weidenfeld, 1963), 39.

10. Leo Bersani, "Is the Rectum a Grave?" *AIDS: Cultural Analysis, Cultural Activism*, edited by Douglas Crimp (Cambridge, Mass.: MIT Press, 1987), 209.

11. Fanon maintains in *Black Skin, White Masks* that Negrophobia is a sexual fear, and that white men who hate black men are in effect displacing or masking a homosexual desire for black men. See Frantz Fanon, *Black Skin, White Masks*, translated by Charles Lam Markmann (New York: Grove Weidenfeld, 1967), 154–56. Quotations from *Black Skin* are referred to by the name Fanon.

12. I think it is quite reasonable to choose this moment even knowing that free Americans of African descent lived in this country and elsewhere throughout the Atlantic African diaspora well before the Emancipation Proclamation.

13. Isaac Julien and Kobena Mercer, "Introduction: De Margin and De Centre," *Screen* 29, 4 (1988): 8-9.

14. Barbara Christian, "Ancestral Worship: Afrocentric Debates in Toni Morrison's *Beloved*," guest lecture for "Issues of Feminism, Gender and 'Race'" class, Stanford University, April 23, 1993.

15. Angelita Reyes, "Reading a Nineteenth-Century Fugitive Slave Incident," *Annals of Scholarship: Studies of the Humanities and Social Sciences* 7 (1990): 465.

16. Toni Morrison, *Beloved* (New York: Knopf, 1987), 273.

17. Speaking of *Beloved* in a 1987 interview, Morrison remarks, "The past, until you confront it, until you live through it, keeps coming back in other forms. The shapes redesign themselves in other constellations, until you get a chance to play it over again." Toni Morrison, "Author Toni Morrison Discusses Her Latest Novel *Beloved*," *Conversations with Toni Morrison*, edited by Danille Taylor-Guthrie (Jackson: Univ. Press of Miss, 1994), 241.

18. The other side of this question might be whether the rape of black women had a kind of systemic effect on the development of notions of African American womanhood—a question which Hortense Spillers has attempted to assay in "Mama's Baby, Papa's Maybe." Hortense J. Spillers, "Mama's Baby, Papa's Maybe," *Diacritics* (1987): 65-81.

19. For an excellent reading of how repressed homoeroticism figures in a fiction of slavery when it was an extant phenomenon—Harriet Beecher Stowe's *Uncle Tom's Cabin*—see P. Gabrielle Foreman, "'This Promiscuous Housekeeping': Death, Transgression, and Homoeroticism in *Uncle Tom's Cabin*," *Representations* 43 (1993): 51-72.

20. See Anthony S. Parent and Susan Brown Wallace, "Childhood and Sexual Identity Under Slavery," *American Sexual Politics: Sex, Gender and Race since the Civil War*, eds. John C. Fout and Maura Shaw Tantillo (Chicago: Univ. of Chicago Press, 1993), 19-57.

21. Fanon makes much of how black men become identified with the *physical* (as opposed to the intellectual or social) symbol of the masculine. "[O]ne is no longer aware of the Negro but only of a penis . . . He *is* a penis" (Fanon 170). But most African American men can attest to anecdotal experience that despite science-haloed denials and arguments to the contrary, many black men number among those who continue to insist on the truth of the myth of black male sexual prowess.

22. See Jacqueline Rose, *Sexuality in the Field of Vision* (New York: Verso, 1987), 94-99. Rose argues that Freud's radical intervention was to challenge the prevailing late nineteenth-century northern European hygienic notion that women were essentially "diseased" by claiming that the central dynamic of hysteria was at the center of everyone's consciousness.

23. "What is important . . . is that with the Negro the cycle of the *biological* begins." And: ". . . For the Negro is only biological." (Fanon 161 and 176.)

24. Toni Morrison, "Introduction: Friday on the Potomac," *Race-ing Justice, Engendering Power: Essays on Anita Hill, Clarence Thomas and the Construction of Social Reality*, edited by Toni Morrison (New York: Pantheon, 1992), xvi.

25. We must, of course, hold in mind, however, as we contemplate this scene, that the knowledge which it imparts is horrible because of its context, not because of the acts themselves, though it might seem so to Paul, and apparently has seemed so to homophobic readers, or to readers committed to forgetfulness.

26. See Judith Butler, *Bodies that Matter: On the Discursive Limits of "Sex"* (New York: Routledge, 1993), 121–40.

27. The possible significance of this fictional *scene* as a pathway to useful knowledge has an eerie contemporary resonance. In 1995, it was reported by the Sentencing Project that one in three African American men in their twenties were in some way involved in the criminal justice system, as prisoners, parolees, or on probation. See Fox Butterfield, "More Blacks in Their 20's Have Trouble with the Law," *New York Times*, 5 Oct. 1995, late ed.: A18. This grisly statistic in important respects echoes the story of Paul D and his experience as a slave and as a member of a chain gang: what is common to all is the submission of black men to the near absolute rule of a white- run system of control and forced labor. (The chain gang is currently making a comeback in some southern states in these law-and-order times.) The experience of being imprisoned is, as we well know, characterized by widespread male rape as well as consensual same-sex sexual encounters.

28. ". . . [W]hat is hidden is aggression as much as sexuality, and the agent of repression is as ferocious as what it is trying to control." Jacqueline Rose, "Negativity in the Work of Melanie Klein," *Why War?* (Oxford, England: Blackwell, 1994), 144.

The Shock of Gary Fisher

Robert F. Reid-Pharr

nigger, youre dead with your zipper open and your dick hanging out

youre dead with a booger hanging out your nose and your zipper open
and your dick hanging out

youre a dead nigger hanging with your dick out and a big booger and
snot hanging out your nose

nigger, yous dead with your guts and your dick hanging out your nose

so, yous dead, nigger, with your dick cut off and hanging out your mouth

so, yous dead with someone elses dick *in* your mouth

so, yous *alive* with someone elses dick in your mouth, nigger
—Gary Fisher[1]

The shock of Gary Fisher and his collection, *Gary in Your
Pocket*, the ugly, unsettling, if strangely erotic effect of poetry
and prose written by an already dead writer who never accessed
print in his lifetime, is the uncanny directness of it all, Fisher's
perverse rationality. One is left speechless by his unassailable
common sense. The nigger is absent even and especially when
his body is present. Dick, booger, snot, and guts notwithstanding, the nigger is inevitably and irrevocably dead. The enumera-
tion of the body's attributes, the articulation of nigger
corporeality, is taken, in and of itself, as evidence of death.
Fisher repeats, then, one of the most regularly articulated para-
doxes of Western modernity. The nigger is not alive, but nonetheless strangely, inexplicably available for animation. Jefferson
writes,

> [The blacks] are more ardent after their female: but love seems with
> them to be more an eager desire, than a tender delicate mixture of sen-
> timent and sensation. Their griefs are transient. Those numberless af-

flictions, which render it doubtful whether heaven has given life to us in mercy or in wrath, are less felt, and sooner forgotten with them. In general, their existence appears to participate more of sensation than reflection. To this must be ascribed their disposition to sleep when abstracted from their diversions, and unemployed in labour. An animal whose body is at rest, and who does not reflect, must be disposed to sleep of course.[2]

For Jefferson the black is always physically available, but nonetheless never emotionally, mentally, or spiritually there. More importantly, this paradox, the notion of a physically present, but socially dead black has infected all arenas of American cultural and intellectual life.

I would argue that even the philosophical and aesthetic ambitions of what has come to be known as African American culture turn precisely on the necessity of establishing a live blackness, a corporeality that does something other than announce social death.[3] To put the matter in the most base terms, life begins for the black at precisely the moment when she takes control of her own black body, wrestles her subjectivity from the hands of white masters in much the way that Frederick Douglass (within the pages of his narrative) wrestles his freedom from the hands of the slave breaker, Covey.[4]

But for Fisher, this model of the slave in conflict with the master, a model that directly references the master/slave dyad within Hegel's *Phenomenology*, cannot be understood as simply noble, or perhaps better put, antiseptic. Instead Fisher forces us to look more deeply into the irony of this struggle. He insists that within the process of creating (black) identity one necessarily traffics in the *re*articulation of the very assumptions embedded within Jefferson and Hegel. There is no black subjectivity in the absence of the white master, no articulation in the absence of degradation, no way of saying "black" without hearing "nigger" as its echo. Fisher writes of one of his many sexual encounters with white dominant men:

Didn't I want to die a hundred times this way? Wouldn't I be happier? I hadn't seen his cock, didn't know it would be so big, so unmanageable — hadn't I always wanted to die this way? He pushed toward my throat, curled me still tighter, and drove my head down on it, still talking about death like it was our only alternative. Maybe I understood this mechanism I'd become the middle of, understood its strength, its unrelenting, its selfishness and selflessness. I tasted his salt, his ooze, and my throat jumped, but I could not dislodge him (Fisher, 65).

What I believe most striking here is Fisher's perfect rearticulation of the master/slave dynamic. The slave is literally kept from speaking so that the master might maintain his fantasy of dominance, his fantasy of having created the nigger in his own image. Fisher's partner continues, "It's okay if you choke Arab" demonstrating that Fisher's silence allows the master to produce a world in his own image, a world in which a black American might be turned into an Arab in the course of a single good face fucking.

I do not want to stray too far, however, from what I believe to be the more subtle, more perverse, more radical aspects of Fisher's aesthetic. As Fisher works to demonstrate the debauchery of his master(s), he never allows the assumption that he is himself an innocent. Indeed, the very fact that Fisher's published words are those that define the exchange between master and slave, black and white, demonstrates agency, articulation, that is not squelched by the masters's cock. More importantly, Fisher is eager to demonstrate that his articulateness is not simply an act of resistance to the master's dominance, but also an effect of that dominance. "My throat jumped, but I could not dislodge him," is a phrase that suggests both that the master's cock stops the Negro's expression, *and* that it is a vehicle of that expression. In this sense, master and slave can no longer be understood as separate subject positions, but instead as complementary components, if you will, in a process of expression.

I haven't read Hegel yet. Why haven't I read Hegel when I'm somewhat in love with this? I'm afraid to know. Half of this is the wondering, the obscurity, the possibility of surprise (and yet the other half is a fixed equation, inevitable — when I get there I'll be able to say I've always known this would happen to me — but I'll come to that admission as through a dream, still half unbelieving) (Fisher, 185).

Gary Fisher dares to know. He confronts — *without* reading Hegel — that which is embedded within Hegel, the fixed equation, the knowledge of both master and slave subjectivity, a knowledge so blunt, so bruising, that it literally can kill. Images of deluded and abusive whites abound in *Gary in Your Pocket*. But this is old hat for Fisher and, I believe, most of his readers. What is more stunning, what shocks is that Fisher says, without flinching, that the black is not inculpable, that she is as much perpetrator as victim. Indeed, as we will see, Fisher's constant return to the erotics of slavery, and his insistence that the black is always an active and potent agent within these erotics not only places him among the most perverse of African American authors, but suggests a model of black subjectivity and black expression that at once masters and deforms some of the most cherished idioms of black American vernacular tradition.

The question that this leaves us with is, How can we read Gary Fisher as a black man? Given my argument that Fisher repeatedly takes up the particularly shocking notion of a Negro racial identity not only produced in direct relation to white hostility, but produced in a manner that takes sublime pleasure in the white's domination, it taxes the imagination to place him neatly alongside Toni Morrison, John Edgar Wideman, James Baldwin, or even the growing number of self-identified black gay writers.

Saturday, November 2, 1985

So I want to be a slave, a sex slave and a slave beneath another man's (a white man or a big man, preferably a big white man) power. Someone more aware of the game (and the reality of it) than myself. I want to relinquish responsibility and at the same time give up all power. I want to, in effect, give in to a system that wants to (has to) oppress me. This made Roy (Southern, white, 40+ man) attractive to me — not wholly this. This made Tony *so* attractive to me. If T.K. had been the least bit dominating (encouraging) I don't know where I'd be now (Fisher, 187).

It is important that we remember how rare this direct (re)articulation of a subjectivity "repressed within itself" is within traditions of African American writing. Indeed, one might have to travel as far as the much maligned Phillis Wheatley to find another author who even comes close to expressing a desire for enslavement, much less an understanding of a (black) articulateness that is dependent upon the interposition of the masters. I suggest that Fisher's contribution to the race-inflected philosophical and aesthetic traditions with which we are concerned is to insist on recognition of the intimate connections between both those practices that exclude the black, kill him, as it were, and those that would resurrect him.

> "Can you get your hand in there? Three fingers?"
> He was pushing my hand, bending my wrist this funny way, telling me to bunch up my fingers— three, no, four—into a tube, "loosen yourself up for my cock." I told him it wasn't possible, that I didn't get fucked anyway, but he kept pushing my own hand into me, making the grunts of enjoyment that perhaps he thought I should be making. Reminding me that I belonged to him— exclusively to him—even more than I belonged to myself, and that I would enjoy this whether I wanted to or not (Fisher, 63).

Again the black's subjectivity is figured as a function of white degradation. Twisted wrist, fingers forced uncomfortably into resisting ass suggest an awkward, unnatural body put to the service of an equally unnatural white master. And yet we also see the fiction of white dominance put on display. The cues of a submissive, repressed subjectivity: those grunts, the reminder of ownership and forced enjoyment, all emanate from the purported master himself while the slave remains infinitely aware of the intricacies of the transaction.

I do not want to rehabilitate Fisher for those wary of perverse black subjectivity. On the contrary, Fisher's genius turns on his ability to spoil all our expectations, to deform our most cherished models of human subjectivity. Even when he reists, Fisher produces nothing like the independent, manly blackness that we see displayed in figures like Douglass. Nor does he articulate a sort of normative black gay subjectivity. Instead, the gesture that Fisher illustrates — the black man with three, possibly four fingers up his ass; the black man caught in an act of self-pleasuring (or self-degradation depending on one's point of view); the black man taking direction from the obviously self-deluded white — is hardly designed to re-articulate our most precious models of black subjectivity. Rather, Fisher offers almost withering critique while also maintaining obvious contact with the idioms of black American exceptionalism, the many ways in which we imagine ourselves as essentially innocent people.

In Fisher's formulation the black is finally whole. The self-pleasuring, self-degrading black gay, brings to mind the figure of the Sankofa, the Akan icon that commands us "Go back and get it!" the very icon that has been taken up by black film makers in both the United States and Britain, and that, indeed, has become the symbol of New York's African burial ground, a powerful symbol itself of the continuity and antiquity of a certain Africanized nobility.

And yet there is a difference. Fisher reminds us that retrieval, including historical retrieval, always involves the very white "master" whom the "retrieval" is presumably designed to reject.

Friday, November 9, 1984

> It felt good sitting on Roy's cock. It felt good being folded in two and deeply fucked by the man. Jamie too with so much rhythm it was all I could do to hold on for him — he was a wonderful fucker. . . . I only have one big regret — that I won't suck a million more, that I won't suck that special one (whoever it belongs to) a million times; that I won't be folded up and made one with a stud (Fisher, 185).

"Folded up and made one with a stud" is the phrase that most intrigues me in this passage. Its resonance with the emblem of the Sankofa is immediately apparent. Again, it forces the notion that the black is made whole, made one, only in the presence of the (white) stud, the master. What distinguishes Gary Fisher's work — what I have called the shock of Gary Fisher — is the manner in which it insists on the *necessity* of the (abusive) white, the master, in all projects of black self-definition.

Others do not see Fisher in the way that I do. In his essay "Gary at the Table," Don Balton places Fisher squarely within a tradition of black gay cultural production exemplified by the work of Marlon Riggs and Melvin Dixon. When one arranges *Gary in Your Pocket* alongside Marlon Riggs's *Black Is/Black Ain't*, it is immediately apparent that both men were eager to integrate the fact of their own sexuality, their own history, and their own impending death, within their respective projects. Moreover, the startling fact that neither was able to complete his work in life, but instead relied upon the assistance of editors to bring their projects to fruition, deserves much more attention than I can grant it here. Still, I would argue that where Riggs's work actively challenges simplistic notions of black identity, it nonetheless continues the assumption of a black seamlessness whereby the black dead come to intercede — and actively so — in the lives, the living experience, of the animated black. I am reminded here of those sequences in *Black Is/Black Ain't* in which Marlon, naked and alone in the forest, follows a path that he tells us has been prepared by Harriet Tubman. We are led to believe, then, that his own death is not an end, but simply a transmogrification of sorts, a return to the past, Sankofa in flesh.

This is not simply a performative gesture, one's own hand being forced up one's own ass as proof of someone else's dominance, someone else's subjectivity. In fact, to produce a too easy relationship between Gary Fisher and his "brothers," men whom he only infrequently hails in the course of his writing, absolutely belies the radical — or perhaps better put — perverse thrust of his writing. Is this black gay male literature? Yes, if the quality of one's literature is simply a factor of phenotype and the reports of one's sexual practice. If by this question we mean to ask, however, whether Fisher participates fully in the established idioms of black (gay) American literary and cultural production, then I must express at least some doubt.

In fact, I think that a better mode of inquiry when examining Fisher's work would be to consider just how thorough he was in his absolute refusal of (black American) normative narratives of human subjectivity. The electricity of the multiple—and sometimes violent—encounters that he has with white dominant men is turned on not simply by pain or racial insults, but also and importantly by his inability to distinguish his own desire to *de*-create from the white's desire to dominate. When he is called "nigger" by a lover, he is never sure how exactly to register the effect. Thus, he rejects the assumptions that that which is performative is necessarily innocent, necessarily outside of the realm of reality, beyond ethical and political consideration. We are not asked to read his work from the vantage point of a well-established cultural relativism. The pain he endures, the semen he ingests, the degradation he faces do have results. Fantasy can kill. "And then, didn't some people become addicted to their own poisons and begin to reason that the disease was the cure, or that their personal cure was hidden somewhere within the topiary of their personal addiction?" (Fisher, 42)

For Fisher, the individual who would know, including the black individual, is never innocent, never wholly separate from even the most ugly truths that he or she uncovers. In order to master fully the intricacies of Western modernity, one must expose oneself to degradation and disease even though the likely consequence of such exposure is death. Fisher believed he contracted HIV as a student at the University of North Carolina during one of his many study sessions in the Wilson Library, that his mastery of his subjects was coterminous with the disease's mastery of his flesh.

> I've amazed myself today by getting just about all my homework done, and atop this I'm understanding it. Calculus was a little puzzling, but I'm getting the hang of it. I whizzed right through some limits. I made short order of my German and English reading by making today a library day. I may as well make good use of my excuse for going to Wilson library every night. I know it's really for the off chance of meeting a

guy who'll have sex with me (hopefully *the* guy). Still, I feel good about getting so much work done. I'll continue to frequent the library because it's as conducive to work as it seems to be for homosexual connections. (Fisher, 139)

The piling on of forms of mastery—literary, scientific, sexual—is so very overdetermined as to seem obscene. The disturbing notion that in coming to know one comes to die, that wisdom is toxic, is an idea that Fisher will continue to rework throughout his writing career. In his last days of life, he comments that he takes the painful, discomfiting treatments meted out to him by his doctor in much the same way that he had taken treatments from his lovers, his teachers. He suggests that his situation is not at all particular, not hemmed in by blackness, gayness, precociousness. Instead, as he attempts to establish a solidity under the sign of Gary Fisher, as he forces fingers up his ass, always with the assistance of an outsider, a nominally proficient master, he comes to create an image of subjectivity that is available to us precisely because it is fractured, uneasy, always in a process of reformulation, precisely because it mirrors the obscene nature of all subjectivity.

Tuesday, May 22, 1979

Hope you've enjoyed it this far, fellow reader. Half of it's in tribute to you! (Fisher, 133)

I think it would be helpful here to invoke Hortense Spillers's useful, if somewhat difficult, distinction between body and flesh. The flesh, "that zero degree of social conceptualization that does not escape concealment under the brush of discourse," precedes the body. Moreover, it is the flesh that has been most insulted in the long nightmare of American race and racialism, the flesh that continues to quiver under the shock of the master's whip.[5] Following Spillers, one might conclude that mastery depends, in fact, on the flesh's immolation.

Fisher takes this insight further, suggesting repeatedly that abused flesh is the very sign of a well-established black subjectivity.

> The better lie — what do I tell Helmut tomorrow? What do I tell him
> tonight when I leave a message on the office machine, or when I dare to
> call him at home? How do I make quick amends for skipping work
> today? What story do I act out? Who do I pretend to be when I step
> into that office tomorrow morning?
>
> The plan — the visual device might involve a bruised lip, a red eye,
> a scratch on my forehead (all of which, right now, are real — real prod-
> ucts of a furious face-fucking I took last night and this morning from a
> leather-clad gentleman . . .) and perhaps a two-inch square shaved
> patch of scalp which I'll cover with a spotty white bandage (this, an
> elaborate, I know, and perhaps unnecessary attention-getter/reality-
> enhancer, as well as a bit of self-immolation/punishment for the acts
> that got me into this situation in the first place). (Fisher, 83)

Fisher is again stunningly direct. His production of a normative
(black) self is absolutely dependent on signs of his flesh's degradation. He is real, believable, only insofar as he is able to access
the abused flesh of his forefathers, to demonstrate a suffering
that literally strikes at bone. Face fucking becomes, therefore,
the emblem of the relation of mastery to flesh that I have suggested. Fisher's own speech is stopped as he receives instruction from the master, instruction that must hurt in order to be
effective, to be learned. At the same time, the master's abuse of
Fisher's flesh (bruised lip, red eye, scratched forehead) allow for
the (re)production of the real Negro, the abused Negro, the Negro who is alive. "So yous *alive* with someone elses dick in your
mouth, nigger."

Indeed, Fisher's work leaves one with the distinct understanding that the white master is necessary to the project of
black historical recovery precisely because his abuse of flesh
(mimicked by Fisher through his "abuse" of language) is what
truly connects the black modern to her enslaved ancestors. Certainly, if it is true that what connects generations of black Americans and other persons of African descent is the fact of some sort
of shared biology and the "white" reaction to the same, then it
becomes clear that each strike against a black body completes
the cycle, returns us to our roots, provides a bridge to a less than
noble past.

Christmas Eve, 1985

I UNDERSTAND this self-slaughter, but it scares me. I'm trying to decreate. Trying to go back; not to an easier time, but a more honest one. Shit, slave, nigger, cocksucker; like the wind and the darkness, the Auroras of Autumn. I'm doing it with sex and society, bludgeoning myself with misconceptuous facts, or the fictive facts that were "in fact" bludgeons *then*. No, I'm doing it with *words* . . . (Fisher, 188–189)

The equivocation in this passage is particularly telling. Fisher seems to not understand what actually produces his "decreation"—is it his (sexual) actions, or the language that he uses to make sense of those actions? He finally settles on words as the vehicle of his own self-destruction cum self-revelation, but here I think Fisher misses how fully challenging his aesthetic actually is. That is to say, he has consistently refused the easy mind/body distinction on which so much in modern western thought and social practice has been established. He has insisted that fucking is not somehow secondary to thinking, but on the contrary, that the two are interrelated and perhaps indistinguishable acts. Thus, Gary Fisher's expression is activated by his white master, the leather-clad gentleman who delivers a furious face fucking. In this way, it becomes impossible to use the phrase "black expression" without recognizing some necessarily physical, sexual, erotic component embedded within it much in the way that we recognize similar components in the child's *expression* of milk from its mother's breast. In this reading Fisher's master is not simply the abuser, the enemy, but the nurturer and provider.

12/11/90 Wednesday (by an hour and a few seconds)

Sperm is perfect nigger food and piss perfect nigger drink and a committed nigger should be able to live, to thrive off this nourishment alone. Piss and sperm nourish the nigger body and feed his black soul. Sperm feeds the wish, the already thwarted potential for the nigger to seek more than a life as a urinal and sperm bank. It feeds the wish but only leads to more wishes, greedier, hungry wishes that only sperm can fulfill. . . . Sperm is more important than the nigger body itself and will ultimately consume him. He must feel toward this purpose, this

> reward to the exclusion of all else. . . . The nigger takes his hot sac-
> rament from the cocks of men who know where a nigger should be,
> why he should be, how he should be, and find pleasure in reaffirming
> that I AM PROUD TO BE A NIGGER. (Fisher, 239)

The shock of Gary Fisher turns squarely on his fierce articulation of what lies just beneath the surface of polite, "civil" American race talk. The life of the nigger is so caught up in the
debauchery of the white master that even when "nigger" is
translated to "black," it is still possible to sense the faintest hint
of the rawmilk smell of cum on the breath.

I have written these comments as a way to make sense of the
curious phenomena of Gary Fisher and *Gary in Your Pocket*. In
particular, I have been struck by how difficult the text seems to
have been for those people—white, black, and otherwise—who
have encountered it. Indeed responses have ranged from righteous indignation toward the text and its editor, Eve Sedgwick,
to a rather maddening inarticulateness, a sort of collective shrug
at a document that demonstrates some of the ugly intricacies of
what is often saddled with the euphemistic label "queer." In this
instance, however, I have tried neither to defend Fisher nor to
suggest anything noble in Fisher's having died before ever publishing a word of his remarkable prose. What I *have* been concerned with, however, is the difficulty that Fisher creates for
those of us that he has left behind. Fisher neither establishes the
fairy-tale black, white, red, yellow, brown beloved community
so feebly articulated by immeasurable rainbow flags, nor signals
a separate resistant black (gay) identity. Indeed, what Fisher
tells us is much more difficult, more shocking than any of this.
Fisher shows that black/white intimacy is necessary and inevitable. More to the point, this intimacy *never* moves beyond the
ugly display of the master's dominance over the slave and the
ugly scene of the slave's yielding to the same. There is no way to
say "black" without hearing "nigger" as its echo. Fisher allows
none of us to remain innocent. That is his challenge and his
promise.

NOTES

1. Gary Fisher, "Being Dead" in *Gary in Your Pocket: Stories and Notebooks of Gary Fisher"* edited by Eve Sedgwick (Durham: Duke University Press, 1996), 69 — 70.

2. Thomas Jefferson, *Notes on the State of Virginia* (1788; reprint, New York: Norton, 1954), 138.

3. This phrase is taken from Orlando Patterson's *Slavery and Social Death* (Cambridge: Harvard University Press, 1980).

4. Here I build on the work of growing number of authors who locate the origins of black literature and culture in the earliest efforts by blacks to refute well-developed notions of black *in*humanity within Western philosophy, especially Kwame Anthony Appiah, *In My Father's House: Africa in the Philosophy of Culture* (New York: Oxford University Press, 1992); Henry Louis Gates, Jr. *Figures in Black: Words, Signs and the "Racial" Self* (New York: Oxford University Press, 1987); Paul Gilroy, *The Black Atlantic: Modernity and Double Consciousness* (Boston: Harvard University press, 1993); Ronald Judy, *Disforming the American Canon: African Arabic Slave Narratives and the Vernacular* (Minneapolis: University of Minnesota Press, 1993). See also my *Conjugal Union: The Body, The House and The Black American* (New York: Oxford University Press, 1999).

5. Hortense Spillers, "Mama's Baby, Papa's Maybe: An American Grammar Book," *Diacritics* 17, 2 (1987).

BROADER NOTIONS

Some Queer Notions About Race

Samuel R. Delany

Race is a fracturing trauma in the body politic of the nation—and in the mortal bodies of its people. Race kills, liberally and unequally; and race privileges, unspeakably and abundantly. Like nature, race has much to answer for; and the tab is still running for both categories. Race, like nature, is at the heart of stories about the origins and purposes of the nation. Race, at once an uncanny unreality and an inescapable presence, frightens me; and I am not alone in this paralyzing historical pathology of body and soul. Like nature, race is the kind of category about which no one is neutral, no one unscathed, no one sure of their ground, if there is a ground. Race is a peculiar kind of object of knowledge and practice. The meanings of the word are unstable and protean; the status of the word's referent has wobbled—and still wobbles—from being considered real and rooted in the natural, physical body to being considered illusory and utterly socially constructed. In the United States, race immediately evokes the grammars of purity and mixing, compounding and differentiating, segregating and bonding, lynching and marrying. Race, like nature and sex, is replete with all the rituals of guilt and innocence in the stories of nation, family, and species. Race, like nature, is about roots, pollution, and origins. An inherently dubious notion, race, like sex, is about the purity of lineage, the legitimacy of passage; the drama of inheritance of bodies, property, and stories.
—Donna Haraway, *Modest Witness@Second Millennium*

I

I don't remember ever being unaware of racial injustice as a major problem in America. My family talked about it constantly. My Uncle Hubert, a New York judge and a crusading politician, fought it passionately. My Uncle Myles, my mother's brother-in-law and another judge in Brooklyn, fought it, too. In 1950, when I was eight, our Park Avenue school sent my whole, largely white third-grade class on a week-long trip up to an Otis, Massachusetts, farmhouse owned by a friendly white couple, George and Lois. Our first night in the country, Lois proposed to entertain us by reading us some Joel Chandler Harris's Uncle Remus tales in dialect. When she was about three sentences into the story of "Brer Rabbit an' the Tar Baby," I raised my hand vigorously. Surprised, she called on me, and I stood up from the rug where we sat listening and announced, "My father says that those stories are insulting to Negroes and are just a white writer making fun of Negro speech so that white people can laugh at us. And you shouldn't do that." Then, among Robert and Wendy and Johnny and Pricilla and Nancy, I dropped back down, cross-legged on the rug.

I'm not sure what response I expected. What shocked me, however, as Lois sat there on a stolid wood-framed chair in her heavy sweater and long winter skirt, was her sudden embarrassment, her quick agreement ("You're perfectly right. I know that . . . I just wasn't . . . Really, I didn't mean to offend any of you—any of you at all." Besides me, there were three black students in my class of twenty-three: Linda, Peggy, and Mary.), and the speed with which she jumped up and turned to go to the wall bookshelf—while, on the rug in the sprawling farmhouse library, among my equally surprised classmates, black and white, I was struck by the presence of extraordinary power, suddenly and surprisingly.

For a third grader, such power is *hugely* uncomfortable.

The discomfort was enough to make me mumble now, with embarrassment, "Of course, *I* don't really care. I mean, it's just my parents . . ." But, with me as their mediator, my parents had already won.

Understand, I knew those stories. My father had read me the "Brer Rabit" tales and had often laughed out loud in spite of himself. Years before, my mother had read me "Lil' Black Sambo." Both had explained why their racial humor was a problem—still, Sambo's tigers melting into a pool of butter around the palm tree had remained with me as a delicious bit of fantasy. If Lois had been prepared to read them, even enjoy them with provisos, caveats, and explanations, I would not have objected. Instead she was doing precisely what my parents had warned me white people did with those tales: present them as language to laugh at and be surprised that such funny speech could actually yield a maxim that made sense, wholly detachable from the human experiences that had taught it. Now Lois slid the orange-covered volume back into the book case and, a moment later, returned to the chair with another book.

The memory of my power, and the strangeness with which it sat—the part of it now mine—in my body for the rest of the evening, blots out all recollection of what Lois finally read that night.

II

Strongly aware of my own homosexual feelings by the time I was nine, ten, eleven, I learned with the feelings themselves, however, that I must keep them secret. About my sexual feelings I couldn't possibly have stood up for myself against another unthinking child's comments, much less an adult's. A couple of times during my adolescence, I had one or another experience when, believing I was discovered, I learned only how anxious and even determined the straight world was not to see or acknowledge such feelings in anyone—and I felt as if I were being given a boon, a gift, another sort of power to aid me in my secrecy.

In 1961, at nineteen I married—a white woman of eighteen, a poet, with whom I had gone to high school. Paradoxically, she was the person with whom I would share these feelings the most. But it wasn't until I was twenty-two, when I'd had what at that point was called a "nervous breakdown," brought on largely by the pressure of having written and sold five novels in three years, and exacerbated by the added pressures of trying to negotiate a heterosexual relationship along with whatever homosexual outlets were available to me, that I began to realize, more than half a dozen years before Stonewall, that the oppression all women in our society in general and gay men in particular suffered was something other than the psychological *Sturm und Drang* Lillian Hellman had portrayed in *The Children's Hour*, but was a centrally political problem.

Since then, both problems have focused a great deal of my thinking and my writing. In June 1998, in Texas, a black man, James Byrd, was chained to a truck and dragged to his death by a group of white men for the crime of being black. Four months later, an openly gay student in Wyoming, Matthew Shepherd, was beaten, burned, roped to a fence on a cold Wyoming road and left to die for the crime of being gay. And the murder of pediatrician Barnett Schlepian in his own upper New York state home by an antiabortionist—made clear how threatening the notion of any structural change in the status of women is to many.

Yet, I have always felt a difficulty in discussing the problems together. The ability to be clear and logical about any one of them at any one time has always come to me as a feeling of power. But the others have tended to stay silent within, a discomfort whose articulation might subvert that power, reveal flaws in its logic, and ultimately negate the socially beneficial authority of my position. The distance between New York, Texas, and Wyoming is, if anything, the allegorical marker informed by the difficulty of bridging the topics throughout my own articulation.

To speak of gay oppression in the context of racial oppression always seemed an embarrassment. Somehow it was to speak of the personal and the mechanics of desire in the face of material deprivation and vast political and imperialist and nationalist systemics.

I remember clearly when to speak of women's oppression in the context of racial oppression seemed to be speaking of something selfish, personal, not large-hearted enough. After all, men took care of women. If you improved the lot of one group of men, wouldn't you of necessity be improving the lot of their women, their children? Pointing out that the very discursive structure embedded in such an argument, such a perception, *was* the locus of rampant abuse to women because it denied them full autonomy in the family, the society, the race—and because it occasioned all mkanner of abuse to women in all the country's races—seemed like moving a millstone up a hill with your shoulder.

Similarly, to speak of racial oppression in the midst of discussing gay liberation was to confront an embarrassing reminder of the huge amount of homophobia that manifested itself most forcefully right at the strongest areas of black nationalism and the fight to end racial power imbalances.

How, then, was one supposed to negotiate, as it were, the road from New York to Texas to Wyoming? How could we look at the highways between them, their intricate and connecting side paths, their main lanes and alternate routes, their service roads, much less their ecological interdependencies?

III

Functioning as a kind of momentary historical vision of the fall of some never-experienced utopia, a childhood story I grew up with, told and retold a dozen times, came from my Aunt Amaza Reed—a woman on my mother's side of the family who, among my black and brown cousins, was blond and had green eyes.

Actually, Aunt Ameza, a second or third cousin, fifteen years or so older than my mother was from a small town near Salem, North Carolina, and her story centered on a town meeting of the then much smaller city, a meeting she attended with her parents when *she* was a little girl of seven or eight—a meeting that must have occurred around 1904, when the subway system opened in New York City and the Jim Crow laws mandating separate-but-equal schooling were first instituted throughout the South. As Aunt Ameza described it, "Salem was one of those little southern towns where everybody was related to everybody else. At the town meeting in the church where they announced that, by law from now on, they would have "separate but equal" facilities, after the mayor explained the 'one drop of Negro blood makes you Negro' rule, he added, 'But we'd go crazy here if we all try to figure *that* one out.' So he told the eighty or so people gathered that night: 'All right, what we'll do is: everybody who wants to be Negro get on this side of the room and everybody who wants to be white get on that side.' Now—" my Aunt Ameza continued—"if cousin Henry was not speaking to Aunt Clem that month, and if Aunt Clem had decided she was white, then cousin Henry was fit to be tied if he was going to be the same race as *that* hard-headed woman—and went over to the Negro side. People went with their friends—and saw it as a fine opportunity to get away from their enemies, their nuisance relatives. That's pretty much how the decisions on who was which race were made. And I'll tell you, by the end of the evening, there were an awful lot of pretty dark people on the white side of the room, and an awful lot of pretty light people on the Negro side. And don't *talk* to me about families! But they took all the names down in a book." Here my aunt grew pensive. "They didn't know, back then, what it was all going to mean, you see. They just didn't know."

By the time I was nine or ten, I had heard the story several times. I'm sure I was not more than ten or eleven when I began to realize that the "single drop of blood" rule, while its intentions were strictly prophylactic, also managed legally to fix the vector of racial pollution in one direction alone. Black contaminates white—but not the other way around. Over the long durrée, then, this seemed certainly a legal mandate that eventually the nation *must* be all black.

IV

I was nowhere near as lucky in my political education about gay oppression. I had no early vision of a prelapserian utopia to fall back on. The topic would have bewildered my otherwise politically liberal parents. What my early education in that matter actually was, was only brought home to me not a full year back at the February '98 Out/Right Conference of Lesbian and Gay Writers in Boston, Massachusetts. One of the Sunday morning programs began with the two questions:

"Why is there homophobia?" and "What makes us gay?"

As I listened to the discussion over the next hour and a half, I found myself troubled: Rather than attack both questions head on, the discussants tended to veer away from them, as if those questions were somehow logically congruent to the two great philosophical conundrums, ontological and epistemological, that grounded Western philosophy — "Why is there something rather than nothing?" and, "How can we know it?" — and, as such, could only be approached by elaborate indirection.

It seems to me there are pointed answers to be given to both the questions — Why is there homophobia? and What makes us gay? — answers it is imperative that we know, historify, and contextualize if gay men and lesbians are to make any progress in passing from what Urvashi Vaid has called, so tellingly, "virtual equality" (the appearance of equality with few or none of the material benefits) to a material and legal-based equality.

By the time I was ten or eleven, I knew why "prostitutes and perverts" were to be hated, if not feared. My Uncle Myles — Judge Paige, a black man who had graduated from Tuskegee, a Republican, a Catholic, and who, as I've said, was a respected judge in the Brooklyn Domestic Relations Court — told us the reason repeatedly throughout the '40s and '50s, during a dozen family dinners, over the roast lamb, the macaroni and cheese, the creamed onions, and the kale (this was *how* I knew I had to hide those sexual feelings; this is what I had to hide them from), from the head of the family dinner table.

"Prostitutes and perverts," he explained, "destroy, undermine, and rot the foundations of society." I remember his saying, again and again, that, if he had his way, "I would take all those people out and shoot 'em!" while his more liberal wife — my mother's sister — protested futilely. "Well," my uncle grumbled, "*would* . . ." The implication was that he had some arcane and secret information about "prostitutes and perverts" that, although it justified the ferocity of his position, could not be shared at the dinner table with women and children. But I entered adolescence knowing the law alone, and my uncle's judicial position in it, kept his anger, and by extension the anger of all right-thinking men like him, in check—kept it from breaking out in a concerted attack on "those people," who were destroying, undermining, and rotting the foundations of society—which meant, as far as I understood it, they were menacing my right to sit there in the dining room in the Brooklyn row house on Macdonnah Street and eat our generous, even lavish Sunday dinner, that my aunt and grandmother had fixed over the afternoon . . .

These were the years between, say, 1949 and 1953, that I—and I'm sure, many, many others—heard this repeatedly as the general social judgment on sex workers and/or homosexuals. That is to say, it was about half a dozen years after the end of World War II. Besides being a judge, my Uncle Myles had also been a captain in the U.S. Army.

What homosexuality and prostitution represented for my uncle was the untrammeled pursuit of pleasure; and the untrammeled pursuit of pleasure was the opposite of social responsibility. Nor was this simply some abstract principal to the generation so recently home from European military combat. Many had begun to wake, however uncomfortably, to a fact that problematizes much of the discourse around sadomasochism today. In the words of Bruce Benderson, writing in the *Lambda Book Report 12*: "The true Eden where all desires are satisfied is red, not green. It is a blood bath of instincts, a gaping maw of orality, and a basin of gushing bodily fluids." Too many had seen "nice ordinary American boys" let loose in some tiny French or German or Italian town where, with the failure of the social contract, there was no longer any law—and there had seen all too much of that red "Eden." Nor—in World War II—were these situations officially interrogated, with attempts to tame them for the public with images such as Lt. Calley and My

Lai, as they would be a decade-and-a-half later in Vietnam. Rather they circulated as an unstated and inarticulate horror whose lessons were supposed to be brought back to the States while their specificity was, in any collective narrativity, unspeakable, left in the foreign outside, safely beyond the pale, a purely masculine knowledge of an asocial horror which was somehow at once presumed to be both in the American male and what American males had to save civil American society (that is, an abstraction that contained both women as bodies, capable of reproduction, and all institutions as systems) from.

The clear and obvious answer (*especially* to a Catholic Republican army officer and judge) was that pleasure must be socially doled out in minuscule amounts, tied by rigorous contracts to responsibility. Good people were people who accepted this contractual system. Anyone who rebelled *was* a prostitute or a pervert—or both. (And he was painfully aware that prostitutes and pimps—if not perverts—were strongly associated in the minds of many in those years, black and white, with blacks.) Anyone who actively pursued prostitution or perversion was working, whether knowingly or not, to unleash precisely those red Edenic forces of desire that could only topple society, destroy all responsibility, and produce a nation without families, without soldiers, without workers—indeed, a crazed, drunken, libertine chaos that was itself no state, for clearly no such space of social turbulence could maintain any but the most feudal state apparatus.

That was and will remain the answer to the question, "Why is there hatred and fear of homosexuals (homophobia)?" as long as this is the systematic relation between pleasure and responsibility in which "prostitution and perversion" are seen to be caught up. The herd of teenage boys who stalk the street with their clubs looking for a faggot to beat bloody and senseless, or the employer who fires the worker who is revealed to be gay or the landlord who turns the gay tenant out of his or her apartment, or the social circle who refuses to associate with someone who is found out to be gay, or the young murderers of Wyoming, are simply the Valkyries—the *Wunchmaids*—to my Uncle's legally constrained Woton.

What I saw in the conversation at Out/Right was that the argument exists today largely at the level of discourse, and that younger gay activists find it hard to articulate the greater discursive structure they are fighting to dismantle. And discourses in such condition tend to remain at their most stable.

The overall principal that must be appealed to in order to dismantle such a discourse is the principal that claims desire is *never* —outside all social constraint." Desire may be outside one set of constraints or another; but social constraints are what engender desire; and, one way or another, even at its most apparently catastrophic, they contour desire's expression.

V

The fall 1993 cover of *Time* magazine ("The New Face of America") most recently morphed that softly brown face of the future, which Donna Haraway, in the same chapter from which I've taken my epigraph, has reread as the face of SimEve. ("Never has there been a better toy for playing out sexualized racial fantasies, anxieties, and dreams.") That face, as Haraway points out, allows us to see the results of myriad micro-pollutions as it cajoles us into forgetting the bloody history of miscegenation that brings it about.

If one of the reasons I am black was because my grandfather, Henry Beard Delany, was born a slave in Georgia (as were six out of eight of my great grandparents), another reason was because black members of my family had been lynched by white people for looking like my Aunt Ameza—even like me.

Two qualities among its many make the concept of race theoretically problematic—and I mean theoretically in the sense of something to be theorized.

First, of the three races of mankind—Caucasian, Mongoloid, and Negroid as they were once known: white, black, and yellow—the black race among them, at least within the bounds of the white United States (thanks to that one-drop rule), at the level of the law functions entirely as a hereditary pollutant.

Second, race is a concept that has no opposite. It has no negative. The word "race" comes from the Spanish "raza"—a large, old family of many generations. By the beginning of sixteenth century, it had spread around the northern rim of the Mediterranean, so that in Italy one spoke of "the Sforza race" or "the Medici race," while on the back of his pen-and-ink drawing with wash over traces of black and red chalk, done between 1510 and 1512, "The Fetus in the Womb," Leonardo da Vinci could write:

> The black races of Ethiopia are not the product of the sun; for if black gets black with child in Scythia, the offspring is black; but if a black gets a white woman with child, the offspring is gray.

Here, the term "races"—and note the plural—simply means the great old families that comprise Ethiopia. That such an observation about racial mixing appears, even before, historically, the term means race, endorses an image of conception, hereditary, and birth that is not without significance.

Not until the eighteenth century was the term, however, "racialized," when writers, Oliver Goldsmith for example, began to use phrases such as "Tarter race" (in *The Natural History of Animals* [1774]). It is not without significance that, along with *The Vicar of Wakefield, She Stoops to Conquer,* and *The Deserted Village*, the works by which we are likely to know him today, Goldsmith also wrote a series of travel letters, presumably from China, that were republished under the title "The Citizen of the World," in 1762. The eighteenth century's totalization of the world begins to pull forward the modern concept of race, that is, "The major divisions of mankind" (as the OED characterizes section "d" of definition 2).

But compare this notion of "race" (a major division of humanity) to the earlier notion, race as family, whether progenitors or progeny. Race as family allows an opposite.

"He has no family . . . All his family are dead . . . She is without family." All these are rational sentences. But once the term becomes racialized, that rationality is precisely what the negative looses: "He has no race . . . All his race is dead . . . She is without race." These sentences are irrational, meaningless. At best (in the case, say, of "his race is dead") they throw us back to the specifically *pre*-racial, family meaning of the term. This is a semantic sign, I would hazard, that race has now become something—an essence—that suffuses the body of the subject and deeply affects the mind, rather than remains caught solely in the process (as with the concept of family) by which the subject is reproduced or reproduces itself.

It would appear, then, that the concept of race develops to assuage the anxiety at the absence of a term for a group larger than a single family, that is specifically not coextensive with the idea of a nation but is nevertheless mediated by heredity rather than by geography.

At this point, the relation of sex to race becomes self evident: You can't very well have heredity *without* sex.

But here we are at the verge of the polluting powers of race. For if family is taken to be the form of the process by which heredity occurs, then race is the thing in the body that is inherited—but the "thing inherited" always turns out to be its own pollutability, which is sometimes called purity. Indeed, even without appealing to the "drop" rule (the United States's historical, if inanely Pyrrhic, method for policing racial borders), we can see that the inescapable imbrication of race and sex via the concept of heredity makes race itself nothing more than a field of potential pollutions.

The polluting power of race is simply another name for the inclusionary power of a great family. One cannot marry out of such families. One can only marry into them. The concept of race arises, however, when the great family becomes so large that it looses locatable boundaries and the relation between members becomes purely sexual—natural, transcendental, essential—rather than contractual; as a corollary to the same transformation, inclusion everts into pollution.

Is it a paradox, then, that in so many narratives of racial impurity, the sign of pollution actualized is the emergence of homosexuality? In the conceptual field of race, a field that has no
necessary existence apart from the threat of pollution, of sexual
infiltration, the dramatic proof that pollution has occurred is the
emergence of men and women whose commitment to heredity,
to preserving the threat of pollution to other races (marked or
unmarked) that maintains the racial field in its stable/unstable
existence, is, at least in the popular imagination where much of
my narrative calculus takes place, radically in question?

The difficulty of speaking of racism and homophobia together is precisely this: Although the machinery of oppression
to both races and sexual orientations is distressingly the same,
the underlying desire to end racism is seen as the desire to lift the
proscription on pollution itself, allowing it to run wild, even
self-destruct, into the micro-pollutions represented by the grid
of constitutive photographs behind SimEve's benign (as a vam-
pire's expression is benign, as homosexual Pater noted of the
Giocanda, the Renaissance model of all-woman) smile. The desire to end homophobia is seen, however, as the desire to remove the stigma on opting out of the pollution game entirely.

Black men coupling with white women—in this country—
extend the black race. Black women coupling with white men
weaken, pollute, dilute the black race. The difficulty of speaking
about the relationship between the oppression of one sex by the
other and the oppression of one race by the other is the fear that
the oscillating system of exploitation of women, white and
black, by black men and by white, that alone is what allows race
to be, will be revealed.

Race exists through potential pollution/procreation.

Same-sex relations threaten to bring pollution/procreation to
a halt.

Woman is the cherished/guarded/enslaved ground on which
this game of pollution/procreation is played out.

What I am doing, is tracing out the negative calculus of desire
underlying the positive arithmetics of the discourse falling out of

patriarchal inheritances. This sense of a contradiction at the level of desire is what paralyzes so many of us in speaking about both oppressions at the same time and relating them in any rational hierarchy. What we can be certain of is that, in any discussion of any one field, however forward looking we believe our statements and position to be, if any discomfort lingers about either of the other two, however silent, then some aspect or other of our articulated positions are, in some manner, acceding to this spurious, fatal calculus.

The power of race is that it grows, strengthens, spreads, reproduces itself, takes all into itself, revels in its ability to include—which, again, is its ability to pollute given another name. (Quite probably for certain white slaveholders, what now and again went on in their black breeding pens, sequestered from the main house, across the fields, played the same discursive role for them as what went on in the European theater did for my uncle, the judge.) To believe that race exists is to believe that its energy—specifically, its sexual energy as a potential for procreation—is a real and potent force, for good or ill. But by the same uncritical calculus, homosexuality is seen as the element that is at once within it but that which, at the same time, denies procreation its all-important outlet. Breeding is, after all, what white slaveowners in the early years of slavery *wanted* their slaves to do. Presumably, having same-sex relationships is what they *didn't* want them to do.

VI

From some time in the '70s comes one of my most vivid memories of this paralysis—well after I had come out—in this case while I was sitting at the blond wood tables of the Schomberg Library on 135th Street. A brother, who had come into the library to read, soon engaged me in a heated and pressing conversation, where I felt I could do nothing but listen: "Don't you realize," he declared, leaning forward and taking my forearm, "homosexuality is the white man's evil—that he has inflicted on us, to help destroy us. Black men ain't gay—unless they've been paying too much attention and listening to white men. There ain't no gay people in Africa . . . !"

Ten years later, again in the Schomberg, I'd been invited to give a reading with Octavia Butler. In the Q-and-A session afterwards, the responses of our community audience were upset by a young man in dashiki and batiked cap presenting the same set of concepts, that evoked mumblings both of disapproval and approval all throughout.

Mumblings, yes—but no one said anything clear and articulate. And the moderator chose that moment to bring the session to a close.

Today, anyone interested can go to the 42nd Street area today (October '98) and listen to the street preaching of a black sect, decked out in leather, turbans, and metal studs, calling itself the Nation of Zion whose preachers stand, flanked by two or more guards. Although their rhetoric begins with a historically reasoned critique of the image of a "white" Christ, they soon move on to exhort openly, as they have almost daily for more than a decade now, the extermination of all mixed-blooded blacks, all homosexuals, black and white, and all blacks with vitiligo (the disease where the pigment producing cells break down and white blotches appear on the face and hands and eventually over most of the skin) because they are seen as unclean and polluted.

Wherever we find it, the hidden calculus supporting this argument remains invariant: Homosexuality pollutes the family, the race, the nation *precisely because* it appears to reduce the threat or menace of pollution *to others*—the mutual menace that holds the boundaries of a given family, race, or nation in tense stability. And "woman" is an undifferentiated, wholly invaginated ground of reparation/procreation that, as it pervades all as an essence, is simply absent on any other level: material, bodily, intellectual, economic, political, an absence often designated in a false positivity by the "social."

VII

Interestingly, the first time I encountered these ideas, and the paralysis they sometimes engender, was, of all places, in Greece—a location that, through the rest of European culture, is historically associated with homosexuality as much as it is, so inextricably, with the origins of European culture through its literature and art.

During the months I lived in Greece, during the mid-'60s (I was twenty-three), one of the places I visited regularly in Athens was a pair of movie theaters, one right next to the other, about three or four blocks off Oimoinia Square. Both screened Steve Reeves-style Italian muscle epics, alternating with American Westerns. To say that one was slightly rougher than the other simply meant there were more young Greek men there, often from the army or the navy, actively hustling the procession of middle-aged Greek business men, in and out. One day I noticed a young man sitting on the balcony in—for that place and time—an uncharacteristic suit and tie—rare among the work clothes, military uniforms, and slouch jackets most of the patrons wore. He seemed a bit too proper for this milieu. But, after observing him for twenty minutes, I saw he knew a number of the people moving about from seat to seat in the balcony—and a bit later, once we had passed each other on the narrow stairway up to the balcony, he came over to talk to me! Petros was a student (was he nineteen? was he twenty?) and turned out to be extraordinarily intelligent. Committed to being a doctor, he was nevertheless a lover of literature. At the movies—and, later, back at the Boltetziou Street room that my three (straight) traveling companions (an Englishman, a Canadian, and another American) and I were sharing—while my roommates were out exploring the city, over four or five days Petros and I had sex some three or four times. "Are you really black?" he wanted to know.

I explained as best I could that, according to American law and culture, I was. His response was to leap on me for another session of love making, which merely confirmed what I'd already learned, really, in France and Italy: that the racial myths of sexuality were, if anything, even more alive in European urban centers than they were in the cities of the United States.

Almost as soon as we finished, Petros asked me would I give him English lessons — though he already spoke the language fairly well. In return, he said, he would help me with my Greek.

Could he take one of the novels I had written home with him to try to read? Certainly, I said. The four or five sessions over which I helped Petros unscramble the syntax of various paragraphs in my fifth novel, *City of a Thousands Suns*, were some of the most useful lessons in the writing of English *I* have ever had.

And for my first Greek lesson, a day or two later, Petros came over to my room after his university classes with a chapbook of Yanis Ritsos's 1956 *'O Sonata Selinophotos* (The Moonlight Sonata). In that high-ceilinged room, with its four cot beds and tall, shuttered windows, we sat down to begin.

"If you are going to learn Greek, you start with very good Greek — very great Greek poetry," Petros explained. "You know Ritsos? A great modern poet."

In some ways reminiscent in both tone and matter of Eliot's "Portrait of a Lady," *'O Sonata Selinophotos* is a good deal longer and, finally, more complex. The speaker, an old woman in a house (which may, after all, be empty), keeps looking out the French windows, wanting to go with someone in the moonlight as far as "the bend in the road — "*'o streve tou dromou.*" No literary slouch, Petros spent an hour and a half explicating the phrase "let me come with you," which tolls repeatedly through the poem, each time modulated in its nuance — the phrase with which, as he reminded me with a grin, he'd first invited himself to my room.

By the end of two weeks, sex had fallen out of our relationship: poetry had taken its place. Then, with a burst of warm weather, now at my excuse, now at his, even the language lessons dropped off. But the friendship endured.

One evening, some weeks on in our now platonic friendship,

Petros and I decided to go for dinner down to the Piraeus—a few stops out on the subway that began at Oimoineia Square, with its dozens of lottery salesmen with their sticks and streaming ticket strips, strolling around the underground concourse.

Along the docks, as the clouds striped the east with evening, we hunted out the smallest and most pleasant of places we could find: a wooden structure, it was built out over the dock boards. Inside, it was painted green, with screening at the windows rather than glass. At places you could look down between the floorboards and see water flicker.

At a picnic-style, or perhaps barracks-style, bench, we got beer and a plate of *mezie*—hors d'oeuvres. As we sat, talking, jabbing toothpicks into oily bits of octopus, artichokes, and stuffed grape leaves, somehow we got into the politics of Greek–American relations.

What pushed up across the transition from the amiable converse of two young gay men out in the purple evening to something entirely other, I've never been able to reconstruct (though it must have been some uniformed, or insensitive statement, or even argument, of mine), but suddenly Petros was leaning across the table toward me, both his fists on the boards. "Even this place—" he was saying. "What could be more Greek than this place—eh? You think, yes? Here on the Piraeus docks? Eh? Well, I tell you—everything you see here is American? The paint on the walls—American! The screening in the windows—American! The nails in the boards—American! The fixtures on the sink over there—American! Even the calendar on the wall, there—even you can see *that's* American!" He pointed to a pin-up calendar, in Greek, advertising Coca-Cola. "The blades that cut the paper mats we're eating on! The machinery that puts the electro-plaiting on this knife and fork. None of that is Greek. Look out the windows at the boats in the harbor. Even if some of them are Italian-built, their hull-paint is American. Everything, the floor, the ceiling, everything you look at, every surface that you see–in this Greekest of Greek places—is American! I *have* no country! You—you Americans—have it all!"

To say I was taken aback just does not cover my response.

Somehow, incensed as he was, Petros, then I, recovered. Soon, we were more or less amiable. We finished eating, then we went for a walk outside by the water. But it was, indeed, as if I had come so far along an evening road, only to round a certain bend and to discover a waterfall or an ocean or a mountain beyond, that I had never seen before, so that, even on the return trip, nothing looked quite the same.

As we walked back to the Piraeus subway station, I told Petros where I had to go the next afternoon—a street that made him raise an eyebrow, then laugh.

It was famous in the city for its cross-dressers. But, I explained to Petros, "No—that's not why I'm going. There's an English-language school down there, where a British friend of mine teaches. Because I write books, he's asked me to come and visit his class. He wants me to read them something of mine. And to talk about writing English with them."

"Will you talk to them about some of the things you spoke to me about, in your book that we read?"

"Probably," I told him.

"Good!" Petros pronounced.

On the dark, ill-lit platform, with wedges of light from above, we caught the subway back to Athens, and I hiked up steep 'Ippocratou to 'Odos Boltetziou, trying to keep hold of the fact that what I was seeing—much of it at any rate—was not what I had thought I was seeing when I'd left to go to dinner.

The next afternoon at twenty to four, I threaded my way out from Oimoineia Square to the glass door with the venetian blinds inside it, hurried up to the second floor of what was called something very like the Panipistemiou Ethnike Anglike; and my British friend John let me into the room, where his fourteen pupils—two girls and twelve boys, all about seventeen or so— had been in session for twenty minutes of their hour-and-a-half English lesson.

The pages I read, from one of my science fiction novels and our discussion of them were nowhere near as interesting as

Petros's exegesis of Ritsos. But the students made a brave attempt to question me intelligently. ("How much money you make from writing of a book in America?" At the time, I made a thousand dollars a novel seven hundred fifty if it was under sixty thousand words. "Are writers very rich in America—they are no so rich in Greece, I think.)" Then my part of the lesson was more or less over, and John turned to other material.

One of the students or John, I don't remember, at some point made a joke about the cross-dressers who would soon be strolling up and down the evening street outside. Then one thick-set, dark-eyed youngster leaned forward. "I must say . . ." he began three times: "I must say . . . I must say, because we have a guest today, I must say—must explain: there is no homosexuality in Greece!" In concentration, his fists knotted on the school-desk table before him, as he leaned with an intensity that mirrored Petros's from the night before—though this young man was a year younger, a head taller, and weighed, I'm sure, half again as much. "There is *no* homosexuality in Greece! The Greeks must not *cannot* do that. It is dirty. It is bad. It is bad and disgusting they who do that. The Greeks do not *do* that. There is homosexuality only from foreigners! It is all the bad and dirty tourists that make—that bring homosexuality in Greece. The Englishmen. The Americans. The Germans. The tourists! Not Greeks—you know, now!"

John knew that I was gay—though I doubt the students did. Perhaps, as someone who had invited me to his class, he felt he had to defend me, though I would have been perfectly happy to let it ride. "That just doesn't make sense to me, Costa. When you all go home from here, the people you see down on the street, most of them are pretty obviously Greek. You hear them talking with one another, joking. That's Greek I hear, downstairs."

"You don't *see* that!" Costa insisted "you don't *see* that! Not Greeks. Not Greeks! If Greeks do that, it is only because of the foreigners. They do it, sometimes, maybe for need money—maybe, that the foreigners pay them. But Greeks not do that. It is bad. It is very bad, Why would Greeks do that? It—how you say—doesn't make sense!"

I watched this impassioned young man. I looked at the other youngsters around the room: one girl in a dark sweater rubbed the edge of a book with a foreknuckle. A boy with a bush of light hair slouched back, one hand forward over the front edge of his desk. Some smiled. Some just looked uncomfortable without smiling. The room's walls were gray. A ceiling fan hung from the center, not turned on. Blinds were raised halfway up the windows. Costa's white shirt was open at the neck; his sleeves were rolled up his forearms. Beneath his desk, he wore dark socks beneath broad-strapped sandals, which now he slid back under his chair. I wondered what surfaces of Greece, if any, I was seeing.

After the class, I walked home with English John—who was rather breezy about it all, though even he seemed troubled. "You know, he manages to make that speech to us almost every other week. I wasn't expecting it today though, but, like he said, we had a guest."

Over the next days, I found myself thinking about both experiences. What was particularly bothersome to me was the way the second seemed posed to obliterate the first—to impugn the very social conduit by which my new vision had been gained. If, indeed, as Costa insisted, I "didn't see that," what was I to make of what I did see?

At any rate, this is certainly the young man I remembered when my tablemate at the Schomberg seized my forearm to insist, so passionately: "Homosexuality is the white man's evil. Black men ain't gay—unless they've been paying too much attention to white men. They ain't no gay people in Africa"; just as, when America takes so much pride in pointing out the influences of black culture on its music, fashion, and language, it was Petros who first alerted me to all the white surfaces that already make up so much of black, melanist culture, even to its most virulent homophobic protestations—by teaching me to see the American surfaces of Greece.

VIII

Because, at the level of cultural myth, in terms of the calculus of desire, within the silent space of discourse, homosexuality represents an opting out of the pollution game altogether, because as far as I can see, the only *uniquely* racial power that exists is specifically the power to pollute (all others can be reread in terms of class, culture, sociality); because the only power to be seized by women is that which directly or indirectly holds stable "the race" (black or white or Asian, it makes no difference), I think that gay liberation is, in its very small way, privileged—in that there can be no advance on that front until there have been advances, changes, and material shifts on the fronts of both racism and sexism. I think this is the explanation of why the gay rights movement followed the civil rights movement and the feminist movement in time as it emerged into postmodern consciousness—even though, as a movement itself, it goes back to the very nineteenth century coinage of the terms homosexual and heterosexual; from here on in, advances on this front cannot proceed much further without advances on the other two fronts.

Conceptually, they are inextricably linked.

On the particular level where the argument must proceed case by case, incident by incident, before it reaches discursive (or counter-discursive) mass, we must look at how that principal operates in the answer to our second question: What makes us gay?

The question, What makes us gay? has at least three different levels where an answer can be posed.

First, the question, What makes us gay? might be interpreted to mean, What do we do, what qualities do we possess, that signal the fact that we partake of the preexisting essence of "gayness" that gives us our gay "identity" and that, in most folks' minds, means that we belong to the category of "those who are gay"? This is, ultimately, the semiotic or epistemological level: How do we—or other people—know we are gay?

There is a second level, however, on which the question, What makes us gay? might be interpreted: What forces or conditions in the world take the potentially "normal" and "ordinary" person—a child, a fetus, the egg and sperm before they even conjoin as a zygote—and "pervert" them (that is, turn them away) from that "normal" condition so that now we have someone who does some or many or all of the things we call gay—or at least wants to, or feels compelled to, even if she or he would rather not? This is, finally, the ontological level: What makes these odd, statistically unusual, but ever-present, gay people exist in the first place?

The confusion between questions one and two, the epistemological and the ontological, is already enough to muddle many arguments. People who think they are asking question two are often given (very frustrating) answers to question one, and vice versa.

But there is a third level where this question, What makes us gay? can be interpreted that is often associated with queer theory and academics of a poststructuralist bent. Many such academics have claimed that their answer to (and thus their interpretation of) the question is the most important one, and that this answer absorbs and explains what is really going on at the first two levels.

This last is not, incidentally, a claim that I make. But I do think that this third level of interpretation (which, yes, is an aspect of the epistemological, but might be more intelligibly designated today as the theoretical) is imperative if we are to explain to a significant number of people what is wrong with a discourse that places pleasure and the body in fundamental opposition to some notion of a legally constrained social responsibility, even as the same view is reduced, under conditions of oppression, to seeing homosexuality as an abnegation of the racial imperative to produce and multiply, rather than a discourse that sees that pleasure and the body are constitutive elements of the social as much as the law and responsibility themselves, and the racial as a remnant of the most hidden, violent, and ruthless class division, between genders and families:

". . . everybody who wants to be Negro get on this side of the room and everybody who wants to be white . . ."

One problem with this third level of interpretation of What makes us gay? that many of us academic folk have come up with is that it puts considerable strain in such a question on the ordinary meaning of "makes."

The argument with our interpretation might start along these lines (I begin here because, after first seeing the polemic against it, the reader may have an easier time recognizing the interpretation when it arrives in its positive form): "To make" is an active verb. You seem to be describing a much more passive process. It sounds like you're describing some answer to the question What allows us to be gay? or What facilitates our being gay? or even What allows people to speak about people as gay? Indeed, the answer you propose doesn't seem to have anything to do with "making" at all. It seems to be all about language and social habit.

To which, if we're lucky enough for the opposition to take its objection to this point, we can answer back: "You're right! That's *exactly* our point. We now believe that language and social habit are much more important than heretofore, historically, they have been assumed to be. Both language and social habit perform many more jobs, intricately, efficiently, and powerfully, shaping not only what we call social reality, but also what we call reality itself (against which we used to set social reality in order to look at it as a separate situation *from* material reality). Language and social habit don't produce only the appearance of social categories—rich, poor, educated, uneducated, well mannered, ill bred—those signs that, according to Professor Henry Higgins in *My Fair Lady*, can be learned and therefore faked. They produce as well what heretofore were considered ontological categories: male, female, black, white, Asian, straight, gay, normal, and abnormal, as well as trees, books, dogs, wars, rainstorms, and mosquitoes. And they empower us to put all those ironizing quotation marks around words such as "normal," "ordinary," and "pervert" in our paragraph describing the ontological level.

Because we realize just how powerful the sociolinguistic process is, we *insist* on coupling it to those active verbs, to make, to produce, to create. Early in the dialogue, however, there was another common verb for this particular meaning of "make" that paid its due to the slow, sedentary, and passive (as well as to the inexorable and adamantine) quality of the process: 'to sediment'—a verb which fell away because it did not suit the polemical nature of the argument, but which at this point it might be well to retrieve: What makes us gay? in the sense of, What produces us as gay? What creates us as gay? What sediments us as gay?

The level where these last four questions overlap is where our interpretation of the question—and our answer to it—falls.

Consider a large ballroom full of people.

At various places around the walls there are doors. If one of the doors is open, and the ballroom is crowded enough, after a certain amount of time there will be a certain number of people in the other room on the far side of the open door (assuming the lights are on and nothing is going on in there to keep them out). The third-level theoretical answer to the question, What makes us gay? troubles the ordinary man or woman on the street for much the same reason it would trouble him or her if you said, of the ballroom and the room beside it, "The open door is what makes people go into the other room."

Most folks are likely to respond, "Isn't it really the density of the ballroom's crowd, the heat, the noise, the bustle in the ballroom that drives (that is, that *makes*) people go into the adjoining room? I'm sure you could come up with experiments, where, if, on successive nights, you raised or lowered the temperature and/or the noise level, you could even correlate that to how much faster or slower people were driven out of the ballroom and into the adjoining room—thus proving crowd, heat, and noise were the causative factors, rather than the door, which is finally just a facilitator, *n'est pas?*"

The answer to this objection is: "You're answering the question as though it were being asked at level two. And for level two, your answer is fine. The question *I* am asking, however, on level three, is: What makes the people go into *that* room rather than any number of other possible rooms that they might have entered, behind any of the other *closed* doors around the ballroom? And the actual answer to *that* question really *is,* That, particular *open* door.

Keep this in mind for a moment, while I turn to the actual and troubling answer that we have come up with to the newly interpreted question, What makes us gay? The answer is usually some version of the concept: We are made gay because that is how we have been interpellated.

"Interpellate" is a term that was revived by Louis Althuser in his 1969 essay, "Ideology and Ideological State Apparatuses"[1] The word once meant "to interrupt with a petition." Prior to the modern era, the aristocrats who comprised many of the royal courtiers could be presented with petitions by members of the *haute bourgeoisie.* These aristocrats fulfilled their tasks as subjects to the king by reading over the petitions presented to them, judging them, and acting on them in accord with the petitions' perceived merit. Althuser's point is that "we become subjects when we are interpellated." In the same paragraph, he offers the word "hailed" as a synonym, and goes on to give what has become a rather notorious example of a policeman calling out or hailing, "Hey, you!" on the street. Says Althuser, in the process of saying, "he must mean me," we cohere into a self—rather than being, presumably, simply a point of view drifting down the street.

That awareness of "he must mean me," is the constitutive *sine qua non* of the subject. It is the mental door through which we pass into subjectivity and selfhood. And (maintains Althuser) this cannot be a spontaneous process, but is always a response to some hailing, some interpellation, by some aspect of the social.

In that sense, it doesn't really matter whether someone catches you in the bathroom, looking at a same-sex nude, and then blurts out, "Hey, you're gay!" and you look up and realize "you" ("He means me!") have been caught, or if you're reading a description of homosexuality in a text book and "you" think, "Hey, they're describing me!" The point is, rather, that anyone who self-identifies as gay must have been interpellated, at some point, as gay by some individual or social speech or text to which he or she responded, "He/she/it/they must mean me." That is the door opening. Without it, nobody can say, proudly, "I *am gay!*" Without it, nobody can think guiltily and in horror, "Oh, my God, I'm *gay* . . . !" Without it, one cannot remember idly or in passing, "Well, I'm gay."

Because interpellation only talks about one aspect of the meaning of "making"/"producing"/"creating"/"sedimenting," it does not tell the whole story. It is simply one of the more important things that happens to subjects at the level of discourse. And in general discourse constitutes and is constituted by what Walter Pater once called, in the "Conclusion" to *The Renaissance*, "a roughness of the eye." Thus, without a great deal more elaboration the notion of interpellation is as reductive as any other theoretical move. But it locates a powerful and pivotal point in the process. And it makes it clear that the process is, as are all the creative powers of discourse, irrevocably anchored within the social, rather than somehow involved with some fancied breaking out of the social into an uncharted and unmapped beyond, that only awaits the release of police surveillance to erupt into that red Eden of total unconstraint. What the priority of the social says about those times in war where that vision of hell was first encountered by people like my uncle, possibly among our own soldiers, is: Look, if you spend six months socializing young men to "kill, kill, kill," it's naive to be surprised when some of them, in the course of pursuing their pleasure, do. It is not because of some essentialist factor in "perversion" or "prostitution" (or sexuality in general) that always struggles to break loose.

It is language (and/as social habit) that cuts the world up into the elements, objects, and categories we so glibly call reality—a reality that includes the varieties of desire. It is a reality where what is real *is* what must be dealt with, which is one with the political: the world *is* what it is cut up into. All else is metaphysics. That is all that is meant by that troubling poststructuralist assertion that the world is constituted of and by language and nothing more that we have any direct access to.

The problem with this assertion is that one of the easiest things to understand about it is that if language social habit makes/produces/sediments anything, it makes/produces/sediments the meanings of words. Thus, the meaning of "makes" on the semiological/epistemological level is a socio linguistic sedimentation. The meaning of "makes" on the ontological level is a socio linguistic sedimentation. And, finally, the meaning of "makes" on the theoretical (that is, socio linguistic) level is also a socio linguistic sedimentation. This is what those who claim the third meaning encompasses and explains the other two are saying. When I said above I do not make that claim, what *I* was saying in effect was: I am not convinced this is an important observation telling us something truly interesting about ontology or epistemology. It may just be an empty tautology that can be set aside and paid no more attention to. Personally, I think the decision as to whether it is or is not interesting is to be found *in* ontology and epistemology themselves, rather than in theory— that is to say, if the observation emboldens us to explore the world, cut it up into new and different ways, and learn what new and useful relationships can result, then the observation is of use and interest, but it is not interesting to the extent it leads only to materially unattended theoretical restatements of itself.

I hope, that without having to go through the same argument again, we can see that at this theoretical level it is the same process of interpellation that "makes us gay" that also "makes us black." Such a process *is* the social construction that everyone so often speaks of and no one seems ever to do anything about. And when race is cut up ontologically — specifically by the science of genetics — we simply find nothing there: the genes for dark skin, full lips, broad noses, and kinky hair are, irrevocably tied neither to each other nor to anything else. They are merely physical traits. They fall together in the people they do merely because, historically, people with those traits have been sexually segregated — so do blond hair and blue eyes, or epicanthic folds and straight black hair. When the sexual segregation is lifted, they flow and disseminate through the population, and reconvene when a few generations of natural selection bring them back together.

I X

Homophobia is not a natural distaste. It is learned. It is supported by lack of familiarity, yes. But, even more, it is supported by a structure of logic. It occupies a place on a conceptual map. That is to say, it is part of a discourse. Such discursive elements are transcendentalized — attached to nature or religion — only when the larger discursive logic is lost sight of. To dismantle such discourses, as a step toward remapping them, requires that we begin by retrieving precisely that overall discursive logic — by showing precisely how it relates to images of man and woman in their functional definitions; of how it relates to the tribe, to the race, to the state, to the nation. However, what is difficult to internalize is that, for the same reasons and on the same theoretical level, homosexuality is no more natural than the homophobia that counters it.

The natural in our rhetorical gallery is directly connected to the good.

If homophobia is "natural," then what it counters — homosexuality — must be bad.

If homosexuality is "natural," then *it* must be good, and attempts to counter it must be bad.

But this, of course, *is* the system that we are fundamentally trying to dismantle—and must dismantle—if we are to institute a more functional conceptual mapping: One that sees homosexuality as pleasurable and useful to a number of people, some of them gay, some of them not, and of no particular consequence to anyone else—though "pleasurable," "useful," "indifferent," just as much as "harmful" and "dangerous," are also all socially constructed categories. The larger social job—which, slowly but surely is coming about—is to demonstrate that in the greater world today, such libertarian ideas leave the whole nation better off and closer to is a more functional and efficient national model. Given our current level of technology (where, indeed, war becomes a far smaller profession of a much more specialized sub group than anything close to the standing armies of the nineteenth century)—and the world's population problem—it seems self-evident that the nations that divorce sex from procreation (and distance themselves from the nineteenth-century discourse in which the country with the largest and the most violent male population of necessity wins out over its neighbors) are the most likely to endure. I also think, by the bye, that a level of international cooperation and assistance must also and of necessity replace the nineteenth-century imperialistic logic that even makes such a statement as the above comprehensible today. But that is an elaboration and we have to start somewhere.

Let me end, however, with another tale, then, from a few months ago.

In Michigan, where I taught last term, a traveling gay discussion seminar came to the women's dorm where the administration had housed my partner Dennis and me. The evening's topic was "coming out." At the beginning of the seminar, a black freshman woman in the audience got up and announced, clearly and strongly, that she felt homosexuality was wrong—contravening the laws of God and nature. If, however, we all understood that she felt that way, she would consent to sit there and listen.

And she did.

I do not know what she made of the discussion from the four young people in the seminar, all within a year or two of her own age, who told of their own fears and moments of bravery in the course of coming to terms with their own homosexuality; of the problems dealing with parents, school mates, friends at home; of the moments of frightening hostility; of the times of unexpected support and understanding. There was one Asian young man on the panel. There was a Mexican woman. One white boy was the son of a minister. There were no blacks. As I sat there, a gay black man of fifty-five, who had spent half of his life before Stonewall and the other half since, listening to them talk, I found much of what they said moving. I found much of it—yes— naive. Some of it I thought was insightful. (I thought, I must confess, one of the women on the panel had all the political sophistication of a clam.) Some of what they said I agreed with. Some of what they said I felt could be further thought through.

But what was probably clear both to me and to the young woman who'd made her initial statement, is that these were sincere young people saying how they'd felt, how the world looked to them. They were clearly people of goodwill who clearly wanted the world to be better for themselves and for those around them.

When we actually change our political ideas, most of us change them fairly slowly. Exposure is as much a factor as logic.

In a democracy, the respect the young woman asked for must be granted if she is ever to change her thinking. That is as much a democratic right as the right of the brave youngsters in the seminar to be heard.

Somewhere, in Michigan then, as it does here and has done before, as it has so many times now, sedimentation continues, sedimentation begins.

NOTES

1. (*Lenin and Philosophy*, by Louis Althuser, [Monthly Review Press, New York: 1971]).

Cornel West on Heterosexism and Transformation: An Interview[1]

Harvard Educational Review

W e've often heard you speak about the connections among homophobia, patriarchy, and racism. Why do you talk about these issues, and how do you see them linked? And would you also talk about some of the personal challenges you face as a heterosexual black man, in taking such a vocal stance against heterosexism?

CORNEL WEST: My own understanding of what it means to be a democrat (small d), partly what it means to be a Christian, too, but especially what it means to be a democrat, is that you're wrestling with particular forms of evil.[2] It seems to me that to talk about the history of heterosexism and the history of homophobia is to talk about ways in which various institutions and persons have promoted unjustified suffering and unmerited pain. Hence, the questions become: How do we understand heterosexism? Why is it so deeply seated within our various cultures and civilizations? We could talk primarily about America, but we can talk globally as well. I think it fundamentally has to do with the tendency human beings have to associate persons who are different with degradation, to associate those who have been cast as marginal with subordination and devaluation. So in order to be both morally consistent and politically consistent, I think democrats have to focus on particular forms of unjustified suffering across the board, be it patriarchy, vast economic inequality, white supremacy, or male supremacy. It's just a matter of trying to be true to one's own sense of moral integrity.

HER: You've taken a very visible, very public stance against heterosexism and homophobia. Are there personal challenges for you in taking that stance?

WEST: Well, no doubt, no doubt. Any time you offer a serious critique of the systems of power and privilege, be it compulsory heterosexuality, be it white supremacy, or what have you, you're going to catch some hell. There's no doubt, both within the black community and the black church, as well as outside, that I tend to catch hell on this issue. There's no doubt about it. But for me, it's fundamentally a matter of trying to highlight the moral ideals that serve as a basis of the critique of homophobic behavior, heterosexism as a whole, as well as their political consequences. I don't think that one can actually engage in serious talk about the fundamental transformation of American society—that is, the corporate elites, the bank elites, the white supremacists, the male supremacists, as well as the heterosexists—without talking about hitting the various forms of evil across the board. The interesting thing is that some of the critiques almost have to take an *ad hominem* form. A person might think, wait a minute, why is he so concerned about homophobia? There must be something going on in his personal life, and so forth.

My view is that I have to recognize deep homophobia inside of me, because I grew up in the black community, in the black church, on the black block, and there's a lot of homophobia in all three sites. So I'm quite candid about the internal struggle that I undergo because of my own homophobic socialization. How do you deal with the feelings of either threat or fear—and, I think, for many homophobes—outright hatred? I don't think I ever, even as a young person, hated gay brothers or lesbian sisters. I think I did associate it early on with something that was alien. And I've often, even in movies, seen lesbian love as very different. I think that, in a patriarchal society, for a man to see two women involved in lesbian activity is less threatening than seeing two men involved in gay activity. When I've seen gay activity on the screen, for example, it does hit me viscerally as very alien and different. That's where my moral struggle comes into play, in terms of acknowledging that difference from my perspective, but not associating it with degradation or disgust.

Rather, it is just a particular mode of human expression that I have been taught to associate with degradation. I simply acknowledge it as different, but I don't have to make that connection with degradation, per se. And in doing so, I have been honest with myself. In an interesting way, people say, well, you're so interested in this issue, maybe you've got a secret life or something. And I say, you know, if one is gay or lesbian, one should be proud of it. There's nothing to hide in that regard, it seems to me. And if one isn't gay or lesbian, one may just acknowledge that others make certain kinds of choices and have different orientations, and so forth. So-called straight persons can go on about the business of living and still fight an antihomophobic struggle along with gay and lesbian comrades.

HER: Your earlier comment about the homophobia you witnessed growing up in the black community reminds me that there's a certain lore about communities of color—not all communities of color, but particularly religious communities of color—that suggests that there is more overt homophobia within these communities than in dominant white communities. Can you speak about this perception? How much of this lore is an attempt on the part of the right to force divisions where there might be alliances?

WEST: Yeah, that's a tough question. That's a very tough question, because degrees of intolerance and tolerance and degrees of hatred and openness are very difficult to measure. I know when I was growing up in the black community, most people knew that, let's say, the brother who played the organ in the church was a gay brother. People would say, oh, that's so and so's child. You know, he's that way. And they'd just keep moving. There wasn't an attempt to focus on his sexuality; he was an integral part of the community. It wasn't a matter of trying to target him and somehow pester him or openly, publicly degrade him. Those who said he's "that way" didn't believe that way was desirable, but they just figured that's just the way he was, that's just his thing, you know. But one of the ways in which he chose to function was to be part of his community. People knew it, but he just didn't make a big deal out of it.

For me, however, it's very important that even closeted sexuality be something that's seriously interrogated, because it can lead toward a kind of internalized homophobia within gay or lesbian persons themselves. I think you get some of that in the great James Baldwin, in his struggles over whether he wants to be gay in identity or to highlight his particular sexual orientation as a public feature of his identity. And that's a tough question. But when I was growing up that tended to be the attitude.

I had always thought that even though homophobia was thick, it was dealt with in such a way that it did not disunite the black community because this was a community under siege, dealing with institutional terrorism, Jim Crow, Jane Crow, and so forth—you had to accent commonality. At the same time, we have seen an increase in so-called gay bashing and lesbian bashing in the country as a whole, including the black community and other communities of color. Here, of course, as you get a slow shattering of community, in this case the black community, then a lot of the paranoid dispositions become more salient and more visible. One of those forms is violence against gays and women, and this is also the case when we consider violence against sisters in the black community. We've always had that, but we've seen also an exponential increase in this violence as the community disintegrates. So I'm a little reluctant to say that homophobia is actually more rampant in the black community than it is in the larger white community. My hunch is that it runs pretty deep in both. But in the past, it was cast in such a way that it was subordinate to the survival of the black community as a whole. As that community now undergoes a very, very deep crisis, if not slow dissolution, we see the scapegoating of the most vulnerable: black women, gays, and lesbians.

HER: With highly charged political and moral issues such as sexuality, how do democratic educators balance a respect for diverse community values with respect for their own democratic ideals, particularly where community values may run counter to them?

WEST: I think it's a tough call. Partly it's just a matter of a certain kind of practical wisdom because I don't think there are any abstract principles that would allow us to make various judgments in each case. There are going to be tensions any time you're dealing with very rich notions of individuality. And by individuality I don't mean the rugged, ragged, rapacious individualism of American capitalism, but of free choices that people make that help them make and remake themselves as persons within a community. Individuality within a community always has a certain kind of tension. I think as democrats, as radical democrats, it's very important that we keep alive a subversive memory of critique and resistance; and therefore, when we talk about sexuality, we understand it as a particular discourse, a particular institutional practice over time and space that has reinforced certain systems of power and privilege. At the same time, there's a tradition of resistance against that system of power and privilege.

Foucault and others have pointed out that the very construct of homosexuality itself comes from the medical community (you know, Westphal's work in 1870), and, as such, is constituted as a disease, and of course, as crime, legally and politically.[3] This is a shift from the discourse of sodomy, which was viewed as a sin against nature. Now this is a very important move because it's an attempt by a set of elites to exert a certain kind of control over how people view their bodies, what they do with their bodies, what the state does with their bodies, and how those bodies are scarred and bruised, internally and externally. But this shift is also connected to other systems of power and privilege, White supremacists, the rule of capital, and so on.

What you actually have then is an attempt to keep alive a certain subversive memory for a democrat. For me, it's impossible to be a democrat and not have a very deep sense of remembrance of the freedom fighters who came before and what they were up against. What was the nature of the systemic oppression that they were responding to? And at the same time you've got a number of these different traditions, each with its strengths and its weaknesses. You've got the black freedom struggle that has historically focused on white supremacy; it has not said enough on issues of vast economic inequality, and has hardly said enough when it comes to homophobia and heterosexism. Then you've got a gay/lesbian freedom struggle that has focused primarily on heterosexism and homophobia, and at times has not said enough about white supremacy. I think in the U.S. context there's always tension when it comes to the legacy of white supremacy, which cuts through every tradition of resistance and critique. That's why somebody like Audre Lorde for me was, and in memory is, such a towering figure. It's so rare to have such a deep artist, on the one hand, and a sophisticated political activist on the other. She was also a progressive humanitarian who could speak to the depths of human suffering and pain that cut across the various forms of oppression and create a common space, a radical democratic common space. That doesn't happen too often, it doesn't happen often at all. To think through the notion of difference in such a way that it becomes a source of strength, rather than a set of obstacles and impediments that reinforce our own paranoid disposition, is rare. We all have paranoid dispositions. For me the important thing, as a Christian, is to recognize that the evil is inside each and everyone of us, in part because of that treacherous terrain called history that has shaped us, and socialized us, and acculturated us. Consequently, it's not ever a matter of one group feeling as if they don't have some white supremacy, male supremacy, or homophobia inside of them. Because we've been socialized in the white supremacist, patriarchal society, those residues are there no matter how liberated one thinks one actually is. It's a perennial struggle, and that's one of the reasons why there has to be a collectivity. You have to organize and mobilize to keep each other accountable. That's part of the democratic ethos within radical democratic groups, because we have to prefigure, in some way, the kind of society that we're talking about within our own movement. The only way we deal with these evils inside of us is to keep each other accountable. I'm not sure we ever fully eliminate them. Audre Lorde says, look inside and then name the forms of oppression working therein, and, at the same time, never be paralyzed by them, never be debilitated by them. She's so honest about her internal struggle against oppression.

HER: What do you see as the limits of identity politics and the struggle for democratic ideals, and what are the strengths? How can people mobilize across and through identity politics?

WEST: I think identity politics, on the one hand, are inescapable and, on the other hand, still too limited. It's inescapable primarily because we have such underdeveloped class-based politics in America. The power of corporate and bank elites is such that it has made it very difficult for fellow citizens to believe that class-based politics can be sustained in a way that these politics would actually meet head-on the tremendous entrenched power of the rule of capital. Consequently, a person falls back on her/his own particular ethnic, racial, sexual identities as a way of sustaining some critique against this deeply conservative society, in which the rule of capital is almost a precondition for democracy to flower and flourish. On the other hand, we have a society that has been so deeply rooted in white supremacy that it makes it very difficult to talk about class-based politics without talking about just how central race and racism have been in the constitution of American identity, culture, and society.

You get a lot of reductionist formulations from the left about this issue. The argument goes: it's really a class issue, it's got to be just a class issue. To engage in that reductionist formulation is partly an attempt to sidestep the challenge of race when we've had this long history of race-based slavery and race-based Jim Crow.

And so I think identity politics have lost sight of a class-based analysis, which makes it impossible for people to conceive of a fight for the fundamental democratic transformation of American society toward more egalitarian distribution of goods and resources. It's impossible to conceive of that fight without beginning with one's own conception of one's pain and suffering as it relates to the most visible scars. The most visible source of those scars for people of color are white supremacists. For women, it has been patriarchy. For gays and lesbians, it has been heterosexism and homophobia. While beginning there, I think one ultimately has to reach a space where there's some overlapping consensus regarding the way in which these various systems of oppression operate. In the economic sphere, you have to have coalition because the powers that be are so strong that individuals will be crushed. We've seen that over and over and over again. For example, any time a gay or a lesbian activist attempts both to accent the critique of heterosexism and homophobia and then to link them to other oppressions, the powers that be become even more hostile. That is true of the black movement, and it is true of the feminist and womanist movement. Democracy — radical democracy in all of its forms — tries to accent the variety of institutional and individual forms of evil and constitutes the most formidable threat to the powers that be. Very much so. And the powers that be are quite serious. No doubt about that. They've got a lot of resources at their disposal to crush people. No doubt.

HER: The question about identity politics is linked to a question about destructive divisions between liberation struggles for people of color and liberation struggles for gays and lesbians. The hierarchy of oppressions — "my oppression is worse than your oppression" — gets in the way of coalition building. What can be done to foster coalition?

WEST: I think the fundamental issue is the difficulty of forging bonds of trust between various communities of resistance. The reason why it's difficult to generate those bonds of trust is, I think, precisely because, at the psychocultural level, the forms of fear and insecurity and anxiety associated with others come from the prevailing systems that socialize us in a way that reinforces the fears and anxieties and insecurities associated with the "other"; for example, gay, lesbian, black, brown, red, and so forth. The powers that be know that as long as there are no bonds of trust or very, very weak bonds of trust, there won't be any effective coalition-building or any substantive alliances among communities of resistance. And they're right. The only way bonds of trust can be forged is when you have enough courageous activists, so-called leaders and so-called followers, who are willing to violate the prevailing lines of demarcation that are in place. But to violate and transgress those lines of demarcation means that those persons have to struggle deeply within themselves to wrestle honestly with their own insecurities and the anxiety that they associate with other people. There's a certain kind of existential honesty and intellectual candor that must go with political courage, both with leadership and so-called "followership," if we're ever going to forge the kinds of bonds of trust necessary to create the coalitions that can present at least a substantive challenge to the powers that be. There's still no guarantee even after the bonds of trust are forged—they've got armies and tanks and a whole lot of other things—but at least the chances are better.

HER: What does that candor look like?

WEST: The candor? Well, it's painful, it's very painful. When I start with the homophobia in me, it's painful. One is ashamed of oneself in terms of how one has been socialized. How does one attempt to overcome it? I would think in white brothers and sisters, when they actually look at the white supremacy in them, it's got to be painful if they're serious democrats, if they're serious about struggle. You overcome it by not just wrestling with it, but also by fusing with others in a context that will keep you accountable in such a way that you will remain vulnerable and, hence, open for growth and development, rather than simply debilitated, paralyzed, and therefore frozen. I think this is true in a variety of the different contexts that we've talked about: the patriarchy inside of us, the class arrogance inside of us, and the homophobia inside of us.

HER: All of that requires a certain level of political courage. So where's the base?

WEST: That's very true. I think the political courage is based on a profound commitment. If you're fundamentally committed to dealing with the suffering and pain, you will be willing to put yourself through some processes. One sign of commitment, for me, is always the degree to which one is willing to be self-critical and self-questioning, because that's a sign that you're serious about generating the conditions for the possibility of overcoming the suffering that you're after. Commitment is fundamentally about focusing on the suffering and trying to overcome it, trying to understand where it comes from, its causes, its effects. At the same time, it is about trying to prepare oneself to sacrifice and to serve in such a way that one attempts to overcome the suffering.

In addition to that, there is a serious intellectual dimension, and that has to do, again, with historical consciousness and that dangerous memory, that subversive memory. Because one of the ways in which one views oneself in process is to realize that you're part of a larger process and tradition that has been going on, and that persons who have raised the same kind of questions you raise struggle in their own ways. You can see it in their lives, their growth, their development, and their conscienticization. It is a complex and perennial process, but it's worth it. I think one of the things that we have to convey is that even given all the pain and suffering associated not just with being victimized, but also with being agents against that victimization, is that there's also deep joy and ecstasy in struggle. It is a desirable way of being in the world because it does, in fact, give you a sense of meaning and purpose. It gives you a sense of camaraderie, connectedness, and relatedness. And a decadent civilization such as our own suffers from what Arthur Miller called the disease of unrelatedness, where people quest for relations and intimacy, and suffer a lack of community and solidarity. It's just a spiritually impoverished way of being in the world. My good friend Stanley Hauerwas says that capitalism tends to produce rather s-h-i-t-t-y people, and he's absolutely right. He's absolutely right. Non-market values of love and care and service and laughter and joy run counter to that seriousness of maximizing personal preferences and maximizing profits. It's just a very impoverished way of being human, you see. I think that one of the things we democrats, radical democrats, have to acknowledge is this joy and ecstasy in pain-ridden struggles. So you get this fascinating juxtaposition of the joy and the pain and the despair and the hope all linked together. But that's what it begins with anyway.

HER: Living out paradox . . .

WEST: That's exactly right. Living in time and space, and that's where for me, the Christian perspective comes in, you see. To my mind, the best of Christianity has been that of a quest to be an existential democrat. See, what the Palestinian Jew named Jesus was all about was, "I'm going to overturn various forms of hierarchy that stand in the way of being connected with you compassionately." You see? And so the common eating, wherein all hierarchies of cuisine are called into question. Everybody come. Everybody use your hands. The same was true of free healing.

The ruling elite in the Roman Empire had to put him to death for a political crime. Why? Because he went straight to the temple. The temple was the center of life. And he turned the tables on the money lenders. Why? Because this market activity, this buying and selling, was getting in the way of a loving, compassionate, sympathetic, empathetic relation with human beings. And you know, he knew he was in trouble; he was in deep trouble. He's got the Roman elites. He's got the top slice of Jewish aristocracy, he's violating their laws and he's speaking to their working classes, right there in the midst of the exploitation of the peasants occurring there across the board, among Jews and non-Jews. So you get this particular Jewish figure who comes in and reforms a dominant tradition of Judaism, provides a critique of the Roman Empire, and ends up on a cross. And his followers come up with a narrative that says that cross is based on his blood that flows, which is that pain and suffering. But love still seems to be piercing through, even at a moment when it seems God is silent and the good is impotent. It still seems to pierce through. And for democrats, existential democrats, that's all we have. The question is: How do we keep that love piercing through our communities in our attempts to create full solidarity? To keep alive traditions of resistance and critique, so that from Stonewall in June 1969, a high moment, a transformation of consciousness, a certain tradition has been kept alive that had been inchoate, but now it's consolidated in a new kind of way, you see.[4] There's this wonderful book by Robert Goss, called *Jesus Acted Up*, that talks about this conception of god, love-making, and just doing, in light of this tradition that I'm talking about.[5] It's one of the most powerful statements that I've read that links my own conception of what it means to be an existential democrat and a radical democrat from the Christian point of view, to the context of the gay/lesbian liberation movement. But Christians have no monopoly on this. The questions are: How do I endure compassionately? How do I continue to bring critique to bear in a loving way with no naive utopian notions that somehow things are going to get better without struggle, or that somehow struggle itself can produce perfectibility, but still be sustained in the midst of very, very dark and difficult times? And, of course, secular traditions have as much access to that compassionate love as religious traditions do, just as religious and secular traditions also bastardize and reinforce systemic oppression.

HER: So how do you reconcile your Christianity with the contemporary Christianity that says love the sinner, hate the sin, when sin is read as "queer"?

WEST: Well, you do have to go back to the various claims to authority that are invoked. That means going back to the scripture, going back to the church fathers, and looking at all of the

302 — D LIAISONS

various ways in which the richness of Christianity has been so thoroughly debased and bastardized in the name of promoting forms of unjustified suffering. For example, in the scripture itself, when one actually looks at the nine references to so-called homosexuality or sodomy, most of them allude to male, same-sex sexual activities — there is only one reference to female. And part of these references are to tribal proscriptions, and part of them refer to male prostitution within Canaanite cults vis-à-vis Judaism. But, at the same time, there are deeply patriarchal, as well as homophobic, elements shot through those who wrote the text. That homophobia has to be teased out as well, in light of the claims of mercy and the claims of justice that are also in the text. As such, the text itself, of course, is polyvalent; it is ambiguous in that regard. For example, the Apostle Paul is concerned about lust and concerned about dehumanized relationships — no matter whether gay or lesbian, or so-called straight. This makes good sense. You want to treat each other as ends rather than means. There's no doubt about it. But, on the other hand, Paul himself is shot through with deeply patriarchal and homophobic sensibilities, being the person he was in his particular time. Now, of course, what's interesting is that most of the religious right, and the religious persons who use scripture to justify homophobia, don't like to admit that Jesus is not only silent on the issue, but he goes about engaging in forms of touch and intimate relation, not sexual that we know of, but in intimate relation in the best sense of sensual, across the board, from Mary to Lazarus, you see. People have said, well, if homosexuality is such a burning issue, how come Jesus doesn't say anything about it? Because if he did, it would have been at least constituted within the writings of the synoptic gospels, you see. And that's very upsetting, very upsetting indeed to right-wing Christian brothers and sisters!

HER: You could catch hell for this one too.

WEST: If Jesus was proclaiming a certain kind of love-centered state of existence that is impinging upon the space and time in which we live, impinging upon history, and if this issue of homosexuality and homoeroticism was such a fundamental sin, he certainly would have highlighted it. And so again, what we get, as in so many other cases, is an attempt to project various conceptions of the gospel that followed after the life and death and resurrection of Jesus, in an attempt to reinforce the very thing that he himself was fighting against. That goes from empire, to vast economic inequality, to the good Samaritan. My God, people don't realize how subversive that was in his day. That's like treating "niggers," and gays and lesbians, and so forth as if they're really part of the family. Now you see, that's just too big a challenge for most Christians who are holding on to such thin and impoverished conceptions of the gospel. And yet, if Jesus would come back and say that the good Samaritan in the latter part of the twentieth century was treating these so-called niggers, and treating these gays and lesbians, and treating these poor white brothers, whom you associate with trash, as part of the family, he would then reveal the depths of their idolatry. He would show that, in fact, what they're really tied to is a set of idols rather than that blood that flowed at that cross from the body of Jesus. It is a very important dialogue in which I think people like Peter Gomes and others have played a very important role: highly visible persons of integrity, who bring critique to bear on this particular form of evil.[6]

HER: The last question that we have for you is, what do you think a lesbian and gay struggle brings to the struggle for a radical democracy?

WEST: There's a new dimension that gay brothers and lesbian sisters bring to the struggle, and that is a conception of the erotic linked to bodies that forces us to accent the cultural as well as the political and economic dimensions of our radical democratic movement. You see, America itself, of course, begins with indigenous peoples being dispossessed of their land, the subordination of indigenous peoples, and hence an attempt to create a Puritanically based conception of a nation with a city on a hill that's special and exceptional. Since the very beginning, Americans have been very, very uneasy with their bodies, and have associated the erotic with the different, the other, the alien. That attempt to escape from one's body and to be open to the variety of different pleasures that can flow from that body has always been associated with anarchy and disorder. This Puritanical culture cuts across race and class and region in America; and even though it has undergone a fundamental transformation, it's still around. Even when you had a Marxist-based movement, they didn't want to talk about the erotic; the Communist Party was often as Puritanical as the YMCA. The big difference was that they allowed for so-called cross-racial relations, which was subversive, culturally subversive. But it still wasn't as subversive as allowing the erotic itself to play a fundamental role. It is partly because the erotic itself has this Dionysian energy that overflows beyond the rational. In that regard, the erotic offers a much deeper critique of radicalisms that are linked to the Enlightenment. To be a serious gay and lesbian activist, or to have learned from gay and lesbian liberation movements, is to engage at this level of a critique of Enlightenment sensibility thinking that it's all about rational control and a rational project. I'm not trashing reason, or trashing the rational. However, the erotic forces us to acknowledge that our radicalism ought to be much more open and much more self-critical. Now there's a sense in which the black movement brought this to bear as well, with the crucial role of the body, partly as a result of an African culture that is much less uncomfortable with the body than a Puritanical one. But, even the African and Afro-American traditions did not accent the degree to which the erotic could be found in same-sex relationships. And that, to me, is a crucial contribution, and also to someone like myself, a challenge, a crucial challenge. Here again, Audre Lorde and others have noted the ways in which the erotic can be empowering and ennobling, enabling and ennobling, and can actually release in us energies that, I think in the end, are indispensable for struggle because they also become forces for hope in a situation in which there is not a lot of hope.

The interesting question is the relationship between the ethical and the erotic. The erotic without the ethical can become just thoroughly licentious in the most flat hedonistic sense. But the erotic fused with the ethical means there is respect for the other, and that respect for the other also means being attentive to the needs of the other given their erotic energies. These kinds of issues seem to me to be fundamental ones because, of course, they affect every relationship. I mean, even in friendships that are nonsexual, there's an erotic dimension. And as teachers of students we know there's an erotic dimension, but it has got to be severed from any use of power for subordination, sexual pleasure, sexual manipulation, and so forth. But if one is honest in one's own humanity and is concerned with a qualitative relation with any significant other, I think one has to acknowledge that there is an erotic dimension. And it's precisely this dimension, among others, but especially within this dimension, that I think gay and lesbian movements have made a major, major advance in radical thought and in radical action.

NOTES

1. Conducted in the fall of 1995 by *Harvard Educational Review* Editorial Board members Vitka Eisen and Mary Kenyatta.
2. The term democrat (small d) refers to the political philosophy rather than the political party.
3. Michel Foucault credits Carl Westphal's 1870 article "Archiv für Neurologie," with presenting the first medical categorization of homosexuals as "species" in *History of Sexuality: An Introduction* (New York: Vintage, 1978/1990), 43.
4. Patrons of the gay and lesbian Stonewall bar in New York City revolted against ongoing police harassment in June of 1969. This rebellion is commonly used to mark the birth of the contemporary lesbian and gay liberation movement in the United States.
5. Robert Goss, *Jesus Acted Up: A Gay and Lesbian Manifesto* (San Francisco: HarperCollins, 1993).
6. The Rev. Peter Gomes is Minister in Harvard Memorial Church and Plummer Professor of Christian Morals at Harvard Divinity School.

There Is No Hierarchy
of Oppressions

Audre Lorde

I was born black, and a woman. I am trying to become the strongest person I can become to live the life I have been given and to help effect change toward a livable future for this earth and for my children. As a black, lesbian, feminist, socialist, poet, mother of two including one boy and a member of an interracial couple, I usually find myself part of some group in which the majority defines me as deviant, difficult, inferior or just plain "wrong."

From my membership in all of these groups I have learned that oppression and the intolerance of difference come in all shapes and sizes and colors and sexualities; and that among those of us who share the goals of liberation and a workable future for our children, there can be no hierarchies of oppression. I have learned that sexism (a belief in the inherent superiority of one sex over all others and thereby its right to dominance) and heterosexism (a belief in the inherent superiority of one pattern of loving over all others and thereby its right to dominance) both arise from the same source as racism — a belief in the inherent superiority of one race over all others and thereby its right to dominance.

"Oh," says a voice from the black community, "but being black is NORMAL!" Well, I and many black people of my age can remember grimly the days when it didn't used to be!

I simply do not believe that one aspect of myself can possibly profit from the oppression of any other part of my identity. I know that my people cannot possibly profit from the oppression of any other group which seeks the right to peaceful existence. Rather, we diminish ourselves by denying to others what we have shed blood to obtain for our children. And those children need to learn that they do not have to become like each other in order to work together for a future they will all share. The increasing attacks upon lesbians and gay men are only an introduction to the increasing attacks upon all black people, for wherever oppression manifests itself in this country, black people are potential victims. And it is a standard of right-wing cynicism to encourage members of oppressed groups to act against each other, and so long as we are divided because of our particular identities we cannot join together in effective political action.

Within the lesbian community I am black, and within the black community I am a lesbian. Any attack against black people is a lesbian and gay issue, because I and thousands of other black women are part of the lesbian community. Any attack against lesbians and gays is a black issue, because thousands of lesbians and gay men are black. There is no hierarchy of oppression.

It is not accidental that the Family Protection Act,[1] which is virulently antiwoman and antiblack, is also antigay. As a black person, I know who my enemies are, and when the Ku Klux Klan goes to court in Detroit to try and force the Board of Education to remove books the Klan believes "hint at homosexuality," then I know I cannot afford the luxury of fighting one form of oppression only. I cannot afford to believe that freedom from intolerance is the right of only one particular group. And I cannot afford to choose between the fronts upon which I must battle these forces of discrimination, wherever they appear to destroy me. And when they appear to destroy me, it will not be long before they appear to destroy you.

NOTES

1. A 1981 congressional bill repealing federal laws that promote equal rights for women, including coeducational school-related activities and protection for battered wives, and providing tax incentives for married mothers to stay at home.

About the Contributors

Reginald G. Blaxton is Vice President for Programs at the Greater Washington Urban League. A native Washingtonian, he attended Colby College, Oxford University and the Episcopal Divinity School. Ordained to the priesthood in 1980, he has been assistant minister in St. George's Parish, LeDroit Park since 1982, and served from 1984 to 1991 as special assistant for religious affairs to two D.C. mayors. He is a founding member of the Washington Metropolitan Community AIDS Partnership. In 1995, he established *Utres Novi* Research and Consultation, which publishes occasional papers on religion, culture, and practice.

Keith Boykin is the author of *One More River to Cross: Black and Gay in America* and *Respecting the Soul: Daily Reflections for Black Lesbians and Gays*. A graduate of Harvard Law School, Boykin served two years in the White House as a Special Assistant to President Clinton. He is the former Executive Director of the National Black Lesbian and Gay Leadership Forum.

Cheryl Clarke is the author of four books of poetry, *Narratives: Poems in the Tradition of Black Women*; *Living as a Lesbian, Humid Pitch;* and *Experimental Love*. Her articles and book reviews have appeared in numerous periodicals and anthologies since 1979, including *Conditions, Home Girls: A Black Feminist Anthology; This Bridge Called My Back: Writings by Radical Women of Color; Kenyon Review; Callaloo; Women's Review of Books; Words of Fire: An Anthology of Black Feminist Thought; Theorizing Black Feminisms; The Black Scholar*. She is currently working on a nonfiction work about contemporary black women poets, and a new manuscript of poems entitled *Corridors of Nostalgia*.

Cathy J. Cohen is an Assistant Professor of Political Science and African and African-American Studies at Yale University.

She is the author of the forthcoming book entitled *The Boundaries of Blackness: AIDS and the Breakdown of Black Politics* and is coeditor with Kathleen Jones and Joan Tronto of *Women Transforming Politics: An Alternative Reader.* Her articles have appeared in numerous publications such as the *American Political Science Review, GQ* and *NOMOS.*

Gary David Comstock is the University Protestant Chaplain and Visiting Associate Professor of Sociology at Wesleyan University. His publications include *Gay Theology Without Apology, Unrepentant, Self-Affirming, Practicing: Lesbian/ Bisexual/Gay People within Organized Religion Que(e)rying Religion: A Critical Anthology* with Susan E. Henking, and *Violence Against Lesbians and Gay Men.*

Samuel R. Delany is a novelist and critic who lives in New York City. For the last ten years, he has taught in the Comparative Literature Department of the University of Massachusetts at Amherst and is the author of *Longer Views* and *Times Square Red, Times Square Blue, The Mad Man and Atlantis,* as well as *Silent Interviews: On Language, Race, Sex, Science Fiction, and Some Comics.*

Martin Duberman is Distinguished Professor of History at Lehman College and the Graduate School of the City University of New York, and is the founding director of their Center for Lesbian and Gay Studies. He is the author of several books, including *Paul Robeson, In White America, Cures, Stonewall,* and *Midlife Queer.* As both historian and playwright, he has received numerous awards, including the Bancroft Prize, two Lambda awards, the George Freedly Memorial Award, and a Special Citation from the National Academy of Arts and Letters.

Barney Frank is the U.S. Representative from Massachusetts' Fourth District. He has contributed to a number of publications including *The Harvard Gay and Lesbian Review, Positively Gay: New Approaches to Gay and Lesbian Life; Acts of Disclosure: The Coming-out Process of Contemporary Gay Men,* and

Improper Bostonians: Lesbian and Gay History from the Puritans to Playland.

Henry Louis Gates, Jr. is W. E. B. Du Bois Professor of the Humanities, chair of the Department of Afro-American Studies at Harvard University, and director of the W. E. B. Du Bois Institute for Afro-American Research. He is the author of several books including *Colored People: A Memoir; Speaking of Race, Speaking of Sex: Hate Speech, Civil Rights, and Civil Liberties; Loose Canons: Notes on the Culture Wars; The Future of the Race* (with Cornel West); and the editor of *The Norton Anthology of African-American Literature.*

Jewelle Gomez is the author of three collections of poetry, and a collection of essays. Her novel, *The Gilda Stories*, was the recipient of two Lambda Literary awards and her adaptation of the book for the stage toured thirteen U.S. cities. She is on the national board of the National Center for Lesbian Rights and is currently the executive director of the Poetry Center and American Poetry Archives at San Francisco State University. Her new collection of short stories is *Don't Explain.*

Tamara Jones is a doctoral candidate in the Department of Political Science at Yale University. Her publications include coauthorship of the essay "Women of Color in the Eighties: A Profile Based on Census Data" in *Women Transforming Politics.* She is a member of the Audre Lorde Project, the Black Radical Congress, and the New York City Coalition Against Police Brutality.

Audre Lorde was a black feminist lesbian writer and activist whose influence continues after her death of cancer in 1992. Contributor to journals and poetry editor of *Chysalis* and *Amazon Quarterly*, she is perhaps best remembered for her autobiography, *Zami: A New Spelling of My Name, The Cancer Journals,* her collection of essays and speeches, *Sister Outsider,* and *Burst of Light*, which won the American Book Award.

Robert Reid-Pharr teaches in the English department of Johns Hopkins University. He was a Phorzheimer Fellow in the English Department of City College, CUNY, and he is the author of *Conjugal Union: The Body, the House, and the Black American* and *GBM*.

Darieck Scott is Assistant Professor of English at the University of Texas at Austin, where he teaches African American literature and creative writing. He is the author of the novel *Traitor to the Race*, and his fiction and essays have appeared in the anthologies *Shade, Ancestral House, Flesh and the Word 4*, and *Gay Travels: A Literary Companion*.

Mab Segrest is a lesbian teacher, organizer, and writer who lives and works in Durham, North Carolina. She is currently Coordinator of the Urban-Rural Mission (USA), an affiliate of the World Council of Churches. She has published two books, *Memoir of a Race Traitor* and *My Mama's Dead Squirrel: Lesbian Essays on Southern Culture*. She is currently working on a third book of essays, *Born to Belonging*.

Barbara Smith is cofounder and publisher of *Kitchen Table: Women of Color Press*. Her articles, essays, literary criticism, and short stories have appeared in a wide variety of publications, including *The Nation, The New York Times Book Review, the Black Scholar, Ms.,* and *Gay Community News*. She has edited three major collections about Black women: *Conditions: Five, The Black Women's Issue* (with Lorraine Bethel), *All the Women Are White, All the Blacks Are Men, But Some of Us Are Brave: Black Women's Studies* (with Gloria T. Hull and Patricia Bell Scott), and *Home Girls: A Black Feminist Anthology*. She recently published a collection of her own work entitled *The Truth That Never Hurts: Writings on Race, Gender, and Freedom*.

Alisa Solomon is a staff writer at the *Village Voice*, where she covers a range of political and cultural topics, and also a Professor of English/Journalism at Baruch College-CUNY and of English and Theater at the CUNY Graduate Center. Her writing has appeared in such publications as *Out, Jewish Forward, New York Times, Ms.*, and *Glamour*, and she is the author of *Re-Dressing the Canon: Essays on Theater and Gender.*

Cornel West is a professor in the Harvard University School of Divinity and the Department of African-American Studies. He has authored *Prophesy Deliverance!*; *Prophetic Fragments*; *The American Evasion of Philosophy*; *The Ethical Dimensions of Marxist Thought*; *Race Matters in Postmodern Times*; *Prophetic Reflections: Notes on Race and Power in America*; *Keeping Faith: Philosophy and Race in America*; and *Race Matters.* His recent work continues his effort to explore the intersections of philosophy, race and culture.